T0121987

A Special Brand of Courage

A mother and her children's remarkable escape from Nazi Germany

Krystyna Louw

iUniverse, Inc.
Bloomington

A Special Brand of Courage
A mother and her children's remarkable escape from Nazi Germany

Copyright © 2010 by Krystyna Louw

All rights reserved. No part of this book may be used or reproduced by any means, graphic, electronic, or mechanical, including photocopying, recording, taping or by any information storage retrieval system without the written permission of the publisher except in the case of brief quotations embodied in critical articles and reviews.

The views expressed in this work are solely those of the author and do not necessarily reflect the views of the publisher, and the publisher hereby disclaims any responsibility for them.

iUniverse books may be ordered through booksellers or by contacting:

iUniverse
1663 Liberty Drive
Bloomington, IN 47403
www.iuniverse.com
1-800-Authors (1-800-288-4677)

Because of the dynamic nature of the Internet, any Web addresses or links contained in this book may have changed since publication and may no longer be valid.

ISBN: 978-1-4502-4401-5 (sc)
ISBN: 978-1-4502-4402-2 (ebk)

Printed in the United States of America

iUniverse rev. date: 1/11/2011

SYNOPSIS

NOTE: *This is a true story, with only the names of the characters changed.*

Hitler's influence on Poland and her people began long before the September, 1939 invasion.

Adam Polek, a successful businessman with strong political ties, is convinced that Germany intends to attack Poland. He runs an anti-Nazi newspaper and falls victim to a brutal attack by a German enemy. On his recovery he accepts a fulltime post in the Cavalry, a move that further aggravates an already tenuous relationship with his beautiful wife, Helena.

When war breaks out, Helena flees East with her two children, thirteen-year-old Marian and nine-year-old Stefa, and Bronek, a part-time student and their chauffeur. Lala, their Maltese poodle goes along with them, later to be instrumental in twice saving their lives.

Added to the holocaust of war, the bombs and the terror, comes – Russian invasion. The suffering of others and her own, together with the new demands made on her, bring about a change in Helena's character. She finds the strength to reject Bronek's love for her and encourages him to flee the country while she and the children make their way back home. Her dread of the NKVD (KGB), the Communist atrocities and their almost certain deportation to Siberia, is far greater than her fear of the Germans.

The long journey home is broken by weeks of work on a farm, by days of concealment in a cemetery tomb. Crossing the river San out of the Russian zone into Nazi occupied territories is fraught with danger on both sides. Helena is wounded but not seriously enough to prevent her from persuading a German frontier officer to set them free.

Back home they find their house occupied by German tenants and Adam's name on the Black List, wanted for anti-Nazi activities. Of Adam there is no sign. Security on her mother-in-law's farm is short-lived. Adam's old enemy and now a member of the Gestapo, presses for the family's enrolment as Volksdeutsch, (German citizens) offering the Dachau Concentration Camp as an alternative.

Under an assumed name Helena braves a visit to the Gestapo Headquarters in Berlin in a futile attempt to obtain visas for Hungary.

With her fluent German and disregard of danger, work for the Polish Underground becomes a natural next step.

In the new year word comes that Adam has escaped to Hungary and wants Helena and the children to join him there. Charged with renewed hope, Helena seeks help from the Underground.

A contact in Vienna, another on the Hungarian border, a leap out of a moving train, and the 'impossible' escape is made. In the jump from the train, Helena smashes her shoulder on a milestone. They are caught and detained in a Hungarian prison.

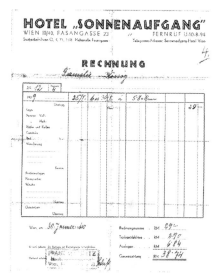

The Commissioner's compassion outweighs his sense of duty and he sends them on to the Polish Consulate still in operation in Budapest.

In their reunion, Adam and Helena find a stronger bond between them than there ever was before.

His diplomatic mission in Hungary is cut short by the increasing number of open Nazi supporters and they leave for the South of France, where Polish forces are being re-assembled for the French Campaign.

With Adam's departure for the front, come the advances of a French Count. Helena discovers he is working for the Nazis and her disclosure of him makes her feel that her work for the Underground is now complete.

France has fallen. Helena refuses to join the evacuees, believing that her husband is alive and will need her. Fifty miles ahead of the German Armies, Adam and his men arrive and together they make a desperate bid for the port of St. Jean de Luz where a Polish vessel is waiting to pick up the last of the Polish troops.

The story ends on the 'Sobieski', a ship that to Adam and Helena seems "like a stretch of free land, with the white and red flag flying high to remind them that all is not lost."

CHAPTER ONE

"War"

Long shafts of sunlight thrust and parried between the avenue of oaks and tall firs and within their branches sparrows continued their chatter, but the air had turned cool and the park was almost deserted. They were sitting on a bench, the tension between them making both oblivious to the serenity around them. Adam turned towards her as if to renew the argument. She heard a thud, he slid off the bench in slow motion and collapsed at her feet.

Helena dropped to her knees next to him. She saw the red stain spreading over his hair... and screamed.

Only a practiced hand could have thrown the stone with such force and accuracy.

A nurse brought her a cup of coffee. Helena grasped it between trembling fingers and swallowed it hot. Alone in the emergency waiting room, she sat on the edge of the couch, the glare from the ceiling lamp accentuating the fine, still-set contours of her face. She looked down, noticing for the first time the blood splotches on the raw silk of her skirt. She ran a scarlet-tipped finger gently over the stain then covered her face with her hands and sobbed. *Dear God, save him.* Her mind became obsessed with the thought that Adam was too young, too vital a life force to be snuffed out by a stone, for God's sake. And beyond that there was the sick fear of losing him, of being left alone with the children. Despite their recent differences she knew now that life without Adam was unthinkable. *Mother of God please save him.*

She had not prepared herself for any other eventuality. "Mrs. Polek?"

Helena jumped to her feet, searching the Doctor's face. "Your husband has suffered an injury to the pyramidal tract," he explained carefully. "This has caused temporary paralysis to the left side of the body."

Numbed, she stood there staring at him. "How temporary?" She finally got out. He pulled her down to sit next to him. "No longer than eight to nine months my dear." He made this sound like good news indeed.

What the Doctor had not counted on was Adam's physical fitness and sheer willpower, fanned by a conviction that the assault had been instigated by Schmidt, a Nazi Party leader. An exposure of Schmidt at this time would provide grounds for his deportation from Poland, so strenuously sought by the Silesian Anti-Nazi League, one of the political groups of which Adam was President. So that it came as no surprise to those who knew him when, two months to the day, on July 29th 1939, fit and impatient for revenge, Adam was discharged from the hospital.

Adam's all-consuming interest in politics had culminated in his acceptance of some obscure but highly confidential post at the Military Base. This was the reason for their argument that afternoon in the park. At the time, Helena saw it as a lighthearted withdrawal from all domestic responsibilities, for it was clear he enjoyed every moment of his political involvement.

She had seen little of him in the past months. Their fast growing Publishing House had been left to the questionable management of Pogolski, a dyspeptic individual who openly resented any interference from the Boss' wife, possibly because he knew she had no illusions about his honesty.

None of Adam's arguments could convince Helena that Poland was threatened with war. Like so many credulous optimists, she believed that Germany's song and dance about the Baltic Corridor, her claim to the port of Gdynia and ridiculous statements to save the so-called 'persecuted' ethnic German settlers in Poland, would never materialize in warfare. Moreover, she believed that by their premature demonstrations of patriotic fervor, the Poles were probably aggravating hostilities between the two nations.

The country seemed to be swept by two conflicting currents: the one uneasy, restless and aggressive, the other eager to be drawn into a comfortable euphoria.

With a mere twenty years of self rule behind them, most Poles wanted nothing more than the simple pleasures that had for so long been denied them: The right to educate their children in their own language, the freedom to print their own books, to establish their own industries and build new homes along modern lines.

Helena had persuaded Adam to invest in a magnificent Afghan carpet for his study. Their bedroom had been redecorated in the latest Swiss pine and she was planning to turn the attic into the childrens' playroom. The last thing she wanted to think about was war.

No sooner was Adam discharged from the hospital than he was back in the thick of it. His paper *The Torch* carried inflammatory anti-Nazi slogans, political meetings led to lengthy discussions that often went on throughout the night. Fortified with beer and vodka, every man fought and defeated the German armies with one sweep of the hand. She saw less and less of him and the nights grew longer and her temper shorter. But because he did his best to devote his Sundays to his family and because they were his most precious possessions, Adam would have been genuinely outraged if anyone had suggested that he was neglecting his wife and children.

This explosive arrangement continued until mid-August, when once again there was a row over his eventual acceptance of a full time post in the Cavalry. Adam broke the news during Olga's visit in the hope that their friend's presence would be a restraining factor on his wife's tongue.

Rozia had served tea with lemon and opened the French windows to let in the afternoon sun. It fell on the thick creamy pile of carpet and caught the burnished tip of Adam's boot.

"The situation has become pressing," he concluded. "I had no choice."

"No of course not," Helena heard herself snapping. "But Michal and Waldek and Piotr do have a choice don't they. And they choose to stay with their families!"

Christ, why can't she stand by me for once, he thought. *Why can't she show some bloody patriotism at least.* Adam's anger mounted and he knew he would regret it if he stayed.

"I don't have to justify my actions and I'm not going to argue with you!" Abruptly he stood up, bowed to Olga and marched out of the house.

Helena followed him to pick up the key that always fell out when he slammed the front door. She took a deep breath and went back to the sitting room, spreading her hands in a half apologetic gesture. There was really no need for embarrassment between them. They were old school friends and if anyone understood, it was Olga. "Sorry about that," Helena murmured.

Waving the apologies aside Olga reached for her gold cigarette case. "Haven't you learned yet that you can't change a man like Adam?"

Knowing her friend was right didn't make it any easier. Nor did Olga's smoking habit. Adam would throw a fit if he saw *her* light up like that. Oh she'd done it, often. Not because she liked the taste of tobacco but purely out of perverseness, to goad him when they argued. He hated to see a woman smoke but was almost paranoid about his wife doing so.

The sight of Olga drawing elegantly on the long ivory holder deepened her resentment. She was hurt by Adam's apparent unconcern at leaving her and the children and deep down there was the feeling of inadequacy that went with having to take second place in her husband's life. She liked to think that she knew him better than anyone. Yet there was this hard, uncompromising side to him that often made a stranger of him.

"Still," Olga was saying with a smile. "You must admit he cuts a pretty dashing figure as an *Ulan* (Lancer)."

"Hm," Helena grunted. "It's alright for you, I mean Frederik..." She stopped in confusion.

"Frederik might be German," Olga concluded amiably, "but he's not a Nazi and if it wasn't for his age I wouldn't be surprised if he joined up too."

"Of course," Helena put in hastily, knowing perfectly well that that would be the last thing Olga's husband would ever want to do. Frederik and Olga enjoyed a cool, convenient relationship, neither partner demanding very much of the other. She was an attractive woman, slim to the point of thinness and surprisingly youthful for her 38 years, while at 50 Frederik had already been taken for her father. A shrewd Art Dealer, he provided her with the luxuries she had always longed for and she, through her impoverished aristocratic background, opened the doors to valuable connections.

Olga watched Helena kick off her sandals and tuck her heels under her. She had always envied her friend's beautiful legs. "Well, all this isn't going to stop me from going to Rymanow," Helena said.

"Are you serious? You don't think Adam's going to let you. Now, I mean."

"Let me? I'm a big girl now remember." Helena wasn't able to hide the peevishness that had crept into her voice. "In any case, I've made the reservations and it's something I've been looking forward to for weeks and so has Stefa."

"I can imagine. Well, you know what you're doing. Where is Stefa by the way? I've brought her a little present."

"Playing in the garden somewhere. I'll call her."

"No, don't worry. I'll see her on my way out. Marian not home yet from school?"

"Sports Day today. Cadets yesterday. Debate or something or another tomorrow. Honestly, I hardly see the boy these days. Wish he paid as much attention to his school work as he does to all those outside activities," she added.

"He is growing up fast isn't he." Olga stood up and they went through to the bedroom. Retouching her face with powder, she caught Helena's eye in the mirror.

"I don't know how you get away with it Helena." "With what?".

"Looking so sinfully good with no makeup and that *tan*. But it's absolutely stunning on you."

"My other friends," Helena smiled thinly, "tell me I shall look like a prune by the time I'm 40."

"Jealousy. See you have a new maid. " Olga went on, pulling on white kid gloves. "It's strange not seeing old Jasia about. You had her for so long she seemed like part of the family."

"Her own sentiments precisely. She was becoming quite impossible you know. Anyway, Adam got her a job at some factory or other. Rozia's not bad, at least so far."

They walked to the front gate. The smell of lilac was heavy in the air. Olga inhaled appreciatively. "I've never seen your tree so full of blooms," she said. "Altogether, your garden is looking beautiful."

"Yes, we've had a good summer," Helena replied, relaxing in spite of herself and taking pleasure in the sight.

Stefa came running up, pigtails flying behind her, Lala, her little white maltese terrier, yapping at her heels.

"Ah, here's my favorite little Goddaughter. See what I brought you from Czestochowa."

Nothing could have pleased Stefa more than the miniature rosary in its exquisitely carved box. Especially since it came from Czestochowa, the city where the Virgin Mary once chose to perform her miracle.

"Oh thank you!" Stefa threw her arms around Olga's neck. "It's the best present ever."

"Glad you like it darling." She kissed them both. "Have a wonderful time at the Spa girls and don't forget to bring me some of that revolting mineral water, not that I promise to drink it."

As Helena watched her friend slide into the low white convertible, heard the six cylinders come to life, she had no premonition whatever of the very different circumstances under which they would meet again.

"Come on Stefciu, let's take a walk around the garden." Helena took Stefa's hand. She felt restless and a little uneasy at the thought of the confrontation with Adam that was still to come.

The sweet scent of the late-flowering rose bushes followed them past beds of giant chrysanthemums. Stefa stooped to smile at her favorite pansies, their variegated faces upturned in solemn greeting. Helena opened the gate to the fruit garden. As always, the apple trees presented them with stunted, sour offerings. Laden plum trees made up for the disappointment, as did the pears and sometimes, if the season was exceptionally good one or two of the peach trees would produce decent pickings. In vain Stefa searched for a ripe cherry. "Bet Marian picked the last one," she muttered crossly. Her face cleared at the sound of rapidly approaching hoof beats.

Helena watched the powerfully built form leap from the saddle in one easy movement and wondered why Adam was returning so soon. Olga's words came back to her. She had to admit that he did look quite "dashing" in that uniform of his. Broad chest covered in an impressive array of medals, sword gleaming at his side and under the peaked cap, the handsome face alight with an almost boyish radiance. Knowing him better than Olga did, she also knew that this radiance shone best when not baulked by opposition. A man of great charm when exerting his own determinism, he could be more than difficult when crossed. They had long ago come to recognize each other's fiery natures and had, for the most part, learned to tread softly.

There was no sign of rancor now. No hint that only a short while ago he'd left her in a rage.

"Pick me up Daddy. Take me for a ride, *please.*" The pleas, the melting brown eyes, usually so irresistible to her father, had no effect. "Not now angel. Run along and play. I have to talk with Mommy."

He tossed the reins over the gate post and gave the big chestnut an affectionate pat. She responded eagerly, nuzzling closer for more attention.

"Didn't expect to see you back so soon." Her voice still held an edge to it.

"Let's go inside shall we? I feel like a drink."

She looked at him quickly. She had seen Adam drink the best part of a bottle of vodka when with friends but very seldom had she seen him take a drink on his own.

"If what you have to say is that bad, you'd better pour me one too."

He handed her a glass of beer, half smiling. "It's not bad. In fact it's the best news yet. We've finally decided to ignore diplomatic pressure from the west and won't be delaying mobilization any longer. I'm being sent to Krakow for a while," he added.

"When?"

"Tonight."

"Then you won't be here when Stefa and I leave for Rymanow." "Surely you don't intend going?"

"Of course I'm going. Marian will be fine with the girl and -"

"Don't be stupid," he cut in. "You know the Germans have been beating their brains out for an excuse to pounce on us and it's just possible they may spring a surprise attack. What then?"

"In that unlikely event, I imagine the Polish troops will manage to hold them off long enough for me to get back," she countered sweetly.

He faced her, his color deepening. Banging the half empty glass of beer on the table he shouted, "Must we always be at loggerheads dammit!"

"As long as you persist in your selfish attitude,"

"Selfish? Now who's being selfish, spoilt and bloody pigheaded on top of it! Don't you realize..."

"Please," she held up her hand. "Here's Stefa. Let's not fight in front of the children."

The argument was dropped but the barrier between them grew more solid.

....

"Gentlemen," he always began in that carefully modulated voice. "And ahem, ladies." This too was part of the ritual and Helena wondered whether the Colonel really did include the ladies as an afterthought or whether the pause was calculated to create some fancied effect on his listeners. "In view of my long military career, I think I am justified in expressing the opinion that there is no danger of Poland being overrun by Germany again."

If it hadn't been for Stefa's nonsense over the veal cutlets, they could have made their escape, Helena thought irritably. Now it was too late. In this company of wealthy businessmen, their pampered, overfed wives and retired Army officials, it would have been unforgivable to leave the table and the main table at that, at the beginning of Colonel Soskowski's pointless and invariably boring discourse.

"What about Germany's threat to take Gdynia from us?" Asked a stout female, fluttering a gem-laden hand in a nervous gesture.

"Nothing but empty talk, dear lady," he summed up confidently. "Take my word for it. But, should Hitler be foolish enough to declare war on us, we will teach him that our Army is not one to be trifled with! And don't forget our alliance with Great Britain and France. No. Hitler doesn't stand a chance and he knows it."

Stefa began to fidget. This conversation had as much appeal to a nine year old as it had for Helena. She bent down to say in an undertone, "Run along then. See you in a few minutes." And gave herself another ten minutes in which to comply with the dictates of good manners.

Not unlike many good Spa Resorts, Rymanow boasted several hot springs, a well-run hotel and beautifully kept, park like grounds. Most of the guests were much the same as the group at the center table, with few exceptions who, like Helena were there for genuine health reasons.

Doctor Sadowski had suggested the waters might be beneficial to a recurrent morning hay fever condition. Whether it was these foul tasting mineral waters coupled with the hot spring baths that were washing away the tensions, or the tranquility of the resort, or a combination of all, Helena could not say. All she knew was that she was feeling more relaxed than she'd been in months. Two weeks had gone by, there was still one more week to look forward to and no sign of hay fever.

She glanced at her watch. The ten minutes were almost up. Theirs was the last table still occupied and Colonel Soskowski was still trying to impress his listeners with the might of the Polish forces. As he paused for breath Helena stood up. This set off a loud scraping of chairs. In a matter of seconds the dining room was empty.

Stefa waited at the foot of a short flight of stone steps. She was hopping from one leg to the other, impatient for their daily walk in the woods, hoping for a glimpse of her favorite squirrel.

"Really," she said in her most grown up voice, "I wish that man wouldn't talk so much. "

Helena laughed. She looked at the small figure skipping next to her and her eyes filled with pride. Stefa was not only a good looking child, she was good company. And bright. Always first in her class. By the time she'd turned five, her natural grace and rhythm had also won her first and second place in her Ballet School. Her artwork was already receiving recognition. Yet for all the attention and admiration that was lavished on her, she remained singularly unspoilt. Above all, little Stefa looked upon herself as a Christian.

They took in their last lingering sniffs at the pine trees and turned back. They were almost at the hotel, hurried on by the sound of the afternoon tea gong, when the impersonal voice over the loudspeaker called Helena to the telephone.

It was Adam. Germany had "declared" war on Poland by proxy of her well-equipped Luftwaffe!

Helena raced upstairs, calling out the news to the others.

Someone turned the radio on in the sitting room. The crackle of static and then repetitive emergency announcements officially confirmed that Poland was under attack.

Pandemonium broke loose. Many of the women lost their poise and broke down and whimpered with fear. The men yelled for porters, for pages, for taxis. Hotel staff and guests collided, tripped over luggage.

Helena threw everything into the one case she had brought. Half way down the staircase she was all but knocked over by the frantically charging Colonel.

They jumped into a waiting cab and caught the next train for Bielsko. Compartments were already crowded. People pushed and shouted at one another, all courtesy forgotten in their own fight for survival. Helena squeezed into a tiny space and lifted Stefa onto her lap. Stefa's eyes had grown enormous, her face ashen. She felt crushed by the noise, by the curses and unleashed emotions, and the stench of fear sweat.

All Police efforts to keep some semblance of order were futile and the same debacle met them at every station along the way. No one asked for tickets.

At Bielsko station the stampeding, confused surge of humanity became frightening. Telling Stefa to hold onto her skirt, Helena pushed through until they were standing on the platform between the carriage exits. A few moments later she spotted Adam elbowing his way towards her with Marian's blonde head right behind him.

Hard as he tried to appear calm, she knew him too well not to miss the desperate urgency in Adam's voice.

"Bronek's waiting outside with the car. Go and collect your jewelry, pack some clothes and drive east. I must get back to Headquarters immediately -- the Germans have already started bombing us. They'll be here pretty soon, so step on it will you?"

"What about the luggage? It's still in the compartment." "To hell with the luggage. There's no time for that."

"But when -- where, shall we see you?" She stammered, real fear gripping her for the first time.

"This shouldn't take longer than six weeks. We'll get reinforcements from the Allies and soon finish them off, don't worry. Go as far as Wieliczka and wait for me at Alex'. Oh yes, you'd better take this with you. It'll come in useful."

He handed her a document stating that bearer, Helena Polek, age: 31. Height 5'4". Hair: Brunette. Eyes: Blue. Was the wife of an Officer in the Polish Cavalry and that the Adler, Registration Number 1840 in which she was traveling, was her property.

"What's this for?"

"Just in case some officious oaf decides to relieve you of your car or gas. I imagine they'll be confiscating unidentified vehicles on the road."

They stood for a moment looking at each other. Suddenly there were tears in her eyes and they were clinging to one another. There was so much she wanted to say. His kiss said it all.

At last he pulled away. He bent to hug Stefa and Marian, gripped Helena's shoulders in a silent gesture of encouragement and was gone.

Before the crowds swallowed him up Helena had a fleeting glimpse of the erect set of shoulders, the familiar back of the neck and all at once felt alone, vulnerable and very young. She looked down at the piece of paper clutched in her hand and was reminded that, as the wife of a Polish Officer, she was expected to show some courage, but up to this day, she had never seriously been called upon to prove her mettle. All at once she was overcome with doubts. She took her childrens' hands, the one tiny and damp with fear, the other firmer but clinging just the same, and left the station.

The tall, lean frame of their chauffeur-cum-gardener stood propped against the Adler. His face creased into one of his rare smiles when he saw them. "I never thought you'd make the first train back, Mrs. Polek," Bronek said, quickly opening the door for her. "It's just as well I didn't take Marian's bet on it, or I'd have lost 50 *Groszy (50c)."* His voice sounded over-cheerful.

Even as he spoke he slammed the car into gear and began to hoot his way out of the parking lot. They covered the four miles from the station to the house in Zielna Street, in record time.

There was little time for packing. Helena searched frantically for the remains of the jewelry Rozia's conscience prompted her to leave behind. An aquamarine ring with matching earrings and pendant were all she could find, out of a sizeable collection acquired over years of succumbing to a weakness for jewelry. Of the girl there was, of course, no sign. Too late to regret her hasty dismissal of honest old Jasia. She thanked God she always wore one or two good pieces on her. The loss of the gold bracelet inlaid with rubies would have been unbearable. Apart from its intrinsic value it was a family heirloom. She threw an odd assortment of clothes into a couple of suitcases, some toiletries, documents and at the last moment, a pair of walking shoes. Marian rushed into the kitchen for salami and sweets. Holding tightly onto her new rosary, Stefa climbed into the front of the car. Lala jumped in the back with Marian, her excited barking adding to the frenzy of it all.

German bombers darkened the sky. The bridge close to the Printing House had already been blown up. As they swept past, Helena had a glimpse of shattered windows. *So much for seven years of hard work.* Even she felt the loss of the business as a permanent thing.

"Drive through Krakow," she told Bronek. "We've got to pick up Eva." Frail and on her own, Helena could picture the state her older sister would be in.

"I don't think we ought to," Bronek's voice was uncertain. "It's a good few miles out of our way and Captain Polek said I was to take you straight to Wieliczka. Krakow's bound to be hit harder than this. I think it's too risky."

"All the more reason why we should take her with us," Helena snapped, annoyed that he should question her wishes yet feeling that he was probably right.

He was. By the time they reached Krakow, it had suffered several raids and the town was in an uproar. They sped along as fast as the traffic would allow, hooting at frantic pedestrians, dodging torn up craters in the roads and narrowly avoiding walls that were caving in all about them. Krakow, the seat of the earliest western culture, one of the most beautiful cities in Europe, unprepared, undefended, blazed and crumbled under the remorseless onslaught. Monumental basilicas, magnificent Gothic Church and Cathedral spires that had towered over the city since the fourteenth century and before, now toppled like matchsticks. They drove through it all as if in a nightmare and straight into the next area under attack. Above and around them bombs whistled to a shriek that ended in ear-shattering explosions.

A Policeman halted them on one of the main streets. "Stop and take cover!" he yelled above the tumult of the bombardment. "The road is almost impassable further on!"

"Don't stop Bronek! Carry on!" Helena shouted.

They had not gone a couple of hundred yards when there was a blast of noise. Helena whipped around to look through the rear window. A bomb had exploded on the spot where the Policeman had stood. She was appalled to see the man's body torn to shreds -- *as ours would have been had we stopped,* her mind screamed.

Next to her Stefa was shaking uncontrollably. She had also looked through the rear window and would long hold the memory of the dismembered body, the arm flying high into the air with the debris. Helena pulled her head down onto her lap to shut out the horrors from her sight. She caught the look on Marian's face in the driving mirror. His eyes were wide with shock. "Don't look Marian," she pleaded. He did not hear her.

They reached the new block of apartments where Eva had stayed. It was razed almost to the ground. Holding Stefa more tightly to her, Helena tried to control the sobs that were chocking her.

They raced on, non-stop now until they came to Wieliczka. The streets were so quiet and empty after the holocaust in Krakow that for a moment it looked as though everyone had evacuated. After a moment Alex and Wanda came out to meet them.

"Thank God you're safe," Wanda breathed. "We heard of the raid on Bielsko. What happened?"

Helena told her. She also told them what they had seen in Krakow. Wanda put a plump arm around Helena's shoulders. "Your sister is all right darling. She came through here yesterday with your brother Henry."

"Where were they going? Why didn't they stay here for heaven's sake?"

"We asked them to but they insisted on going further east. They'll be fine, don't worry. Now come and have some supper, then off to bed with the lot of you. You all look done in."

"Marian, you've been eating liquorice again. Go wash your hands and face before you come to the table." She sent him off with a playful pat on the bottom, her eyes following him adoringly.

Wanda's normal behavior brought back some of the sanity that seemed to have deserted the world around them. Of all Adam's family, cousin Alex and his wife had always been the closest. Their own happiness and joy in living touched all who came to visit them and Helena could only remember happy moments under their roof. A middle-aged couple, they became Marian's slaves at the Baptismal Font. As his Godparents they claimed and spoilt him during all school holidays.

A dentist by profession, Alex had chosen to settle on this smallholding and attend practice twice a week in Krakow. Initially it was for his wife's sake that he had decided to buy property in Wieliczka, the village where she was born. It was the one thing he could give her to make up for his inability to give her a family. But it wasn't long before he too felt more content in his small consulting room at the back of the house than in the elaborate surgery that he and his partners had built up in the city.

Regardless of anyone's tastes or wishes, supper consisted of sour milk and mashed potatoes mixed with chopped fried bacon. It was a country dish peculiar to this region and Marian's favorite.

The girls were given the spare bedroom overlooking the orchard. As always the beds were freshly made, ready for the unexpected guest. Stefa was asleep the moment her head touched the pillow. Framed by a tousle of unplaited hair, her flushed little face betrayed the torture of fresh memories. Gently Helena tucked the eiderdown around her, forcing her own mind away from these memories.

She walked over to the window and pulled the curtains aside. Fifteen years had made little change to the scene before her. Except for its cloak of another season, the orchard looked the same. In the dusk she could see the old pear tree. Even that hadn't changed. It still looked productive and was still capable of evoking nostalgia.

She and Adam had found themselves in the same party of young hikers that summer, 15 years ago. She remembered thinking how much better he would look with some hair on his head. Later she learned that in his clique, a shaven head for the summer was the hallmark of a true sportsman.

She had been perfectly aware of her own good looks and popularity with the boys but having been told that girls played no part in his man's world, she was flattered by Adam's attentions. By the time they stopped over at Wieliczka and he had asked her up to the house to meet his cousin, she knew that he was as much drawn to her as she to him.

It was here in the orchard, under the pear tree, that he took her hand in his, and solemnly began to read her fortune. She remembered liking the way her small hand looked in that no-nonsense, square shaped palm. She remembered his deep frown of concentration and the words, "No doubt about it. This line shows a long and happy life ahead of you."

"Just a minute," she interrupted him, amused, wholly enchanted. "What qualifications do you have for fortune telling, anyway?"

"Don't ask silly questions and listen. I haven't finished. Do you see that intersection with the larger crease? Well, that means you will marry a fair and devastatingly handsome man. I see a name, yes, here it is, the man's name is Adam Polek." And he stopped her laugh with the first kiss.

The last part of his prediction had come true of course, for two years later they had come back here on their honeymoon.

And yes, it had been a happy life, if you didn't mind an unpredictable existence. If you didn't mind your husband being involved in all sorts of "sure fire" schemes and partnerships, running for local office, involving himself in politics. The success of his candidature for Mayor of Bielsko had been imminent, before Hitler's own plans intervened. But she would be lying if she said that Adam's preoccupations had been to the total neglect of her and the children, until recently that is.

She sat at the dressing table and automatically began to brush her hair. It bounced back, thick and glossy, cut into a shorter style than Adam liked. So where did the blame really lie, she asked herself. If there was to be blame attached to the discontent that had marked the last few months of their marriage. Knowing him, could she honestly have expected Adam, a man so addicted to patriotism, to ignore the growing demands his country had made upon him? And, to take the argument closer home, had she not shown a deplorable lack of interest in his activities? Activities which now proved to have been more than justified.

She gazed into the blue depth of her eyes without seeing them. Adam had been right, she was a selfish, spoilt bitch, she told herself evenly. It's not as if he went after other women as so many of his so-called friends did.

The pink satin nightgown that she pulled out of the suitcase seemed ridiculously out of place now. She put it on anyway, sat on the edge of the bed and went back to the first part of Adam's prophesy. A long life. A tremor went through her. Right now, longevity seemed such an unbelievably rash promise for anyone to make. Stefa stirred. Bending over her, Helena's throat tightened as she caught the words, "Daddy, don't go. I'm so scared Daddy."

*

CHAPTER TWO

"A Journey of horror"

Polish and German radio communiques deteriorated to a torrent of ever-contradicting facts. While Poland was sinking in a sea of devastation, the conscience of the outside world seemed mute. It seemed that all the treaties made with allied nations weren't worth the paper they were signed on. Towns and villages laid to waste, thousands killed. So great were the enemy forces that in the course of a few days they had attacked and penetrated all of Poland's northern and southwestern fronts, broken up her armies and were rapidly approaching Krakow. One armored brigade confronted by nine German Panzers -- twelve valiant Cavalry brigades pitching their horses against enemy tanks! On top of which the Germans had over fifteen hundred modern aircraft to support their armies on the battlefield. Poland never stood a chance.

On September 6th, the Polish radio station in Krakow made its last broadcast. Announcements were later resumed in German.

Krakow had fallen.

Alex got up heavily and switched off the set. "Time you folks got out of here. The Nazis will be in Wieliczka any moment."

"No," Helena told him. "Adam said I was to meet him here."

"No hope of him coming now, better get away Helena. With Adam's reputation with the Germans... They're sure to take it out on his family."

Marian agreed with him. Bronek too, nodded his agreement. Still she hesitated. Seeing her indecision, Wanda turned to Helena in her quiet firm way. "Well, come and help me get some food ready for the road."

"All right then," she decided. "But you two are coming with us."

"We'll be all right here," Alex said. "In any case my car's in Krakow and it would be too much of a crush if we all tried to fit into yours."

"Nonsense. We can all fit in. Stefa can take turns on our laps."

Helena would never forget that first part of the journey, in all its grim detail. Faithful horses still pulling their load... a cartful of dead peasants... a baby crying in the arms of a mother who would never again feed it... a missionary convoy with the bodies of Nuns and children sprawled halfway out of carriage windows, bullets spewing into the ones that tried to escape the burning coaches. There was no stopping to help these people. There were too many injured, too many dead and everyone's haste to escape from it all, too great.

Every so often, as they saw enemy planes approaching, Bronek drew the car to the side of the road and they took cover under the sheltering branches of the nearest trees. Almost against her will, Helena found herself looking up at the callous faces of the pilots as they swooped low, machine-gunning anyone in sight. She lost count of the number of times they had to scramble out of the car and run for the trees.

Then it happened. Alex and Wanda, always the last to reach cover were still running across the field when a volley of shells hurled them to the ground. And the bullets kept coming long after their riddled bodies had stopped jerking.

Helena pressed her face against the bark of the tree and fought against hysteria.

Later, in that awful silence that always followed the Stukas' departure she became aware of Marian's retching and Stefa's wails.

It was Bronek, white-faced and trembling, who drew them away and hurried them back to the car, giving the bloody scene as wide a berth as possible.

Helena took Stefa onto her lap, steeling herself to stay calm. "Now listen, crying won't bring them back," she said. "We've got to keep our wits about us or we'll all end up the same way. We must carry on as though they never came with us, you understand?"

Bronek turned to look at her. She didn't like the way she sounded either. But she also knew this was the only way to handle it.

Marian gulped hard a couple of times and nodded.

"That's my boy. Now come on Stefa. Look, even Lala's upset by your crying."

They both tried. She couldn't ask for more. It had hit Marian the hardest. She hated to see that strange bitter look on his young face.

A moment ago she had said crying wouldn't bring them back, now she had to tell herself that neither would remorse. If only she hadn't insisted on taking them along —

Stefa took out her rosary and began to tell the beads in a soft, broken undertone. Bronek drove on without a word, his knuckles showing white on the steering wheel.

The roads were a mess, with the Artillery, Infantry, Cavalry and Army supply columns all trying to push past hordes of refugees. Military Police halted them a number of times but upon producing the document that Adam had had the foresight to draw up, they were immediately allowed to move on. It was at the moment when they were caught in the middle of the road, blocked in by traffic, dead horses and shattered vehicles, that the untiring Luftwaffe chose to return to the attack, giving them no chance to seek cover.

"Drop to the floor!" Bronek shouted.

Planes roared back and forth above them. The noise was deafening, made worse by the unceasing rattle of machinegun fire. A bomb exploded close by, shaking the car as though it was made of cardboard. A neat row of bullets smashed the left rear window, indicating how low the aircraft were flying.

Helena felt the sweat break out all over her body. This time there could be no escape. The air that seeped in through the broken glass smelled of dust, freshly upturned soil and decay. Stefa's Hail Marys turned into a desperate incantation and the next few moments became a lifetime. Miraculously the roar of the planes grew softer, soon to drift to a distant whine.

Bronek raised his head. "Everyone all right?"

One by one they climbed back into their seats. Helena let out a shuddering sigh. "Thank God," she whispered. Apart from a few punctures in the bodywork and the broken window, they had come out of it unscathed. Bronek's face relaxed when the engine responded to the first touch of the starter. He pressed the hooter to get the car in front of them to move. The vehicle wouldn't budge, yet in the early dusk a form could clearly be seen sitting at the wheel. "Christ" Bronek groaned, getting out.

He was back almost at once, the stark look on his face showing quite plainly why the man behind the wheel was incapable of moving his car. He tried to reverse then, only to discover that the occupants of the car immediately behind had also been killed.

Bronek saw it as their second narrow escape. Now the odds were stacked against them, he thought as he climbed back into the Adler. Again he leaned on the hooter in an attempt to attract the attention of a passing Sanitary Squad. He had seen several along the way and each time had turned quickly away, unable to confront the load that they carried. A battered old truck equipped with a crane finally got to them and managed to move the obstructing vehicles out of their way.

Bronek turned on the fan and opened up the engine. As soon as the stench of death was behind them, Helena unpacked the sandwiches. Only Lala still had some appetite left. The couple of bites that Helena took shot straight back and she reached the window barely in time to save the upholstery. She sat back, mopping her brow, glad of the respite that came after a nausea attack. Temporary as the relief was, it was enough to give her the strength to carry on. She'd been sick four times since they left Wieliczka that morning.

"Good, it's getting dark," Bronek broke a long silence. "The bastards won't find their targets so easily now."

He decided to leave the main thoroughfare for the less congested country roads. Not daring to switch on the headlamps, he maneuvered along the potted, bumpy roads in semi-darkness.

Helena tried to ride the bumps but each jolt brought on another attack of nausea. When she couldn't hold it in any longer, she hung her head out of the window. Nerves and car sickness explained her condition to the others. She'd never been car sick in her life and she kept her growing suspicions and alarm to herself. The symptoms were the same as with both her other pregnancies. It was obvious by now that with or without allied aid, it would take a good deal longer than six weeks to defeat the new German power and the thought of going through another traumatic pregnancy in their present circumstances, made her groan aloud.

"Are you all right?" Bronek asked, using the accepted formal term "Pani" (Madame). He couldn't see her face but sensed the strain she was under. "Shouldn't we stop for a while?"

For no apparent reason Lala began to whine, resisting all Stefa's efforts to pacify her.

"She's afraid of something. I can tell. Hadn't we better go back?" Stefa said in a trembling voice.

Bronek's even temper snapped. "Try to keep that confounded dog quiet, will you?"

Lala answered him with a blood-curdling howl.

Helena picked the dog up, felt the peculiar rigidity of the little body and said, "Perhaps you had better stop Bronek. You know, animals are supposed to have some sort of sixth sense."

Reluctantly he jerked the car to a standstill, climbed out and began walking to check on the road ahead. A moment later and he was running back, obviously shaken. "Lala was right," he panted looking at her strangely. "The road ends in a precipice. In this light we would probably have gone clean over the bloody thing!"

"How did she know?" Marian's voice was filled with awe.

"Because dogs do have a sixth sense." Stefa told him. "Look, she's quite happy now that we've turned back."

An adjoining road finally led them to a small village and a Parish house.

The aged, half deaf Priest welcomed them in as one family. Waving aside Bronek's objections, he left them in a two-bedded guest room, with God's blessings.

Bronek reached for a blanket from one of the beds.

"Where are you going with that?" Helena asked him.

"The car. I can sleep there."

"Rubbish. This is no time to stand on ceremonies. Anyway, after all the driving you've done, you're in need of a bed more than any of us. You and Marian take the one and Stefa and I will share the other."

They undressed in the dark and climbed into bed in their underwear. Helena had packed pajamas for them all but no-one had thought to bring in the cases.

21

Her aching body wouldn't allow her to lie still. Her mind raced from one thought to another. She felt exhausted and over-stimulated all at the same time. "I feel like a drink." When was it she'd heard Adam say these words? It became important to remember. *Oh what the hell.* She turned over. *Nothing's important any more.* She saw the broken bodies of Alex and Wanda and blood everywhere. She sat bolt upright, eyes wide open, heart pounding. No! She mustn't let her mind wander, not to that. She made herself lie back quietly. Jasia had once told her of a cure for insomnia "Look at black, see nothing but black, turn all your pictures into black..."

When she woke up, the boys were already at the car, looking over the damage. An old man servant called them into the kitchen for breakfast. After quietly disposing of the scrambled eggs, dark brown bread and coffee into the outside toilet, Helena went to look for the Priest. She found him in the little garden, picking strawberries.

"They're not the best of crops," he said, "but they are sweet and will be good to eat on the road."

He walked with her to the car and when they said goodbye, he wished them a happy journey and blessed them with the sign of the cross.

"Bet he doesn't even know there's a war on," Marian whispered.

"Probably not," Bronek agreed. "Lucky man."

They had decided to make Buczacz their destination. It was as close to the eastern border as they could go and luckily, it was also the home of Adam's old friend, Teodor Gronski.

Dozens of abandoned cars along the road bore witness to the critical shortage of gas. Bronek had provided for this and most of their luggage space was taken up by odd tins of the precious stuff.

The further east they traveled, the less they saw of the Stukas, making it possible to keep to decent roads again with comparative safety. For the most part, they drove in that torpid state which comes with long hours of traveling. Occasionally Stefa followed Lala's example and dozed off, always to wake up with a frightened start.

Marian sat gazing absently out of the window, blind to the fields of lupines, yellow and sweet smelling, or the dense, harvest-ready corn fields, glistening golden in the sunshine. Momentarily animated by a passing troop of soldiers, he'd look closely, hoping to see his father's face among them, then sink back into his seat, more discouraged than ever, his thoughts straying to Wanda and Alex. After the grief had come a wild fury that rocked him, that made his ears sing and blinded his vision. He had never experienced anything like it before. Somehow, he managed to control it inside himself but his knuckles were still bruised from his grinding teeth. He had come out of it spent and depressed. Useless. He was useless, sitting here running away from the fight. It would have been better to have fallen in battle like a man. After all, he wasn't a child any more. He was almost thirteen.

Absorbed in his own thoughts, Bronek's long profile seemed etched in even sharper lines. He looked worn out. For the first time in three years Helena was getting to know him. Adam had engaged him, paid his wages, saw to his welfare. She had merely used his services. Admittedly, he had never been very communicative and when not working would bury himself in his books. Adam had mentioned what he was studying for but it hadn't registered. Quite often she used to hear Jasia chatting away to him as he worked in the garden, his monosyllabic responses trying the woman's patience to the point where she would stamp back into the house, muttering something about still waters running deep.

"How old are you, Bronek?" Helena asked him. "Twenty-six."

"I thought you were older. Tell me, why haven't you been conscripted?"

He gave her a rueful smile. "Didn't you know? I failed the medical. They don't need bad hearts in the Army."

Of course she should have known. She murmured her regrets, remembering that Adam had told her about some kind of treatment Bronek was undergoing. The extent of her selfish unawareness of others made her squirm. She studied him covertly and decided to leave the question of his education for another time.

Despite the difference in their ages, Marian and Bronek had become good friends. Anxiety over the car provided a common bond, as did the plotting of their itinerary. Marian's sense of direction had always been extraordinary and he had a knack for taking the right short-cuts. A decision had to be made whether to take a longer but better road to the next town or a shorter, rougher one. Swayed by Helena's state of health, Bronek insisted on the longer route.

"Damn," he swore. "We're over-heating. And we're right out of water. Marian, check how far to the next village."

"Don't have to. There it is on our left. I can see the Church from here."

As they turned into the dirt road leading to the village, Marian also spotted the first enemy planes they'd seen in several hours.

There seemed nothing in that scattering of poor cottages, nestling against a windbreak of poplars, that could possibly warrant wasting a bomb on, yet one of the planes was obviously intent on making it a target and the villagers hared for the sanctuary of their little Church. Bronek stopped outside this, the only brick building and they found themselves being bundled inside with the others by a young Priest.

Above the whistle of the bombs and the din of explosions, the deep, steady voice of the Priest continued, pausing at intervals for the congregation to rumble the words after him. This was no conventional recitation but the most positive and inspired prayer Helena had ever heard. She looked down at Stefa. Her eyes were closed in prayer but her face was calm, as if she knew that no harm could befall them in the house of God. As she held her closer, Helena felt her warmth and realized she was drawing strength from the child.

When the world outside returned to normal, or as normal as it would ever again be for these people, they began to leave. Helena wondered at the total absence of panic. Solemn-faced they walked out of the Church with dignity, the men holding their hats or caps in both hands, their women behind them, scarfed heads bowed, children clinging to their hands or to the folds of ankle-length skirts. The Priest stayed on his knees, head and shoulders bent low as though all the strength had been sapped out of him.

Helena pulled Stefa to her side and they followed the silent crowd. As they went through the doors she stopped, aghast at the scene of total devastation before her. Not a single cottage had escaped the effects of the incendiary bomb that leaves nothing but rubble and ashes in its wake. Incredibly, the Church alone remained intact. Behind every miracle she believed there must be the power of faith or positive thought or call it what you will. Whatever it was, it had been there for the Priest and his flock and it had communicated itself to Stefa. She turned to the woman standing next to her.

"What will you do?"

The woman shrugged. "We have relatives in the next village. They'll help us put our houses up again."

Sheltered within the inviolate field of the Church, the Adler sustained negligible damages. Bronek studied the one or two extra scratches in the bodywork, a dent on the roof and thought, *third time lucky.* He filled up with water and, still dazed they drove off.

Helena's impressions of the next few days became vague. At times she was too tired and too ill to care what happened or where they slept. She only knew that every night found them with a roof over their heads. Bronek had been aware of her predicament for some time and drove more carefully, going round bad patches in the road, stopping as soon as visibility became poor and delicately avoided the subject of her nausea.

It was late afternoon when they drove into Buczacz. It had been years since Helena had visited this uninspiring city, with its depressing architecture and narrow streets. Nor had she seen anything of Mr. Gronski since that time. Nevertheless, when they turned up at his door, his welcome was as warm as ever. She had almost forgotten how very large he was and being aware of his predilection for red wine, was not surprised to see that his complexion had become even ruddier and that a persistent twitch had developed over his right eye. A veterinary Surgeon of (according to Adam) exceptional skill, he lived alone in his double-storey house with only an ancient peasant woman to do the chores and Jacek Kowal to look after him and the garden.

"So!" He boomed. "It's taken a bloody war to bring you back on a visit." He kissed Helena's hand then reached out and gave her a hug. He stepped back to look at Marian with sheer delight. "Jesus the boy's grown."

Marian returned the man's handshake with equal spirit.

Stefa politely showed no outward signs of alarm when this bear of a man picked her up. "And this, I take it, is the new addition to the family."

"Not so new any more, as you can see," Helena laughed.

"Fine looking child. Image of her father, eh?" He put her down with surprising gentleness and in his blunt way gestured towards Bronek. "And who's this?"

"This is the man responsible for bringing us here in one piece," Helena said, introducing them.

"In that case you are more than welcome young fellow."

"There's plenty of room and beds for all, but don't know about sheets and stuff. Browse around Helena and see what you can find will you? Get old Magda to give you a hand. Time she did some honest work for her keep. If you're short of anything, go and buy it. Here, this should cover anything you might need," and refusing to hear her protests, he pushed a wad of notes into her hand.

"Strange man," Bronek remarked when their host left them. "Wait till you see him at dinner. If he has dinner with us, that is."

"Why Mom?" Marian wanted to know.

"You'll see," was all they could get out of her.

Teodor Gronski did join the party for supper that evening, armed with two bottles of red wine. Having witnessed the man's formidable capacity for food, Helena was interested to see the reaction this feat would have on the others.

Unaware of the sensation he was creating, their host stripped a whole, large chicken clean of meat and then proceeded to gnaw at the bones, crunching them in his teeth and chewing them up as though they were pieces of crackling. Marian was clearly impressed. It reminded him of the stone-age models he had seen at the Museum. Bronek had his reservations. Sensitive by nature, Gronski's gross behavior made him feel uncomfortable. Apart from that, he judged the older man to be in his forties and wondered how long his teeth could take that kind of treatment.

Gronski noticed Helena was picking half-heartedly at the food and at once became solicitous. "What's the matter Helena? Aren't you well?"

"I think I'm too tired to eat right now."

He nodded. "A good sleep will fix you up. Have some wine then."

When she convinced him that she couldn't possibly, he pushed the bottle towards Bronek. "Come on young fellow, drink up. First class insurance against all ills this!" And he threw back his head and laughed. Bronek needed no encouragement and soon a glow began to spread across his cheeks.

Their host emptied what was left of the second bottle into his glass. The meal over, he got heavily to his feet and bade everyone a curt goodnight.

At other times he was urbane and eloquent, making them forget for a while what had brought them to his home. Often he spoke of Adam, treating his guests to amusing, at times exciting anecdotes of the time when they had fought together against the Bolsheviks. Barely out of his teens himself, he had taken Adam under his wing during the Poles' struggle for independence at the end of World War I.

"Now *there* was a true Eaglet of Lwow," he chuckled. "If I remember correctly, he was recruited by the Legionnaires on the strength of falsified documents. He had not only added a couple of years to his age but had also produced his mother's 'signed' permission for him to join up." He shook his head at the memory. "Too small to have a uniform fit him but big enough to hold a rifle."

"Did he shoot a lot of Russians?" Marian asked eagerly.

Gronski laughed. "Don't know if he shot any. Mostly he was our runner. Don't look so disappointed Marian. Your father was the bravest young lad I ever came across. It takes guts to run messages on the front line, you know." He lit a cigarette and settled back in his chair.

"One morning," he went on, "we found him nearly frozen to death. He had discovered the body of one of the Sentries, so he takes up the gun and stands sentry for the rest of the night. Poor kid nearly lost his toes, they were so badly frostbitten. You see, there were no boots to fit him either."

For all his eccentricity, Helena couldn't help but like the man. She was touched by his attachment to Adam and she was grateful for the moments of peace his hospitality afforded. It was the disturbing news brought by the increasing number of defeated Polish troops that reminded her that the war was anything but over. To hold up the overwhelming predominance of the enemy as long as possible, the various armies went on fighting independently. The young Polish Navy was holding out valiantly in the Baltic. Warsaw was performing one of the most renowned feats of heroism in the history of Europe. The capital refused to surrender and fighting continued while day after day a rain of shells and bombs spread devastation through the city.

The soldiers that came into Buczacz had been crushed by incalculable odds. They were worn out, some wounded. There were those with no more fight left in them, whose only thought was of escape over the borders into Rumania. Then there were Adam's type of men who desperately tried to form a new Army and return to the attack. Helena knew them only too well. Men who don't know the meaning of surrender, who fight to the limit of endurance and beyond and who are awarded their medals posthumously. And it was this knowledge, coupled with her own weakening condition, that strained her own powers of endurance and kept her awake in the lonely hours of the night.

At times Bronek would come in to keep her company or to read to her from their host's large collection of literature. She discovered that Bronek had been studying for his Bachelor's Degree and his love of the Polish language was nothing short of reverence. It worried her to see him looking pale and thinner than ever, but he insisted that there was nothing wrong with him, nor would he be persuaded to make a bid for the border. Often she caught him looking at her intently and instinctively avoided the eye contact.

The vomiting continued, confining her largely to the house. On her brighter days Helena did whatever she could to make the place a little more comfortable. She got Magda to bring feathers and made up cushions for the hard, wooden chairs. She brightened the huge, cold sitting room with flowers from the garden. Honest, practical Magda lacked the so-called finer touches. She fed them mostly on a concoction of cabbage and potatoes with chunks of bacon or sausage thrown in. When she felt up to it, Helena prepared the meals, to the delight of everyone it seemed, except Gronski. He didn't appear to notice what was put in front of him. Quite frequently he would not turn up for meals at all.

The days, colder now, dragged on. A great number of new civilian refugees poured into the town from the west, all with the same tragic news of defeat. What of the Anglo-Polish treaty of alliance so recently entered into? What of France's promised support? There was no reliable source of information but worst still, not the slightest hint of hope.

On the evening of the 17th of September, news broke out that the Russians were moving into Poland. Most of the Poles believed that they were coming to help them fight the Germans, but there were those who maintained that their entry was in keeping with the Molotov-Ribbentrop pact. A pact shrewdly connived by Germany, whereby a demarcation line had been drawn for the partition of Poland. They would keep western Poland and Russia could have the territories east of the River San.

Early the next day the Bolsheviks entered Buczacz.

Women who ran out to welcome their "Liberators" with flowers, dropped their offerings and fled behind doors -- children cried as their parents pulled them roughly off the streets. For the tanks that crawled through the city menacingly pointed gun nozzles this way and that. These were followed by the ferocious looking Cavalry, commanding instant obedience of their mounts with brutal short reins. Then came the Infantry in their ill-fitting uniforms; stocky bodies that would have looked more dignified behind a plough. Even so, they held their carbines ready for action. And so the inexorable procession continued, leaving no one in any doubt as to their intentions.

*

CHAPTER THREE

"A dubious refuge"

The small Infantry unit stationed in Buczacz, maintained an uneasy truce with the local population. Broad faces reflecting all the curiosity and suspicion but little of the friendliness of their race, they strode the streets in awe of the imagined opulence around them.

As soon as it became evident that the Russians presented no real danger to the public, the people began to move freely among them on the streets and even to engage them in conversation. But before they stopped to speak to anyone, the soldiers made sure they weren't being spied upon and as soon as any of their colleagues joined the group, they began to praise all that Russia stood for, with exaggerated emphasis on the glorious might of Stalin and the Peoples Party.

It was clearly a source of wonder to them that people could buy an unlimited amount of goods. Some asked if the articles had come from America. Within a few days they had either confiscated or bought up most of the stocks in the larger stores with their worthless Rubles. They showed a child-like delight in brightly colored silks and high-heeled shoes, but their greatest joy was to adorn themselves with timepieces of all shapes and sizes.

The soldier that walked past Helena proudly sported an alarm clock on the front of his tunic. She could have spared herself the trouble of controlling her face and the laughter that bubbled in her throat. The man didn't as much as look her way. He was wholly captivated by the ring of the alarm which had at that moment gone off. She was wondering how a simple man like that could possibly emulate these people's reputation for brutality, when her attention was caught by the sound of an angry Russian voice inside a jewelers shop. She stopped to listen. The similarity between the Polish and Russian spoken language made it possible for her to make out the gist of what was going on. Through the open door she could see the soldier grab the little shopkeeper by his lapels.

"You whoring son-of-a-bitch! What do you mean by selling me a watch that isn't working."

"Please let me have a look at it and I'll see if I can fix it."

The Russian let go of the poor man and grudgingly handed over his novel possession. It didn't take the man long to discover that the watch had not been wound. Without embarrassment or apology, the soldier snatched the "repaired" watch out of the shopkeeper's hand. He held it to his ear, smiled to himself with satisfaction and strode out.

The little man caught her eye. "And those are our new rulers?" was all he said.

Within a week the Security Police moved in, with the inevitable hammer and sickle on the sleeves of their civilian suits, rifles slung across their shoulders by bits of string. They set up an organized Depot where every citizen had to report with his credentials. At the same time they began to search private homes officially looking for firearms, yet in the wake of such visits, leading members of the community -- doctors, lawyers and professors disappeared without a trace. Everyone knew that they could only have been deported to Siberia, as slave labor.

Owners of private cars were questioned at length, before their vehicles were confiscated. Bronek had had the presence of mind to leave the Adler on a deserted strip of road some distance from the house. Within hours of the invasion the car had disappeared.

Meanwhile, all refugees from the western parts of Poland were asked to call in at the Magistrate's Offices. A census was being conducted to "gather data for administrative purposes". A neat phrase for what turned out to be a cross-examination by the dreaded Soviet Secret Police, better known as the N.K.V.D. Once they had your name down, your fate rested in the careless hands of some official whose actions depended largely upon his mood at the time. If you were unfortunate enough to become classified as a reactionary suspect, accused of spying against the

Union of Socialist Soviet Republics, you were lost. A favorite tactic was to wrench children from their parents and toss them into separate cattle trains. It would be weeks before they reached their destinations -- some labor camp in the vast, ice-packed reaches of Siberia.

The methods employed by the N.K.V.D. in their interrogations had become common knowledge. Their demon-inspired devices varied only in degrees of bestiality.

Her turn would inevitably come. Helena knew that and she was determined not to subject herself to such an interrogation. She thought of leaving Buczacz but knew she would not have the strength for it. Why in heavens name did she allow herself to fall pregnant? She, who had always said she didn't want more than two children.

She stood up to help Magda clear the table.

"You didn't finish your dinner again," Magda told her. "Times like these you've got to keep your strength up."

"Yes I know. I'll have it tomorrow. Teodor, do you think you could get hold of some old clothes for us?"

He nodded, reading her mind. "Good idea."

"What do you want old clothes for?" Marian wanted to know.

"Well, judging by their own appearance, I imagine the Russians would be more in sympathy with the under-privileged." She thought of Marian's fine wool jacket, Stefa's angora sweater, her own fashionable three-piece suit and silk blouse. "The stuff I brought with us might well classify us as despicable bourgeois, if not rotten capitalists."

Later that evening, Gronski produced three worn coats as well as a couple of head scarves.

Bronek had already discarded his city clothes for a loose fitting peasant shirt and baggy pants. He'd also cultivated a permanent three-day stubble. But no amount of camouflage could hide the refined features or the "City Aura" as Gronski put it. So much so that he was adamant the younger man should not show himself in town.

Now that Helena felt a little safer to move about the town again, it was becoming increasingly more difficult for her to leave the house. Morning sickness stretched to spasmodic bouts of vomiting throughout the day, until the afternoon when Magda found her stretched out in a swoon in the bathroom.

"Have you seen a Doctor?" Were the old woman's first words when she brought her to. Helena shook her head, too spent to speak. "Then I'm going to fetch one right away," she snapped, helping her into bed. "Not that it needs a Doctor to see you've just had a miscarriage," she added. She gave Helena a knowing look. "Did you do something?"

"No, I didn't."

Helena lay staring at the ceiling, hands clasped tightly together across her chest. Her body was shivering under the warm eiderdown. She was trying to understand the emotional turmoil that was gripping her. The embryo couldn't have been more than a few weeks old, she reasoned. *But it was my baby and I didn't want it. I didn't want it!*

Her senses dulled with anguish and as the mother's instinct and the guilt took over, she gave way to racking sobs. "There's nothing bad that doesn't turn out for the best." She looked up, half expecting to see her mother standing there, saying the words that she used to say. Yes, this was for the best, not only for herself but for Marian and Stefa. As she concentrated on that thought, she began to feel herself calming down and by the time the knock came on the door, she had managed to dry her eyes.

In spite of his workman's overalls and grimy, bearded face, Helena recognized the Doctor as one of the few friends Teodor Gronski had brought to the house.

He examined her briefly and confirmed Magda's diagnosis with a frown. "Why didn't you tell me about this before?"

She shrugged. "Had you been a quack I might have."

"There are times when even the most scrupulous doctor will see fit to take the law into his own hands, you know."

"Oh well, nature provided the solution, thank heavens," she said tiredly. He felt her pulse. "And none too soon either. You're in a deplorable condition. "

"That's what I told her. She's been sick ever since she came here and wouldn't say anything about it," Magda put in.

Why can't they leave me alone? Her mind screamed. *All I want is some sleep and they keep harping at me.* She closed her eyes but couldn't hide the tears that seeped through.

"Magda, I want you to come with me and see that Mrs. Polek takes the tonic I'm going to give her. Keep her in bed for a few days and for the love of God try to feed the poor woman on something better than cabbage and potatoes."

The old woman's respect for the Doctor didn't prevent her from muttering that there was nothing wrong with cabbage and potatoes. She'd been brought up on it and had never known a day's illness.

To her credit, Magda did do her best to vary the diet. Three days under her able care and Helena felt like a new person.

Shopping in town became an ordeal. Robbed and abused by the Russian troops, the shopkeepers tried to make up their losses on the local customers.

Helena hated to haggle over each purchase but neither could she afford not to. She and the children were on their way home from the worst wrangling match yet and Marian hadn't stopped complaining. "I wouldn't mind if you could at least eat the beastly apples, but all that fuss over cooking apples, huh!"

"But you'll eat them anyway," Stefa pointed out.

"Yes, but..."

"Shsh," Helena put her hand up to listen. From the school building across the road came muted calls. Looking up they saw a sea of hands, some waving, some stretched out in supplication.

"Mother of God those are our Airforce prisoners," Helena cried. "They must be starving!"

Without thinking, she waved back, intimating that help was on the way. "Quick Marian, fetch some rope from the house."

He was back in moments. They tied one end of the rope to the handle of the basket of groceries, while Marian threw the other end up as high as he could towards the prisoners.

Eager fingers caught the rope and Marian was about to heave the basket up when the Guard appeared.

"What the devil do you think you're doing!" He pushed Marian roughly aside and strode towards Helena.

The soldier's menacing demeanor was too much for Stefa. She burst into tears. Incredibly, the man turned to her and patted her on the head. "Don't cry little one," he soothed. "Here, *you* can send the basket up if you like."

Helena learned that the man also had a little girl, somewhere outside Minsk. He was a simple farmer, drafted into the Red Army without warning and, from what she could make out, wanted nothing more than to be allowed to return to his farm, his daughter and the wife who waited and kept the top of the stove warm for him.

The rest of the prisoners of war were held in the Market Square in the open, sitting or lying on the ground, hands tied, faces pinched with cold and hunger. No provision was made for the wounded, nor were they afforded special consideration.

Civilians were forbidden to get too close to the prisoners but Marian always managed to get near enough to see that his father was not amongst any of the newcomers. He had been going to the Square every day since the first batch of prisoners were brought in and with each passing day he had become more moody and depressed.

"I just don't know what to do about him," Helena confided in Bronek. It had been a rotten day for her. Tired from lack of sleep, she couldn't shake off the feeling of impending danger. And Marian's attitude made her all the more aware of her impotency to deal with it all.

He moved away from his habitual post at the window and sank into the cushion she'd just finished for the last of the club chairs. "He'll come right don't worry. The kid's going through a rough time you know."

"Yes I know, but aren't we all?" She shook her head. "I've never seen him like this Bronek. Remember how good mannered he always was, how easygoing. He's even started to bite his nails again," she wailed.

"It's worse for him I think" Bronek said. "All this has probably accelerated his growing pains. Mentally, I mean."

They looked up as Marian walked into the sitting room, his blonde hair tousled, his face sullen. He threw his cap onto the table. "What's for supper?"

"Marian, I wish you wouldn't behave like a thug," her gentle voice took him by surprise.

"Oh, sorry," he murmured. Picking up the cap he headed for the hallway.

"How about a quick game of chess before supper?" Bronek called after him.

Marian stuck his head around the door. "What've you got to bet on?"

"Half the pudding?"

"You're on!"

Helena wished women could take their minds off their troubles as easily as that. Thoughts of the massacre of the Polish Cavalry had been haunting her; the N.K.V.D. kept haunting her. There wasn't a day without fear or a night that wasn't broken with sleeplessness or unimaginable nightmares.

Automatically she went on folding scraps of left-over material into neat squares. How would it all end?

"I prefer your hands without the varnish," Bronek interrupted her thoughts. "They look more -- elegant."

"My dear Bronek, one *puts on nail* varnish to look more elegant," she said, taking a quick look at her fingers, secretly pleased with the compliment. But the mood didn't last and her thoughts went back to the problem of staying in Buczacz. One of these nights there would come the tarpaulin-covered truck, the loud hammering on the door and they would be marched out before prodding bayonets, just as they stood, with no time to pack a thing. Worse still, they might be separated. She shuddered as she thought of it.

"You all right?" Bronek asked, studying her, concerned by her pallor and the dark rings under her eyes.

"Yes, yes I'm fine. I was just thinking it might be better to take a chance on getting back home."

During her childhood, western Poland had still been annexed to the Austrian Empire. Independence came only after the First World War. As a senior official with the Bielsko Municipality, her father had been virtually obliged to send his children to a German-speaking school and it was not until she had reached her fourth grade in high school that she was enrolled into a Polish College. She hoped her fluency in German might now stand her in good stead.

"It's been on my mind too," Bronek said. "I think we should talk to Gronski about it tonight."

"Yes. He's been living on borrowed time too. In fact I can't understand why he hasn't left yet." She looked up at him. "The children will miss you Bronek. So will I." "What do you mean? I'm coming with you."

"No Bronek. I couldn't drag you all the way back there. You wouldn't stand a chance with the Germans. From here you can at least try to get into Rumania."

"And what chance will you have, all on your own?"

"Better really, I think. But let's discuss this with Teodor later." She stood up, smiling at him, curiously unsettled. "Now I must go and make that pudding you so glibly bet Marian on. It'll be custard again so I'm sure you won't mind losing."

It seemed that Teodor Gronski had finally reached the same decision as Helena. The time had come to flee. That same evening he produced a bottle of "Sliwowica" (plum brandy) from his cellar and called a meeting immediately after supper.

"Tonight I must leave Buczacz," he began. "Things are getting a bit hot for me here." His eyelid twitched violently for a moment. With an impatient gesture he drew his forefinger over the offending eye and continued, rubbing at it absently as he talked. "I'm joining a group of Polish soldiers in the forest."

"What soldiers?" Marian shot out. "I didn't know we had any free soldiers."

Gronski broke into a beautific smile. "They're ex-prisoners of war, actually. We're going to attempt crossing the Carpathians into Rumania. My advice to you Helena, is to take the children and return home. Your German should be of help."

"Yes, I've already decided to do that."

"And I'm escorting them back," Bronek put in firmly.

"No you're not. Look, it's not that I don't appreciate your concern because I think it's the most unselfish, the most selfless..." she stopped to regain composure, shaking her head helplessly. "But I've already told you Bronek, I honestly think we'll be safer on our own. The Russians won't pay all that much attention to a woman and two children."

"That's as I see it," Gronski nodded agreement. "Now listen, here's my plan. Jacek is leaving for his village tomorrow morning by cart. I've already spoken to him about you and he's willing to take you along with him providing you travel as his family." He turned to Bronek. "And you, young fellow, you're coming with me. I need you." There was a finality to his tone that no one could argue against.

He walked over to the sideboard from which he took out a linen blouse, a brightly printed shawl and a full, almost ankle-length skirt for Helena and a similar outfit for Stefa. For Marian there were boots and a scarf. He dumped the clothes into Helena's lap with a wry smile. "You ought to make a pretty convincing peasant family in these."

She looked up at him with gratitude, touched that he should have worried about them when he himself had been walking a tightrope. So that's what kept him away from the house all those nights -- the ex P.O.Ws.

Delighted with her new clothes, Stefa wrapped the shawl about her shoulders and went into a pirouette.

"Splendid!" Gronski applauded. "A proper little milkmaid if ever I saw one."

He refilled the three glasses and held his high. *"Na Zdrowie* or should I say, here's to the damnation of our enemies!"

They all drank to that.

"Well Helena, I'll say au revoir. Perhaps we'll meet again when all this is over. You'd better get some sleep now. Jacek will be calling for you at four in the morning."

He lifted Stefa up. This time she hugged him in return. Next he turned to Marian and had him almost staggering under a volley of affectionate back thumps. Then he took both Helena's hands in his huge fists and raised them to his lips. "God's speed," he said, leaving abruptly.

Unable to sleep, Helena had left the curtains open and was lying propped up in bed looking into the moonlight. It must have been about midnight when he knocked gently and walked in. She had been expecting him and her heart gave a lurch. He held her gaze while he sat on the bed and took her hand.

"Helena, I can't leave you," he got out, pressing her hand to his lips.

"I know Bronek," she whispered. "But you must."

"You don't understand. I've never loved a woman before." He threw his arms about her and buried his face in her hair. Involuntarily she patted his back. He drew back, gripping her shoulders hard.

"I'm not a boy, Helena. I'm a man -- the only man you now have to take care of you and the kids and can't you see? I want more than anything to *be* your man!"

As his mouth pressed against her lips, parting them, she felt the response stir inside her. For a brief moment she held him then pulled away.

"No Bronek. This is madness!"

"No my love, this isn't madness. This war's the only madness. We must live and love while we can."

He reached out to kiss her again but she held him off.

"I can't. Not as long as there's a chance that Adam is alive."

"Jesus, what chance do you think..." She put a trembling hand against his lips. "Don't. Please."

"Forgive me." He took her hand and kissed it. "You do care for me though. Admit it Helena."

"Yes of course I care for you. I've grown very, very fond of you Bronek. You've been a wonderful friend and companion. But don't you see? I can't allow it to go any further. We'd both regret it."

"Never!"

"Listen to me Bronek. We've been through a lot together. We've lived more closely than most. We've shared fears and dangers. Life and death. All this can draw people together in, in a kind of desperate passion to the exclusion of everyone and everything else."

His face tightened. "I'm sorry you see it like that. I'm afraid I can't get so analytical about it."

"I didn't mean to belittle your feelings. You're too dear to me for me to hurt you. I was only trying to put things in their right perspective. And there's no doubt at all in my mind that your best chance of survival is to go with Teodor. And our best chance is to make it alone."

He regarded her with a deep tender sadness, the gray eyes almost black in their intensity. After a while he said, "If that's what you really want, there's nothing I can do is there? I just want you to know Helena, that whatever happens I'll always love you."

He stood up then, bent to kiss the top of her head and murmured, "Thank you."

She saw the door close behind him through a blur. He had nothing to thank her for.

...

Jacek's stocky form was barely distinguishable in the half light as he bent down to help them onto the cart, pulling Marian up beside him on the driver's seat. Wordlessly they drove off.

Lala lay curled up against Stefa. The dog was strangely subdued, showing none of the usual excitement at the prospect of a trip. Helena stared at her uneasily. What sixth sense was guiding her now? They'd never before had to drag Lala from under a couch to make her come with them.

*

CHAPTER FOUR

"Under the Communist yoke"

A chill wind sprung up bringing with it a light drizzle.

"There's a rug at the back of the seat," Jacek called out over his shoulder. Helena wrapped it around the already shivering Stefa and tucked her long skirt closer about her own legs. Their threadbare coats were no proof against this kind of weather. Her heart went out to the man when she saw him share his mackintosh with Marian.

The moment they left town Jacek pushed his horse to a fast trot, taking rough, circuitous roads that sometimes narrowed to nothing more than tracks. Soon Helena felt as though every bone in her body had been shaken loose. It hadn't occurred to anyone to cover the rough planks they had to sit on.

With the first rays of light she was able to distinguish Jacek's craggy profile. He was a man in his thirties, muscular and stolid looking, his back already stooped from long hours of work in the fields. Sensing her eyes on him he turned and smiled, his cheeks crinkling into a mass of corrugations.

"We'll stop over at Jazlowiec," he said. "My elder brother will put us up there for a while and you can rest. He's a well-read man," he added as an afterthought.

By late morning the sun fought a losing battle and the gathering clouds took away what little warmth there was to the bleak countryside. Helena gazed absently at the passing fields. A broken-down car reminded her of their lost Adler. Adam had been so proud to drive it home, spanking new. He even tried to teach her to drive. She could now think of that fiasco without resenting his impatience with her. But at the time she swore she'd never touch the bloody thing again. That's when he employed Bronek. Poor Bronek. She let her mind drift. Her heart leapt at the thought of last night, of her almost overwhelming desire to be loved, to belong. The blood rushed to her face when she thought of Adam. One thing is certain, she decided, she couldn't tell him about this. He'd never understand.

She looked up. Marian was watching her. "What's wrong Mom? You look so worried."

"Do I? No, it's nothing. We'll be all right."

He nodded and turned his attention back to the big gray. He loved the strength behind the rippling muscles. No comparison to Dad's chestnut of course, but a fine farm horse nevertheless. Maybe Jacek will let him have a turn at the reins.

Stefa was curled up on the seat, her head pillowed on her mother's lap.

The road seemed smoother. The cart groaned out a steady rhythm. Helena closed her eyes.

When she woke they were turning into the driveway of a large farm and Jacek was saying, "We're here."

Stepping down from the cart Helena looked up into the brightest of blue eyes shaded by bushy white eyebrows. A hand was thrust out to her and she felt a firm grip.

"And who might your company be Jacek?" The elder Kowal asked.

After the introductions he said simply, "You are welcome." He then took Stefa's hand and led them towards the house. In the doorway stood a little woman, as round and wholesome looking as a rye loaf.

"My wife," said the man, as though immensely proud of the fact.

Helena was fascinated by these people's economy of words which somehow didn't detract from an attitude of sincere friendliness. The little woman called her daughter-in-law to look after them while she went to prepare a late lunch.

Twenty-year old Zofia was a typical Ukrainian country girl, sturdy, rosy-cheeked and brimming with good humor and pregnancy. She had been married less than a year when the war took her young husband away but, blessed with the faith and acceptance of the inevitable so characteristic of her people, she had no doubt that God would sort everything out in the end.

The farmhouse, a rambling red-bricked affair, had the usual loft accessible by means of a ladder. There was a cellar and a large all-purpose kitchen where the family evidently gathered to eat as well as to relax in. At night, and during the cold season, the kitchen also served as sleeping quarters for the old couple. In addition, there were two extra rooms, one was Zofia's and the other was made available for the guests. The warehouse, laundry and toilet were outside as was the pump which supplied water to the house.

The meal that the old lady prepared for them was simple and would have tasted as good even if they had not been as hungry. There was real pleasure in her face as she watched Marian scoop up the last of the meat sauce with his bread. Helena said nothing about his lack of table manners.

After they had eaten, Zofia went out to fetch water. Marian saw her lightly carrying the two great wooden buckets filled to the brim and ran out to give her a hand. She passed them both over to him. He staggered and nearly dropped them, the expression of bewilderment on his face sending the girl into shrieks of laughter.

"Eh Marian, you'd better give them back," she giggled.

He clenched his teeth, flexed his muscles and marched on.

"Good lad you have there," Kowal remarked, watching him through the open door.

"Yes," Helena agreed but what she didn't tell him was that she would have been truly surprised to hear him say this only a short month before. She smiled, remembering how cleverly Marian used to avoid any type of work and school work in particular. *The war's changed us both.*

Jacek spent the rest of the day on repairs to the cart. Two wheel spokes had cracked and were on the point of falling out. This meant fashioning new ones by hand and fitting them on. When six o'clock came and Jacek was still not too happy about the job, Mr. Kowal insisted that they stay the night and start off first thing in the morning.

"That would be best," Jacek agreed. "My village is quite a long way from here and I wouldn't want anything to go wrong with the cart while we're on the road."

Helena had been told that his village lay somewhere near Monasterzyska and wondered how they would carry on from there. Poland suddenly seemed a very large country and she would have given anything to have her car back.

Marian brought in their suitcase and Zofia came to sit on Helena's bed while she unpacked their few belongings.

"Ooh! I've never seen the likes of them," she breathed, pointing to the lace-edged knickers. Sensually she ran the silk across her cheeks. "But I think you'd better hide your things. You never know, the Russians might just drop in and that'll be the last you'll see of them, the pants I mean."

Helena took what later proved to be good advice by hiding their clothes under the mattress.

It had been an exhausting journey and they couldn't wait to get between the clean white sheets. Helena and Stefa shared a wide, soft bed. Marian barely noticed the hardness of his wooden cot. He hadn't slept since long before dawn and he drifted off almost immediately.

It was Stefa who lay awake, troubled by the fact that Mother Mary hadn't yet come to tell her that Daddy was alive. She knew he was, of course, but she needed reassurance. She looked towards the wall next to the bed on which hung a vividly colorful picture of the Virgin Mary. She could not see it now but knew exactly where it was on the wall. *If you keep him safe dear God and dear Holy Mary, I promise to say my prayers every single night for the rest of my life,* she bargained earnestly. She curled up into the fetal position, feeling the warmth of her mother's body against her back. She knew God would answer her prayers. Hadn't He made Mom better?

Towards one in the morning Helena woke up to the sound of loud voices and the stamping of boots. She listened, her heart thumping. She could make nothing of it but was immediately alert to the danger. She was already out of bed and getting dressed when she realized that all was quiet again except for the sound of a truck driving off. She sank onto the bed. *Does anyone ever get used to this sort of thing* she wondered, hating the weakness that had overcome her body.

"Is it all right Mommy?" Stefa whispered.

"Yes love. Go back to sleep."

No mention was made of the night's disturbance until after breakfast. Kowal finished his second cup of coffee and said, "The Russians were here last night. Wanted to know who the strange cart belonged to. I told them my old sister had come to stay with us."

"What happened to Jacek?" Helena asked, worried that there had been no sign of him that morning.

"We managed to get him away. You see, all our younger men are... removed." He paused to light a pipe, regarding her gravely. "I know you want to get back to your home Mrs. Polek, but now Jacek isn't here to take you. They'll come again and if they find my "sister" isn't here, God knows what they'll do."

"Yes of course. We can stay as long as you think it's necessary but I don't want us to be a burden on you..."

"Please --" he held up his hand.

"No, I'm serious," she went on. "I know there's always work on a farm, especially now with your labor shortage. You must let us do something to earn our keep."

He smiled. "Don't you worry, we'll find a job for you. Just one thing though. A fine looking woman like you isn't safe out in the fields. We've had several cases of outrage in the district by these devils. And in any case you're supposed to be my old sister, so you'd better try and make yourself up to look the part."

Zofia produced a brownish tint used for dyeing fiber, some flour and charcoal. Stefa added her own artistic expertise and between the three of them they managed to change Helena's image so dramatically that Marian swore he would not have recognized his mother if it wasn't for her hair. She would have to keep that under a scarf.

Since Stefa was too small to be of any real help on the farm, Kowal suggested she be sent to the nearby Convent. It seemed like a good idea at the time and the next day Helena took her to see the Mother Superior.

Sister Klara's gentle voice gave no hint of the strength of character that lay behind the direct gaze. Her small square hands were in proportion to the rest of her body and she used them with an unconscious grace.

Helena explained that she wished to enroll her daughter as a temporary day pupil.

Penetrating eyes stripped her face of its make-up. "Are you in trouble?" The Nun asked bluntly.

"Not at the moment. Why do you ask?"

"Because we can accommodate you here for a while if that would help."

"That's very kind of you Sister, but I think we'll be all right where we are. We're staying with the Kowals."

She nodded. "The Russians are already showing an intolerance to any religious teachings." She tapped an officially stamped letter on her desk. "This is our first directive: No corruptive catechism lessons to be included in our syllabus, no prayers, no Christian symbols to be displayed, and a number of other similar prohibitions."

She saw Helena glance at the Crucifix hanging above the door and smiled imperturbably. "As long as I am here, no changes will be made."

When she left, Helena felt secure that she was leaving Stefa in the care of an exceptional woman, someone she could trust absolutely.

True to his promise, Kowal found plenty of work for his two guests and soon came to marvel at their unexpected tenacity. He had always thought of city people, especially the womenfolk, as weak. This one was proving him wrong. He watched them both agonize over their labors. From Helena's earliest struggles to straighten an aching back after picking sugar beet, he saw her gaining strength until she was able to put in almost a full day's work without apparent effort. He watched Marian thrash hay in the barn until there wasn't a breath left in his body and saw his muscles grow and harden.

With some pride Marian often relieved Zofia of her water buckets. He was maturing fast. The soft puppy fat had disappeared and his voice began to break. Occasionally Helena would catch something in the turn of his head, a gesture or smile that would remind her so strongly of Adam, she'd want to cry.

Her own body had never been as fit. It was good to feel the firm tone of muscles and the control behind them. She had cut her nails short and didn't care about the roughened skin of her hands. She knew that when all this was over she would emerge a different woman, and the thought cheered her.

Some afternoons Helena would walk up the hill to collect Stefa from school, glad of the extra pair of walking shoes she had packed. She'd make a point of going earlier, to enjoy a cup of tea and a chat with Sister Klara.

In the evenings they sat in the kitchen, made cozy by the large warm stove, the lingering smells of home cooking and the glow of a paraffin lamp. Stefa and Helena vainly tried to match Zofia's quick, expert fingers plucking geese feathers for down. Conversation during those moments invariably steered back to the subject uppermost in everyone's mind -- their present hopeless position, their plans for the future.

Kowal never spoke much but what he did say showed a profound knowledge of human nature as well as the affairs of the country and those of the neighboring states. His conversations certainly bore out his brother's remarks that he was a "well read man."

"I've seen any number of invading troops pass through the streets of Jazlowiec in my day," he told them, "German, Austrian and Russian, but this deportation of masses of people and separating children from their parents, this I've never come across before."

His words sent a chill through Helena. It was this that had always terrified her the most.

"It won't be long before they seize all the farm produce, cattle and poultry they can lay their thieving hands on," he went on. "We must eat and store all we can, while we still have the chance."

The deep pits he had dug in his garden and barn in which he stored salted meat and other preservable foodstuff was ample proof that the old man knew how to act in the lean times of occupation. But against the inhumane conduct of the new regime he had no solutions.

More Russian soldiers began to appear in Jazlowiec and as predicted, they soon requisitioned all the livestock in the district.

The women were in the fields when the Kowal's farm was subjected to its first foray. Later they heard the story from a bitter Kowal. Not only had they taken every single bag of wheat that Helena and Marian had so laboriously pounded, sorted and sifted, but the pantry looked as though a swarm of locusts had been through it. Nothing edible had been left behind. A quick check revealed that they had not found the other and even better stocked pantry under the floorboards in the passage. All the rooms had had a thorough going over and many articles which took their fancy had disappeared, including Marian's watch. It was some consolation that they hadn't thought to search under Helena's mattress. What infuriated her was the wanton damage to the doors, furniture and holy pictures -- and the spittle on the floors.

From his occasional trips to Buczacz, Kowal brought back news of the latest developments. Posters had been displayed on walls and billboards, stating that elections were to be held for the inclusion of the Ukraine to the Soviet Union. A farce so pointless as to be almost funny.

October 31st was announced as a day for rejoicing. The people of the Ukraine had, by virtue of their unanimous vote pro the Union, regained their freedom from the oppression of the Polish rulers and henceforth, their land would lawfully become part of the U.S.S.R. Speeches of gratitude for the so-called liberation followed in a special broadcast addressed to Stalin -- an election comedy that was repeated in November.

"I don't know who they think they're fooling," Helena said, wiping her hands before accepting a mid-morning cup of coffee from Mrs. Kowal.

"Their own people," Kowal replied, reaching for his own mug. "I could do with a slice of bread," he smiled at his wife.

"Me too, please," Marian called out sprinting past the house for the toilet.

The outside facilities had never bothered him. In fact, knowing that his sister had a highly developed sensitivity to smells that went unnoticed by most people, he had tried, quite unsuccessfully, to convince Stefa that the smell there was superior to the flushed variety. It also allowed you to leave your door open since the entrance faced the open fields. He was looking out now, wondering how long it would take for the rain clouds to reach them, when he noticed two army lorries driving up the hill towards the Convent. Fear numbed his fingers and he ran out still buttoning up his fly.

Kowal had also spotted the lorries and was trying to calm everyone down. "I expect they've come to confiscate their provisions," he said, but as he looked at Helena his eyes grew troubled.

She ignored his words and started off down the driveway. "I'm going up there."

"Don't be a fool woman!" Kowal pulled her back. "There's nothing you can do. You'll only make things worse if you try to interfere. Wait until the school comes out and if Stefa doesn't turn up, then we can worry about it."

He was right of course, and so they waited, eyes glued on the hill. Marian's thumb began to throb. He had bitten too deep into the nail. Almost two hours later they saw the lorries drive off. No-one thought about lunch. Helena counted the minutes to 3 o'clock at which time Stefa usually came home. At 3.30 she walked to the door.

"I'm going," she said firmly. "No Marian, you stay here." "But Mom?"

"Right. I'm going with your mother," Kowal announced with authority. "You do as you're told Marian. Look after the women here."

They were leaving the gate when they saw Stefa running towards them.

"Mommy!" her breath came in rasping sobs. "I don't want to go back to that school -- it's horrid. They've taken the Nuns away!"

"It's all right darling, it's all right. I won't let you go back," Helena led her into the house and sat her on her lap. "Now, slowly, tell us what happened."

She told them that the entire Convent staff had been removed and replaced by Russian teachers and the first thing they did was to pull down the crosses and all the holy pictures, substituting these with portraits of Stalin. Their mid-day meal consisted of "kipiatok" and since this was nothing but boiled water laced with stray potato peelings, no-one would touch it. Tearfully she recounted the incident.

"The teacher brought the cross into our class and told us to pray to God for food. We said our prayers and then he asked us if God had answered us. Some of the kids said no, but most of us just kept quiet. Then he made us repeat after him. It -- oh Mommy, it was a prayer to Stalin!"

Kowal and Helena exchanged looks.

"When, when we finished, lots of food was brought in, sweets too and the teacher broke the cross into little pieces." Overcome by sobs she could not go on.

"What happened then," Kowal prompted, in a hard tight voice.

"Th-then the teacher said, You see you have proved it for yourselves. There is no God. Stalin is your pro-protector or something, and is good to anyone who is loyal to him and loves him."

"The swines," Marian ground savagely.

To Stefa, in her deeply religious phase of life, this sacrilege was more bewildering than terrifying. The terror came later, when she described how Sister Klara dared to defy the authorities by refusing to relinquish her command over the children. Still unbending, she was beaten to the ground, kicked, her rosary and cross torn off her and the gold ring ripped from her finger. Her hands were tied and she was dragged out and thrown into the back of one of the lorries, together with the other Nuns.

Helena pictured those firm little hands tied helplessly together and that seemed worse than the beating.

After their initiation to an anti-Christ doctrine and to control and punishment, the children were given their play break, only none of them felt like playing.

Re-assembled again, the children were then subjected to their new Headmaster's enlightening lecture. Stefa may have repeated it in more simple terms but she had not failed to grasp the essence of the message. It was perfectly clear that the talk was on the merits of joint endeavor, on the duty of every child to conform to the dictates of the glorious Party, irrespective of family ties or difference of opinion. In short on all those spurious qualities that make up Communism. In the same breath he reviled western policy of class discrimination, western degeneration, western capitalism, democracy -- anything and everything western.

Listening to Stefa, Kowal felt the first twinges of fear at the monstrous methods these people stooped to in an effort to convert the children of Poland.

From that day on Russian soldiers became frequent visitors to the farm. As was customary, under pretext of looking for firearms they walked off with butter, cheese, honey and even clothing. During these visits Zofia and Helena hid themselves in the hay stacks, the field or at the back of the house. Someone always stood guard to give the easily passed-along warning signal, three loud sneezes.

It was more difficult to avoid them in the late evenings, when the younger ones liked to pay their calls. Some were little more than boys, reminding Helena of children playing at soldiers, in their baggy uniforms and enormous boots. One evening, unable to make a quick enough exit, she was caught sitting on a stool in the kitchen. Her heart began to hammer and all she could do was hope that her makeup, the shadowy corner and stooped posture would create the desired impression.

Three uniformed men swaggered in, all very young, very boisterous and very much at home. Evidently this was not their first visit to the house. Without bothering to remove their caps or greet anyone, they pulled out chairs and sat at the table.

"Where's the coffee mother?" The heftiest of the three called out. "Remember how we like it -- strong and sweet, same as our girls." Gales of laughter from the other two.

Without a word Mrs. Kowal poured out three cups from the percolator that always simmered on the stove. They drank greedily, slurping and making loud smacking noises of appreciation.

"Now what about some of that bread of yours, with lots of butter, eh comrades?" The coffee lover turned to his mates.

"Cut nice and thick," said the second one.

"And don't forget the honey," added the third.

Having given their order, the three bears sat back comfortably, oblivious of the hostility of their hosts.

Kowal went on smoking his pipe, deliberately taking no notice of the intruders.

"There is no honey," Mrs. Kowal said.

"Don't give me that shit old woman. You think I don't know you're hiding it?"

"Then find it, because I can't," came the reply.

For a moment he seemed undecided what to do, then turned to the others. "Do we look?"

"Oh leave it," said the big one, obviously in command. "As long as she puts enough butter on. We haven't time, anyway."

One of the soldiers became aware of Helena's presence. He peered at her, screwing up his eyes to penetrate the gloom.

"Who's this you have here?" He asked finally, jerking a thumb at the bent form.

Kowal stirred. "My old sister. She's sick."

The hefty youth must have fancied himself as a wit for he kept up a rapid stream of wise cracks that seemed to amuse his two companions to the point of hysteria. Helena managed to catch a word here and there and from what she could make out, their brand of humor was coarsely juvenile.

They ate as they drank, noisily and with relish, stuffing great big chunks of bread into their mouths. When they'd had their fill, they belched loudly and left, with a promise of another visit soon.

"Barbaric young louts!" Mrs. Kowal spat out as soon as the door closed on them.

"At least they didn't raid the place," her husband remarked.

"I suppose these lads must also get homesick," Helena ventured. "They can't all be as tough as they make out they are. Look at those three for instance. Anyone could see they were putting on a big act."

Mrs. Kowal snorted. "Then why must they behave like pigs?"
"Possibly because they don't know any better."

This was met with another snort, but her husband seemed to have more liberal views.

"I agree, the Russian as an individual is a decent enough person," he said. "Perhaps more generous and kind-hearted than most, especially the older folk, but what chance have they got under the new system? Everything's become collective -- work, family life, even personalities. There's nothing more soul destroying than mass identification and that's what those crazy beggars have let themselves in for."

"Mm," Helena nodded. "Communism."

"Communism is fine in theory but it just doesn't work in practice. People aren't all the same. They know that, so they have to use force to keep them in line. Deprived of freedom of speech, thought and ambition, how long can humanity last?"

"Sounds to me you're trying to make excuses for them Kowal," his wife accused. "I say they destroyed their souls the day they renounced the good Lord."

"That may be mother, that may be." He had already spoken at greater length than he was accustomed to and was quite happy to let the matter drop.

By breakfast time the next morning Kowal had made his decision. He turned to Helena and spoke with obvious reluctance. "You know how welcome you have been here, but for your own sake, I think it would be better if you made a move now." He didn't have to remind her of the brutal treatment his neighbors had suffered only the day before. The wife, still very young, had been assaulted, the farmer a cripple, dragged off heaven knew where.

"Yes, I suppose it's time we left. When do you think we should make a start?"

He walked to the window and looked up at the clouds. "Tomorrow night. It should have cleared by then. I'll take you to Monasterzyska."

"But will the women be all right here on their own?"

"As safe as they can be. The wife, I hope, may be too old even for the worst of them and Zofia -- well, she's showing plainly enough now. In any case, what protection can I give them these days?" He added bitterly.

By the next afternoon, the weather had turned fine and sunny. There was an air of calmness about which transferred itself to them all. This, and the birds chirping on the window sill and Lala's silent delight in them, all conspired to rob Helena of her usual alertness. Between moments of daydreaming and watching the old lady prepare what seemed like a month's supply of food for their journey, she was sewing linen bands for the three of them. This was to conceal the money that each would carry so that should the worst come to the worst and they became separated, at least none of them would be left destitute.

Kowal and the children were in the fields while Zofia was busy raiding the hives, determined that they take some honey with them.

"Holy Mother of God!"

Helena looked up at Mrs. Kowal's horrified gasp. Two soldiers were stealing up behind Zofia.

Mrs. Kowal rushed outside. Helena followed as far as the doorway and stopped when she saw one of the men knock the old lady to the ground with his rifle butt. The other was dragging the girl behind the hedge, his hand clamped hard over her mouth. She bit him and her short scream was drowned by his savage curses. Then all was quiet.

Helena's stomach knotted. Her only thought was of escape. She ran out through the back door and hid in their haystack with its secret entrance. Trembling and crying, she felt more anger now than fear and she heard herself muttering curses she'd never used before. She cursed her own helplessness. She cursed the barbaric louts that would club an old woman. God Almighty! The old lady may be lying out there bleeding to death and all she could think of was her own skin. With a sob she tore out of the hiding place to call for help.

As she ran around the side of the house she saw Mrs. Kowal staggering under Zofia's weight. Her first concern was for the old woman whose whole head seemed to be covered in blood.

"No, I'm all right. See to Zofia," she gasped.

The poor girl was doubled up with pain and moaning, "Oh Mother of God, oh Jesus, my baby, my baby."

Supporting her as much as she could, Helena took Zofia up to bed. Then she took a closer look at Mrs. Kowal's head. Satisfied that the wound was only superficial, she left them and ran out to look for Kowal. She remembered Marian saying something about fixing the broken door to the barn and made for that.

She was out of breath by the time she found them. "Zofia needs a midwife," she panted. "Quickly!"

"Marian. Down the hill, third house on your left." Before he could tell him to hurry, Marian had already jumped the fence to the road.

"What happened?" He asked sharply.

"They..." Helena looked at Stefa's ashen face and pulled herself together. "It's a miscarriage," she said.

"Oh my God," Kowal got out, running for the house.

Kowal sat hunched over his knees, staring into the fire. He had aged ten years. Helena looked up at the dragging hands of the clock and got up to make him some coffee. She couldn't control her shaking hand as she passed the cup to him.

"Thank you. Better sit down and have some yourself," he said, not looking at her.

Finally Mrs. Kowal appeared, her face torn with anguish.

"She'll be all right. But she's lost the baby. Our first grandchild."

Her husband went over to her, took her in his arms and gently placed the good side of her head against his chest. Helena left them rocking in their grief and ran up to Zofia's room.

She was turned to the wall, her hands clutching the sheet so hard that the knuckles showed white.

Helena looked questioningly at the midwife.

"She'll be fine. As strong as a young mare the girl is."

Apart from a few nasty bruises, Zofia had apparently suffered no serious injuries but she knew that shock might set in and that it would help if she could get the girl to talk about it. She took Zofia's hand and made her recount exactly what had happened. She remembered little after she had bitten the soldier's hand for he had struck her with his fist. She had been conscious enough however, to know that only the one man had raped her. As she talked, tears began to flow from underneath the tightly shut lids. Helena held her, tears running down her own face. Gradually the girl's hands relaxed their hold. Helena was sure then that Zofia would soon recover.

Even so, she didn't like the idea of leaving that night but her offer to stay on was flatly rejected. "They can't hurt my family any more than they've done already," Kowal pointed out in a tired voice. "But your turn might come next."

She hated to see him like this. All the strength and confidence seemed to have ebbed from him, leaving a defeated old man. And there was nothing she could do or say to help.

"I think it would be best if we left straight away," he went on. "We might cause more suspicion if we travel by night."

Helena applied more make-up, packed their suitcase, the food hamper and within the hour they were ready to go.

Despite her searing experience, Zofia remembered that she had not managed to get the honey for them and insisted that they take a jar she had hidden under the floorboards. Marian and Stefa had said their goodbyes. Now Helena stood at the foot of the bed. Her heart ached for the young girl lying there, battered, humiliated, yet stoically calm. Zofia's eyes opened.

"You're going now?"

"Yes." Helena came round and took her hand. "How are you feeling?"

"I don't feel. There's nothing. I feel nothing. God must have his reasons. I don't know..."

What could she say to that? She didn't know either. She bent down to kiss the girl. "Thank you my dear for all you've done for us. And, and look after Mrs. Kowal."

"Yes, that I will. God go with you."

Kowal had covered the floor of his wagon with straw for them to sit on but Marian begged to share the driver's seat with him. They set out on deserted country roads. Some of the farms that they passed showed no signs of life at all. Even the dogs had lost interest in protecting a property that had neither food nor master.

A sharp bend brought them onto a better road, flanked by an avenue of poplars. Helena concentrated on the play of sunlight through the trees -anything to draw the thoughts away from the farm. That incident had done something to her as well. It destroyed the last shred of naivete and made her lose all compassion for those poor homesick boys that looked like toy soldiers and behaved like brutes. She even dismissed Stefa's friendly guard's help in Buczacz as the unpredictable act of a savage. But more than anything else, her flight to the haystack left her feeling like a coward. She had not run because it was the optimum thing to do, she had run because she was *scared*. She vowed never again to let fear get the better of her.

"Halt!"

The unexpected command jolted her nerve ends to a quiver and the sudden appearance of two mounted soldiers out of a dense section of trees, had a similar effect on the horses. It took all of Kowal's strength to keep them under control.

Both men had mean-looking eyes, flat noses and prominent cheekbones. The only discernible difference between them was the ugly scar that the one carried along the side of his face.

For the second time that day Helena felt the awful tightening of the stomach.

"Where are you going?" Scarface demanded.

"My sister here has been so poorly that I'm taking her to see a doctor in Monasterzyska," Kowal was quick to reply.

Both men took a good look at her. She sucked in her cheeks, half drooped her eyelids and gazed back at them vacantly.

"Hm," the man grunted in automatic disbelief. "Where are you from?"

"Jazlowiec."

"You have a farm there?"

"Yes."

"Then why isn't the boy tending to the fields?" He shot out, darting a swift look at the other man to make sure he had not missed this brilliant display of cunning.

But Kowal was ready for him. "My sister might need treatment for a few days and there'll be no-one to look after her in town. I figured I could leave the kids with her and get back to the farm myself."

Scarface turned to his companion with a leer. "You want to lay that sick old cow?"

The other spat in disgust.

"On your way then old man!" The Russian barked.

They didn't follow the good road for long after that, but once again branched off onto narrow, out-of-the-way paths. The going was slower, far less comfortable but probably safer.

The skies were clear, the moon and stars bright. Visibility was good enough for them to move on throughout the night. They stopped only to rest the horses.

Marian got his chance at the reins while the old man took a short nap. The horses were easy to handle and Kowal made no objection when Helena also took her spell in the driver's seat.

Towards sunset of the following day they drove into a small wooded grove and made camp for the night. Marian led the horses off to graze along the bank of a stream nearby, while Helena cut slices of bread and cheese for their supper. As soon as they had eaten, the family wrapped themselves in blankets and snuggled into the straw. Kowal set out for Monasterzyska, now only a few miles away. He knew the district well, every road and clump of trees was familiar to him and he also had many friends here.

It was past midnight when he returned, dog-tired but from the expression on his face, Helena guessed he must have good news for them. She poured him a mug of coffee, sweetened it with Zofia's honey and waited until he was ready to talk.

Cradling the warm mug in both hands, he took a few sips and, in his own slow pace proceeded to tell them that a great number of the *Volksgenossen* (Polish citizens of German descent) who had settled in this part of the country, were being brought to Monasterzyska from where, on Hitler's orders, they were being sent on their final journey back to their Fatherland.

"It's ridiculous," he commented, "because some of these folk have been here for generations. I know several families and they're as much Polish today as I am."

Such a transport was due to leave the very next day.

"With your fluent German," Kowal concluded, "you should be able to lose yourselves among the repatriated without much trouble. That should get you safely as far as Lwow, at any rate."

Helena's last thought before falling asleep was that Luck was still with them. *Not luck, God,* she corrected herself.

She was first up the next morning, washed herself in the stream, scrubbed the rest of the make-up off her face and changed into her own clothes. Envigorated by the sharp cold water and feeling more like herself again, she raced Lala back to the camp. She made Stefa change as well and, with the exception of their coats, gave the country outfits to Kowal to take back with him. It was his idea to put Lala into a sack which Marian could carry over his shoulders.

"Mr. Kowal," Helena put her hand on his arm, not knowing how to bring up the thing that had been gnawing at her. "If only I could have done something..." she said lamely.

He patted her hand, knowing what was on her mind. "My dear, I have never taken you for a stupid woman. Had you done anything else, I would have had to reverse my opinion."

She was glad he turned away then, because she knew how uncomfortable women's tears made him feel.

After breakfast they drove to the station, to be surrounded almost at once by hundreds of Germans loaded with their belongings: Huge kists, blankets with bundles of pots and pans tied to them, dogs, bird cages and a variety of household paraphernalia such as they'd never seen before.

At the entrance to the platform they were stopped by the Russian Militia. Helena explained in German that her husband was following them with their luggage and Kowal confirmed the story in Russian.

"What the devil are *you* doing here then?" The Russian asked him.

"I'm a relative and I'm only seeing them off."

The man let them through and they took their places among the horde of passengers.

"Come on Marian," Helena urged him. "We'll never get a seat unless we push."

He did not need to be asked twice. Pushing his elbows out as he had seen his father do at Bielsko station, he forged a throughway straight into a compartment. They settled into a window seat and searched the platform for their friend. He spotted them immediately.

Shortly before the train was due to leave, Russian soldiers came aboard to check on everyone's personal documents, identity cards and other *Passierschein* that the people had been issued with. This was something neither she nor Kowal had anticipated. Helena's thoughts raced, forming a plan that just might work.

She quickly briefed Marian and Stefa so that when the men were within hearing distance they made a big issue of not being able to find their papers. Helena told the officer in charge that her husband had left the day before with his parents and their luggage and had forgotten to leave their papers with her. Kowal hastened to corroborate the story and Stefa put the finishing touches to the scene by weeping with great conviction. The bemused officer took it all in, stroked Stefa on the cheek and said reassuringly, "Don't worry, you're sure to meet your Daddy at the station in Lwow." His German was good.

Helena leaned out of the window to say goodbye to their friend. Stefa had already thrown her arms about Kowal's neck and continued crying. Marian stood back, blinking his eyes furiously. She couldn't help but draw comparison between that first time Kowal held her hand so firmly, and now. She looked into the blue eyes, no longer bright, and choked back the words she had meant to say, instead she bent forward to kiss him.

As the train began to pull away, they had a last glimpse of a broken old man rubbing awkwardly at his face with the back of a sleeve.

*

CHAPTER FIVE

"Unexpected friends"

Their Military escort traveled noisily in a separate carriage checking the papers of all newcomers who joined the passengers at the larger stations. With every stop the delays became longer and more harrowing as the people tried to fit themselves into the already overcrowded compartments. Helena had no idea there were so many German residents in this part of Poland and now understood Hitler's concern over his *Volksdeutsch*.

The Poleks shared their four-berth compartment with a solidly built woman and her four children. Her husband, together with numerous stout relatives and friends kept popping in, forcing Helena to heave Stefa on and off her lap to make room for them. This, coupled with the loud babble of their incessant talk and the screech of the children, did nothing to endear the Germans to her.

Marian made friends with a couple of older boys from an adjoining compartment and the three of them spent most of their time in the corridors. Lala maintained a silent vigil under Helena's seat.

At mid-day they were unexpectedly treated to hot vegetable soup with thick slices of bread and the same fare for supper. The nearer they came to Lwow, the better the food became and on the second day meat was included on the menu. Helena carefully rationed their meals. Wrapping bread around chunks of meat, she stored away whatever they could do without, for future emergencies. No one was deceived into believing that this solicitous treatment was prompted by any nobler motives than those of propaganda. For the moment, Russia and Germany were firm 'friends'. But whatever their reasons, the food was more than welcome. Even Lala perked up when she was given a bone to gnaw on. However, she drew the line when it came to fraternizing with her canine co-passengers.

Stefa showed the same aloofness, a behavior that was so completely alien to her nature that it worried Helena.

Tante Helge pushed her large form through the door and smiling broadly, asked if she could sit down next to her sister for a bit. Helena once again pulled Stefa onto her lap.

"It's the smell, Mommy. I can't stand it," she whispered. "Those kids are full of wee wee."

Helena smiled with relief. "I had noticed it but it's not all that bad."

"You don't have to sit right next to them," Stefa pouted. "And the little one keeps asking me to pick her up!"

"Never mind darling. The mother's bound to change them soon. She looks a clean woman. Come and stand next to the window." Stefa leaned her forehead against the window pane and soon became absorbed in her new game of spotting a tree and counting its branches before it flashed past.

Meanwhile, *Tante* Helge and her family monopolized Helena's attention. Believing them all to be in similar circumstances, the Germans were friendly enough and spoke openly. The older ones spoke German, some with difficulty but the younger generation knew only Polish and a Rhuthanian dialect. They had settled in these parts and had grown to regard the land as their birthright, remaining German in name only. They felt unhappy and uneasy at the Fuhrer's insistence on this migration of communities. They would find it hard to become German citizens overnight.

Helena also felt uneasy, but her immediate problem was how to get around the Russians once they reached Lwow. She tried to think of some workable solution, between constant interruptions from her garrulous neighbor.

On the afternoon of the second day, the woman's chatter was cut mercifully short by the announcement that they were coming into Lwow. The train pulled in to a siding from where the passengers had to be moved to the Central Station to board the train scheduled for the west. Russian trucks were parked outside, waiting to take the Germans to the Central Station. Before the trucks could be boarded, each person was once again made to produce his papers. There was no hope of escape from Soviet censorship -- the Military Police were everywhere. Helena had had two days in which to worry over this problem and that's all she had been able to do, worry over it. No solution had presented itself.

Still without a firm plan, they managed to move away from the line of passengers.

She had not been to Lwow before, but knew that Adam had many friends in the city, dating back to the days when he had run away from home as a boy to join the Resurrectionary Forces in Lwow. In that desperate bloody but victorious battle, men, women and children fought to overthrow the Bolsheviks. Lwow had been freed in November of 1918 but it would be 3 years before a definitive peace treaty was signed between Poland and Soviet Russia.

Adam had brought Marian here to attend the anniversary celebrations of the twentieth year of independence. A year later and those same enemies were again reducing the country to nothing more than a buffer state between East and West.

The name so often mentioned by Adam came back to her. "Do you know where the Muszumanskis stay?" She asked Marian. "Yes, in Lyczakow Street, number 26. Of course! that's where we should go."

"Pray that we can," she told him bleakly.

Their friendly officer was now swearing at some poor unfortunate for a crime of which the culprit himself seemed quite unaware. The innocent look on the victim's face evidently incensed the Russian, for he ended his tirade by giving the man a blow that sent him staggering against the Guard standing behind him. Whereupon the officer lost interest in the case and ordered the man to be taken away.

Helena hesitated to approach the officer after this display of brutality but the expression on his face had already returned to normal and she pushed her way towards him.

He smiled in recognition and asked why they were not with their party.

"I can't find my husband," she said worriedly. "He must be staying with our relatives in town and didn't know the time our train was due to arrive. What are we to do now?" She fixed him with an imploring look.

"Sit down on this bench and don't worry. I'll arrange everything for you," he promised, marching off with long, purposeful strides. No one could have shown more sympathetic understanding.

The capricious nature of the Russians never ceased to amaze, and disturb her. You never knew where you stood with them. Dr. Sadowski used to say that the crazier the person, the more unpredictable his behavior. If that was the case, then these people were quite mad, she decided.

"I think we should get out of here," Marian was saying.

"And how do you propose we do that - simply walk out?" She snapped, betraying her own fear.

At that moment the train with its load of Germans began to shunt slowly past. Helena looked up and there was her sister's face at one of the windows. Hardly able to believe her eyes, she waved frantically and ran after the carriage. But the train had gathered speed and Eva had not seen her. Helena could only guess that she and Henry had been more successful than she was in getting them included in the convoy. But how did they think they would be able to disembark before it reached Germany? Eva had looked pale and drawn. She didn't want to think of what her sister might have been through since leaving Krakow. Slowly she walked back. Marian came up to meet her.

"Who was that? Who were you waving to?" "Eva," she said, staring after the train.

"Aunt Eva? But how on earth..." then he noticed the tears in her eyes and tried to be reassuring. "They'll be all right Mom. At least they're on the train, which is more than we are."

She didn't have the heart to tell him that that was precisely what was bothering her.

"Mom, I think Marian's right," Stefa was saying in a tight voice. "We must get out of here."

"Quiet," Helena hissed. "The officer's coming back."

With a benign smile he beckoned them to follow him. Outside, a Taxi was waiting. Helena had a few bad moments wondering whether the driver would be a Pole but was reassured as soon as the Russian began taking down the man's life history and that of his nearest of kin, before asking her for the address where her husband was supposed to be staying. This she gave him without hesitation as number 13 Lyczakow Street. She was taking no chances.

"Now listen, you Polish son-of-a-whore," the Russian snarled at the cabbie. "These people are our German Comrades, understand? Drive them to number 13 Lyczakow Street, collect her husband and parents and take them immediately to the Central Station. I don't care how many bloody trips you have to make, but you're to bring all their belongings. You will then report to me at 7 sharp, on platform 4 and if I'm satisfied, you'll get your pay. And remember," he added, pointing to the revolver at his side, "a bullet through your thick skull if my orders aren't carried out!"

The driver's thin, tight-lipped face remained immobile under the harangue, although he nodded several times to indicate that he understood perfectly and Helena thought she detected a spark in the dark eyes. She decided she liked this face very much.

The moment they left the station behind them, Marian leaned over the cabbie's seat and asked him if he was really Polish.

"Yes of course," came the curt reply.

"We aren't Germans either. We're Poles," Marian explained eagerly. "Lwow is Dad's favorite town. He fought here and belongs to the *Eaglets of Lwow,* though we come from Silesia."

The man half turned, regarded them coldly and said nothing.

"Look, you've got to believe us. We can't go back to the station!" Marian was desperate.

Helena nudged him to keep quiet and whispered, "The Muszumanskis will convince him. You just tell him where to go."

No one spoke after that and the cab rattled along the near-deserted streets. Lwow presented a dismal sight, with its torn streets and gutted buildings. A far cry from the bright and busy city Adam had described. Out of the ruins, the chimneys stood out starkly against the darkening sky. One of the ten major Polish Military bases, Lwow had also been an important commercial and industrial center, a tempting target for the Luftwaffe.

Helena gazed at the ruins and her mind went back to Bielsko. She had not thought of her home since that first day of September. Now she wondered if the house in Zielna Street was still standing and if she would ever live in it again. She remembered with irony the hours spent in selecting wallpaper to match their new bedroom suite, the months spent over the crochet hook on lace curtains. The sittingroom was to have been redecorated in the new year. Peach slips had been planted in the garden. They needed careful tending against the frost and she couldn't imagine anyone bothering about those. They would perish, together with how many of their friends? She dare not think of the family.

"It's not here," Marian said. "Carry on a bit further. I'll tell you when we come to the Muszumanskis."

Helena had already come to respect Marian's unerring navigational sense, and now that they were on their own, he had assumed his share of command with an ease and confidence that surprised her.

The man looked at the boy curiously but still said nothing and drove slowly on. "Isn't it here perhaps?" He asked presently, in a more friendly voice.

"Yes. The second house on the left. Number 26."

The driver told them to leave their things in the car while he made sure that there was someone at home. He returned with the caretaker who pointed to a ramshackled old outbuilding in the yard and said that was where Mrs. Muszumanska lived with her family. Marian argued that she didn't stay in the yard but on the first floor.

"Yes, yes," the man said shortly, "but now she lives down there."

With a snort of disgust Marian marched towards the outbuilding and rapped on the door. A careworn woman in her early thirties opened the door. In the dim interior of the room behind her, three children were playing on the floor, a solitary bed occupied the one corner. A few wooden boxes, a paraffin stove and lamp completed the dreary picture.

"Yes?" The woman said indifferently. Then her eyes flickered as she caught sight of the cabbie.

"Don't you recognize me, Mrs. Muszumanska?" Marian asked, holding out his hand.

"Good Lord it's Marian. Polek's boy!" she cried, kissing him on both cheeks. "Where's your Dad, child?"

"We don't know, but here's my Mom and sister Stefa."

"Helena. I'm so glad to meet you at last. Adam was always talking about you."

"Well," Helena returned her smile, "he had plenty to say about you."

"And this is little Stefcia. Amazing both your children take after their father, don't they?" She took Helena's arm and led her inside. "And this is my little family -- Janek, Krysiu, Wladziu, come and be introduced."

The Taxi driver leaned against the doorway. "You might as well introduce me too," he said, smiling at Anna.

"Oh, Alfred. This, as you will have gathered, is Helena Polek. Adam's wife. Alfred's been a godsend to us. I don't know what would have become of us if it hadn't been for him."

She pulled out a chair from a dark corner for Adam, gesturing for the others to join her on the bed. She then went on to tell the story of how her husband Olek had been locked up in the local goal the moment he returned from the front, that she and the children had been thrown out of their apartment and made to live in this hovel and that it was Alfred who helped them to survive by bringing food whenever he could. Helena also learned that Alfred went as far as to sneak food parcels to the political prisoners in goal.

Alfred laid a hand on Marian's shoulder. "I apologize for disbelieving you," he said, "but one has to be so damned careful with strangers these days, however innocent they may appear and especially when they're introduced to you as German Comrades. How did you swing that one, by the way?"

By the time Helena finished telling her story, she had them both laughing and congratulating all three of them on their acting abilities.

"And now," Alfred said, moving towards the door. "I want you to wait here with Anna until I can find you somewhere to stay. You obviously can't all fit in here. And don't worry," he added with a wink at Marian, "I shall never permit the family of an *Eaglet of Lwow* to perish."

When he had gone Helena asked Anna to tell her more about the man, and learned that he was an old friend of her husband's and that Adam had also known him. "They all fought in the same regiment in the defense of Lwow."

"And so did you, I believe," Helena put in quietly.

"I was a courier, well behind the lines," she said, smiling at the memory. "They wouldn't believe I was old enough to carry a gun."

"And were you?"

"I thought I was, at 12. But I was telling you about Alfred. He became a very successful Architect, one of the reasons why he has so many contacts in the city. Goodness knows how he came by that uniform he's wearing today though. He's one of the most resourceful men I've ever known. You're lucky to have come across him like this."

Anna's words brought home the phenomenal coincidence of having Alfred's cab waiting for them at the station. She felt her scalp tingle. How differently it could all have turned out if he hadn't been there.

"Let's hope our luck holds," she said, turning away to unpack her little bundle of leftovers. "Untie Lala, will you Marian."

Anna's eyebrows shot up first at the sight of the meat then the dog.

"With the compliments of our Russian benefactors," Helena said, passing her the food while she explained where it came from.

There were still Stefa's and Marian's hoarded rations to fall back on.

Anna's brimming eyes told their gratitude. Suddenly she laughed. "I must say I admire you, holding on to your pet like this."

"She's part of the family," Helena pointed out. "Aren't you Lalusiu?"

Lala's "whoof" was so clearly meant as a reply that the children crowded around her and wouldn't let her alone until she 'spoke' again. Lala obliged and her fondness of children even allowed them access to her upturned belly.

Helena watched as Anna's children devoured the buttered bread with pathetic eagerness and noticed that the mother barely touched the food herself. The sight of the woman's wasted form made her speak up. "It's not going to help them if you let yourself get run down, you know."

Anna nodded and helped herself to a piece of meat.

Alfred was back within the hour. His eyes fell on Lala and a frown creased his brow. "This your dog?"

"Yes but don't worry," Helena said. "She's more intelligent than a lot of humans. In fact she's already saved our lives." And so the journey to Buczacz had to be recounted in detail.

Time fled and it was evening before Alfred said they must go. He told them he had found a house for them in one of the back streets next to the Lyczakow Cemetery.

Not suspecting that this would be their first and last meeting, Helena left Anna with a cheerful "See you soon."

During the short drive to their new home Alfred warned them to be on the lookout for any cars, trucks or lorries that might stop outside or close to the house.

"It's become common practice for them to load a truckful of Poles and disappear. And don't imagine they spare the children, either."

"Don't I know it," Helena said in a thin voice. "So what do we do if we see them coming?"

Alfred smiled at her in the rearview mirror. "It's quite simple," he said with an eloquent hand gesture. "At the first sign of danger, nip out by the back door and hide in the Cemetery. You'll be safe there."

Stefa gripped her mother's hand. This was a solution that didn't appeal to her at all.

They pulled up outside a derelict looking building with planks nailed across the front door. Alfred showed them in through the back and left immediately, promising to return as soon as he could.

A quick search of the house produced nothing but the barest of furniture, some dishes, half a packet of porridge and a couple of onions. The house seemed deserted but for one locked door. This intrigued Marian to the point where he had everyone looking for a key that might fit.

Stefa was the first to lose patience. "Oh come on Marian, you'll never find that silly key. Your turn first to cavey by the window. Mom and I are going to take a bath."

"The trouble with you is that you lack imagination," Marian told her with brotherly venom, but nevertheless took his post at the window.

Finding the geyser on had been a wonderful surprise and the soak in the hot water utter luxury. Helena had no qualms about using one of the sheets as a towel.

Alfred returned at 9 o'clock. He looked tired and a little older in the worn serge suit that had replaced his taxi driver's uniform.

"I'm famished! You wouldn't by any chance have anything resembling food around the place, would you?" He asked in jest, flopping into a chair.

"Yes, if you don't mind left-overs," Helena said.

"Mind? Mind? My dear lady, I am ready to devour garbage, if you can supply it."

"Wait a moment and you'll get something better than that," she promised, hurrying to the kitchen.

The onions gave added flavor to the train left-overs. Pleased to be able to do something in return for his kindness to them, Helena proudly placed the plate of food in front of him.

"Lordy this looks good. Mmm and smells good too. You're a genius, a miracle maker and a fairy godmother and I won't ask you where the food came from in case it turns into thin air."

From the way he attacked the food, it was evident that the man had not eaten a square meal in days. And yet, she thought, he had provided for the Muszumanskis as well as the prisoners in goal. Adam had always maintained that the Lwowians were the jolliest, the most kind-hearted people in the world. She now understood his affection for them. She was beginning to understand many things about Adam, she reflected.

As soon as his plate was empty he pushed back his chair and stood up. "I kiss your hand Madame. Can't remember when I had a better meal. Must go and see the chaps next door now."

"Oh yes. Who are they?" She asked.

"Two of the most brilliant and the most wanted brains in Lwow. Believe me, the less you know about them the better for you."

When he came out of their room his face was grave but as he did not volunteer any information no one asked any questions.

"I must be off. Thanks again for the meal."

"What are you going to do now?" Helena asked him. "I mean, aren't you in trouble for disobeying the Russian's orders?"

He grinned. "Nothing gives me more pleasure than to disobey their orders. But I'm no longer a Taxi driver. My occupation as of now, is much more down to earth so to speak. Forgive my rudeness and permit me to make a belated introduction." He bowed over her hand with exaggerated flourish. "Lazarz Tombs, grave digger, at your service."

Marian laughed till the tears came to his eyes. Lazarz, patron saint of beggars, couldn't have suited him less, nor could Tombs for that matter. There was nothing beggarly or tomblike about Alfred.

Once again he warned them to be on the alert for passing vehicles and said he would be back the next day.

Despite the apparent peacefulness of the night, Helena could not relax the tension that grew with each distant sound of an engine. Wrapped in blankets, she and Marian took turns to keep watch at the window. Stefa slept soundly right through the night and was able to relieve them after breakfast while they tried to catch up on their sleep.

When Alfred did not return that day Stefa became jittery and it was Marian who managed to reassure her. "It's not so easy for a man on the run to always keep his appointments," he said knowingly.

"I suppose not," she conceded."As long as that officer doesn't start looking for him."

It didn't occur to him or to Helena that Alfred would ever let himself be caught. The confidence that this comparative stranger inspired, amazed her. In a matter of hours he had, in effect, become their source of security -- and only hope.

It was 1 o'clock at night when the sound of car engines brought Helena out of a light sleep.

"They're coming this way!" Marian shouted. "Let's go!" He was pushing Lala into her sack and running for the door.

Helena grabbed the blankets and pulled Stefa out of bed. They made for the Cemetery, hiding behind a monument some 300 yards from the house.

Huddled close to the ground, they were oblivious to the fact that corpses lay immediately below them, or that the ground was cold and damp.

Loud Russian voices, screams, a woman's cry... these awful sounds continued for what seemed like hours, before the cars drove off.

The silence and darkness that followed deepened the silence of the graveyard. The whole thing seemed like a bad dream, slowly brought to reality by frozen limbs and mud covered clothes and hands.

" Think it's safe to go back now?" Marian asked in a whisper.

Helena answered him by getting to her feet. She put her arm around Stefa and they began to pick their way back over the tombstones.

The house was a shambles. Furniture thrown about the rooms, doors broken, crockery lying smashed on the floor. She looked at her watch. They had been out of the house for no more than 20 minutes.

She walked over to the stove and groped behind it. The raiding party hadn't found the porridge she had hidden there. She was about to cook some of it to warm them up when one of the tenants appeared.

"You must leave the house immediately."

"But why?" She asked. "They've already searched it."

"And found ample proof that it is occupied," he pointed out. "Come with me."

Without another word they took up their blankets again, Marian flung Lala over his shoulder and they followed the man through the Cemetery until he stopped under a willow tree.

He looked around carefully before picking up a stone and tapping it against one of the grave slabs. The slab slid to one side and he motioned for them to follow him inside the tomb.

Marian climbed down eagerly enough but Stefa cried out that she didn't want to be buried alive. Helena knew exactly how she felt, but managed to persuade her that here they would find shelter from the Russians. *Or a convenient, ready-made grave.* Cold fingers of fear crawled along her spine as she followed Stefa down the narrow steps.

*

CHAPTER SIX

"Life in a Tomb"

Halfway down the steps the air turned thick and dank. Helena heard Stefa's quick intake of breath and tightened her grip reassuringly on the small shoulder. Her own mind began to conjure up pictures she didn't want to think about either and she forced herself to focus her concentration on the physical construction of the tomb.

As the light grew brighter, she saw that this must be the resting place of a wealthy family. There was room for four coffins at least and sufficient sitting space for perhaps a dozen people. Four rows of roughly made benches stood against the walls and there were four or five people sitting there now. Food supplies were wedged in the alcove that had been made to house a child's coffin. The stone slab leading into the tomb rested on wooden rollers which enabled it to be slid back easily from the inside. The outside of the tomb was so well camouflaged that no one could have guessed it served as a hiding place for the living.

A distinguished looking man greeted them, introducing himself as The Digger. Despite the name and the disguise, his impression of a grave digger was anything but convincing. He explained that for the safety of all concerned, there were certain rules which every inhabitant had to abide by.

"The first and most important rule is that someone must always be in the tomb to open the slab for the others, in response to this code knock." He rapped four times on a bench. "The grave diggers are our men and they use their spades to indicate the all clear or danger signals. Watch for these whenever you are outside." Again he demonstrated: A spade held upright meant 'all clear', when held across the shoulder it indicated 'danger'.

"Everyone must be inside by nightfall when silence, as far as possible, has to be observed." The tired lines of his face broke into a smile. "That's about all. You might find the benches a little hard to sleep on at first but you'll get used to them."

Helena spread the blankets on the benches, thankful that the place was warm enough not to need them as covers.

Marian untied the sack to let Lala out. Helena saw the look of horror that crossed the Digger's face but before he could voice the protest that she saw coming, she assured him that the dog was well trained and would make no sound.

"Come now, how can you vouch for a dog's silence. Don't you realize that the life of every individual here is at stake?"

"And do you think that I would endanger them and my own children, if I could not answer for my dog with absolute certainty?"

He studied Lala for a long moment. She returned his gaze, permitting herself one wag of the tail. He looked back at Helena and left it at that.

The children fell asleep right away. Helena lay awake, trying to ignore the close atmosphere and the tightening of her chest. A faint light flickered in the furthermost corner of the tomb, lending an eerie animation to the shadows. She closed her eyes and the last thing she remembered was Lala's warm nose burrowing into her hand.

Sometime during the night they were woken up to make room for others. Women and children sat down beside Helena and a man said in a hushed voice, "Move up as close as you can, we've got four extras tonight." Everyone was sitting up now, with not an inch of space between them.

There were hushed whispers all around. With morbid aptitude for detail, people retold their own frightening experiences and those of their relatives and friends. Helena found it hard to believe that the Bolsheviks would resort to such inhumane extremes as to smash babies' heads against walls so that their mothers could be taken away for labor. Yet these people had no reason to lie. They had lost everything they possessed, including their families in some cases and had nothing left to cling to but their obstinate will for personal freedom. Considering themselves lucky to have been given the choice, they preferred death, if necessary, to enslavement.

The voices droned on and on until her mind began to spin and weakness threatened to overcome her. The atmosphere was so close that she began to gasp for breath. She wiped the perspiration that covered her brow and upper lip. Never at ease in confined spaces, Helena was convinced she wouldn't survive long in this place.

Life became meaningless and faded further and further away. She had the crazy notion that if she could only keep count of her heartbeats she wouldn't pass out.

All at once there was a hush as the now familiar knocks were repeated overhead. Out of the sepulchral silence Helena's name was called.

When the slab slid open, she gulped the fresh air like a grounded fish, rapturously feeling her senses clear.

Stefa was the first to reach Alfred and taking hold of his hand whispered urgently, "When are you going to take us away Mr. Alfred? It's so awful here, and it smells so musty and, and I'm so scared!"

Impulsively he hugged her to him. "Don't be afraid Stefciu. This is the safest place in all Lwow right now. You aren't here alone you know. There are more than a hundred people hiding all around you in tombs just like this one. Children too. But I'll do my best to get you out as soon as I can, I promise."

He turned to Helena and said he could do nothing at the moment as he had to see to the Muszumanski's children. Anna had been arrested while taking food to her husband in goal.

"If I don't return within a couple of days, one of my friends will take care of you and help you leave the city."

When he said this she knew instinctively that they would not be seeing Alfred again. "Oh God," was all she could say to him. The realization that they would have to stay on in this hell-hole made her feel so wretched that she had no thought for Anna's plight.

On the way back to their bench she staggered, feeling dizzy again. The Digger put out a supporting hand.

"I'll get you some water," he said. He watched her gulp it down, recognizing the symptoms. He'd seen many sufferers of claustrophobia in these tombs and he felt for her.

"Thank you," she said. "I, I'm sorry."

"Nothing to be sorry about my dear." He hesitated then reached for a child of five or six who was sitting on the edge of a bunk. "Do you think you could look after this little one for me?"

Helena looked into the dark-rimmed eyes, saw the great weariness in the thin little face and put her arms out. Without a word the child clung to her. Helena looked up questioningly at the man.

"She seems to be mute but not deaf," he said. "The last group of people brought her here. Someone found her wandering the streets."

Her heart twisted. You poor mite, she thought. You must have gone through hell. She took the child's hand.

"Come and meet Lala," she said with a cheerful smile.

The man ran his fingers through his gray hair. Jesus but he was weary. He couldn't remember when last he'd had a decent night's sleep. It should work, giving her the child to take care of. He noticed the difference almost immediately. From the start he had recognized the inner strength in the woman. Always did want to be a psychologist, he thought ruefully. There had been little challenge and less joy in Law. Even now he was more useful to society than he'd been all his life in his profession. He dimmed the small paraffin lamp and closed his eyes, resting his head against the stone wall.

"And then the frog turned into a Prince and they lived happily ever after. Now go to sleep." Stefa finished all in one breath.

Obediently the child curled up in her corner and closed her eyes.

It was their second day underground. People came and went but still no message from Alfred. If no news came by nightfall, they would have to make their own way out, Helena resolved. It wasn't the claustrophobia any more, she had more or less learned to deal with that. It was the inactivity and the constant fear of discovery that frayed the nerves. Yes. She'd speak to the Digger tonight.

Helena watched Stefa tuck the little girl in. Between them they'd managed not only to bring some life back into her but her voice as well. She had never been mute. She'd been in shock. The child had taken to the family instantly and now Helena didn't know how she would be able to leave her on her own again.

And what happened to the Muszumanski children? She knew Alfred would have provided for them somehow. But what of Anna? *Oh God, she probably tried to get the meat to him.*

"Good, isn't she?" The Digger said behind her.

Helena jumped. "Oh, I didn't know you were there. Yes, yes she's a lovely child."

"I've arranged for a friend of mine to take care of her until we can trace her relatives, if any."

"Wonderful. Takes a load off my mind," Helena admitted. "I've been worrying about her."

"Yes, I know."

"There is something else I wanted to talk to you about. It's-" She stopped at the sound of the code knock. The Digger hurried to open the slab.

"Is Mrs. Polek with you?"

She heard the whisper and ran towards the man. It was a stranger. "Alfred?" All her fears were in the question.

"He's all right," the man reassured her, "but on a special job on the border. He asked me to see to it that you get out of town safely."

"I'll get the children,"

"No," he interrupted, "not today. Be ready early tomorrow morning."

That evening a woman came for the little girl. There were tears in every eye when she left but the agonized look that she gave Helena, stayed with her deep into the night.

The man came before daylight bringing with him a small boy of thirteen or so.

"This little chap will show you the way to the station. You will catch a train as far as Jaworow, right?" Helena nodded. "The Lwow-Jaworow line is a short goods route and no one will trouble to check on your documents." He seemed to know what he was talking about so she nodded again. "Then from Jaworow it's about 25 miles to the River San. That you can walk quite easily, right?" He ignored her startled look and went on calmly. "There are any number of villages along the river bank and the people are very friendly and helpful, but try Krakowiec first, it's the nearest to Jaworow."

He smiled for the first time. "I'm sure you'll have no trouble in getting someone to take you across the river. Most of the villagers own fishing boats."

She couldn't tell whether his optimism was meant to spare her unnecessary worry in advance, or whether he was genuinely ignorant of the difficulties then involved in crossing the San. The river that had become the border between German occupied Poland and the Soviet 'Protectorate'.

She tried not to show the relief and happiness that filled her when she said good-bye to their host. "I don't know how to thank you," she began.

"Well don't," he smiled. "There's no need. The best of luck to you my dear. I'm glad I was wrong about your pet." He handed her a small parcel. "You'll need a little food for the road."

Knowing the straits these people were in she didn't know what to say. She reached out to embrace him in silent gratitude.

Their young guide darted in and out of the dark side streets of Lwow like a cat through well-known alleyways. Marian followed a few paces behind, carrying their suitcase. Then came Stefa. Helena brought up the rear with Lala's tense body in her arms. Every now and then Stefa looked back to make sure that her mother was following.

A train was waiting at the siding to which the boy brought them. He saw them on board and with a cheerful wave of the hand was gone, his thin little figure lost in the early morning gloom of the city. Helena wondered what would become of the boy. As though in answer, Stefa said flatly, "I have a feeling he's going to be caught."

"You shouldn't say things like that!" But the disturbingly prophetic ring to the child's voice made her shudder.

It was market day and the town buzzed with a noise and activity that seemed ridiculous in relation to the meager produce on display. A few soldiers and Security Police mingled with the local crowd. Helena kept well out of their way and eventually took refuge in a small restaurant.

The owner served them an unlikely breakfast of steaming sour cabbage and slices of equally sour black bread. The man hovered over them, wiping his hands on a dirty apron and repeating how very lucky they were to have the last portions out of the food quota allocated to him for the day, which he should really have reserved for his Russian customers. Helena took the hint and overpaid him.

They hurried out of the town, following the sun towards the west, but no sooner were they on the open road than they hastily reversed their steps. Military Patrols were stopping all road traffic. Helena talked it over with Marian and between them they decided to follow a narrow path leading out into the fields.

There seemed no end to the open country ahead. Catching his mother's eye, Marian gave a sickly grin. "Looks like we're in for a nice long hike, doesn't it?"

His poor joke gave her an idea. "Tell you what," she said brightly. "We'll make a real hike out of this. We'll stop after a bit and sit on the grass and have a picnic. How's that?"

Neither could have shown less enthusiasm and it wasn't long before Stefa asked for a rest, then another and another. Her shoes hurt, her feet were sore, her knees wanted to buckle under her. Marian took over. He bullied, cajoled, threatened and used every trick he knew, so as to keep her going. When they came to a cluster of trees, Helena called a halt. They stretched out full length on the grass.

Groaning, Stefa took her shoes off to reveal broken blisters on both heels.

"See? Blood!" she pointed triumphantly. "I wasn't shamming."

"Who said you were?" Marian asked.

"You!"

"No I didn't. I said you're acting like a spoilt brat, that's what I said."

"It's the same thing."

"Pity you weren't made to work in Mr. Kowal's fields like we were, then you wouldn't be making such an almighty fuss over a bit of walking."

Too tired to stop their bickering Helena nursed her own sore feet. The work on the farm had not prepared her for this type of exertion and she knew Stefa would not be able to carry on much further. She scanned the countryside. Ahead of them was a slow rise of hill.

"The village is probably just beyond that hill," she said.

"Hm. Depends how far beyond," Marian muttered, unconvinced.

The wind whipped at their clothes as thick clouds began to gather overhead. Helena tore narrow strips off the bottom of her petticoat and wound these around Stefa's heels.

"Come on," she said, getting to her feet. "It shouldn't be too far now and we don't want to get caught in a storm."

For all his banter, Marian made Stefa climb onto his back, while Helena struggled with the suitcase.

Lala ran on ahead, sniffing at the air. She stopped after a while, gave a tiny whimper and ran back to Helena, jumping up against her legs.

"Don't tell me *your* feet are sore now!" Marian scoffed.

But Lala was trying to tell them something and no one paid attention.

The other side of the hill that Helena had counted on dipped into a small ravine. Instead of the village, it hid a group of Russian Cavalrymen. They were all dismounted and busy studying a map.

For a split second Helena stood exposed on the ridge of the hill before throwing herself to the ground and dragging Marian and Stefa down with her. Too late. One of the men gave a shout and there was a scramble up the bank towards them.

On the spur of the moment Helena made out as though they had just sat down to attend to Stefa's feet. Unraveling the makeshift bandages quickly, she saw with satisfaction that there was blood on them. She made sure that this would be seen by whoever came up.

The Cavalryman was young, with a strong hard face and the body of Atlas. He had expected anything but this calmly preoccupied domestic scene and he stopped short, speechless, the gun limp in his hand.

"Well don't just stand there," Helena said in German, barely giving him a glance. "Haven't you got a knife or something to cut this knot with?"

That was too much for him. He waved an arm and shouted for the others to hurry up. There were four men altogether. Two of them officers. The young one's eyes were the palest of blue and cold and wary. Helena noticed his rank was that of Lieutenant. The other, a tall figure, had the unmistakable aura of being in command. He carried himself very straight. A thick-set broad-faced lad took his position next to Atlas.

The Captain came forward.

"She spoke in German," the athletic one informed him in an undertone.

"Who are you and what are you doing here?" The officer demanded in Russian, ignoring the soldier's remark.

"Look, I don't know what you're talking about," Helena said to him in German.

"Very well, I shall ask you again in your own language, *Wer bist du und was machst du hier?*"

She managed a smile. "Thank goodness there is a well-educated man among you. If I were Russian speaking I don't think I could ever pick up another language. Yours is so intricate but really lovely to listen to." *My God I sound idiotic,* she thought miserably.

He gave an impatient shake of the head. "That doesn't answer my question."

"Well, to use your own description, we are your, uh, German Comrades. Unfortunately we were separated from our party. You know, one of the repatriated groups and thought we would be sure to find a station further along and meet up with --"

He silenced her with a gesture, his heavy eyebrows making one solid line over the unsmiling eyes. "Why didn't you wait wherever it was that you say you were separated? And is that all the luggage you have? *And,* why walk through the fields when you could take the road?"

She was defeated. She knew it and he knew it.

"Well?" He prompted. "What have you to say for yourself now?"

"Only that you could take pity on these children and leave us alone!" She burst out, hugging Stefa to her.

Stefa didn't need to understand the conversation to realize that they were in deep trouble. Involuntarily she whispered a frightened *"Oh Boze"*

The men looked at each other.

"What was that your child said?" The officer demanded.

"She said 'Oh God'. It, it's Polish of course, but you must understand that we've lived in these parts for years and as a matter of fact they hardly know any German."

Again they exchanged glances. She had a strong feeling that something was wrong here. What? Their whole attitude worried her. It was nothing like their standard behavior. No one had demanded to see her papers, nor did it look as though rape was on their minds. She could only think that these men represented a special branch of Soviet Security.

"Stay where you are," the Captain barked. He took his men aside. They talked for a while in lowered tones and obviously came to some agreement, for now the Captain addressed her briskly in Polish.

"Your story is full of pitfalls. An imbecile could see through it. You are obviously Poles. No, don't try to deny it, you'll only make things worse for yourself, believe me. I have yet to meet the German who mentions his God in any language but his own and in any case, your daughter has a typically Polish face. Now, are you ready to tell the truth, or do I have to take you for interrogation by the N.K.V.D.?"

The very mention of the Soviet Secret Police was enough to make her admit to the truth. The last thing she had expected were the whoops of joy that met this admission. All reserve gone, the men crowded around and she could have kicked herself for the farce she had staged, that could have ended in disaster. But how was she to know that they were also Polish.

"Well," the Captain beamed. "You couldn't have picked on a better group of Russians if you tried. I don't have to tell you what we're doing in the Red Army."

"No."

"But isn't it very dangerous?" Marian asked. "I mean, say they recognize you as Poles."

A spark of amusement touched his eyes. "Did you?"

"No. You were terrific! I don't mind telling you, you had me scared stiff."

The man laughed and turned to Helena. "I take it you were on your way to the San? Quite. Well, we can give you a lift but will have to leave you a couple of miles short of Krakowiec."

Atlas rode ahead as the lookout man. The broad-faced lad rebound Stefa's feet before carrying her down the ravine and lifting her onto his horse. Helena was helped up in front of the Captain. Marian and a very uncertain Lala jumped up with the Lieutenant.

The night turned pitch dark but the storm had passed them by. Riding at a fairly slow pace, they covered almost ten miles before a halt was called.

"This is as far as we can take you," the Captain said, lifting Helena off his horse. "Follow this path, it will lead you straight to the village." He clicked his heels and kissed her hand in a decidedly un-Russian-like manner.

A moment later and the men were out of sight, leaving the three of them to grope their way along a barely discernible path.

"What a stroke of luck, meeting up with those fellows like that," Marian mused. He stumbled and swore softly under his breath. "Why didn't I bring a torch along, after that chap *said* it was such a long way from Jaworow."

"I doubt if we could have bought one anywhere."

"I wasn't thinking of buying one."

"Oh." She grimaced. Marian was certainly learning to cope.

At the sight of the first glimmer of light they quickened their steps. The shrubs thinned out to reveal a small cottage. Helena knocked on the door. There was no reply. In response to Marian's louder knocks, the door finally opened a fraction and a pinched, frightened face peered out from under a hurricane lamp.

"Yes?" The woman croaked.

"May we please come in. You can see we're perfectly harmless," Helena said.

Reluctantly she made way for them, latched the door firmly as soon as they were inside and set the lamp on a long table in the center of a mud-walled room.

A revoltingly acrid odor assailed their nostrils. It was hard to distinguish the stench of cow shed from chicken run, for they both came from the passage leading off the main room. The animals and their owners undoubtedly shared the same roof. Helena noticed that Stefa's face had gone pale and she was breathing hard behind her hand. She had always known the child had a 'thing' about smells but until now, she hadn't realized how bad it was. Within seconds Stefa had it under control and Helena turned to the woman.

"I'm sorry to disturb you so late at night but we've come a long way and I was told that I would find someone here to take us across the river."

This seemingly harmless remark produced the most extraordinary reaction. The woman gave a start and shook her head so hard that long wisps of gray hair loosened from the carelessly tied bun at the nape of her neck.

"No! my old man won't do that anymore, not for anyone!" She shrieked. "The Russians have been searching all the cottages and attics and barns for people trying to get across and they caught some this very morning. My man's hiding out until things quieten down."

Before Helena had a chance to say anything the woman rounded on her like a witch, beside herself with fury.

"And it's all because of the likes of you, shitty gentry!" She screamed, baring her gapped teeth. "All the comings and goings! Not satisfied to sit on your fat arses you come here, then you want to get back at the expense of our men's lives!" She raised her fingers. "Three have been killed already because of you people. You hear? Three!! And my brother one of them." She broke off with a choking sob.

*

CHAPTER SEVEN

"Challenge across the River San"

As though motivated by some capricious force beyond her control, the old crone's fury as suddenly and as unexpectedly turned to abject remorse. She fell before one of the many holy pictures ranged along the walls and piously crossed herself. "The good Lord forgive me. I didn't mean to say all those things. Oh God, deliver me from evil, Merciful Jesus, deliver me from Satan." Striking her breast she muttered. "My sin, my sin, my very grave sin."

Cleansed to her satisfaction, she stood up. Her attention riveted on Stefa, whom she approached as carefully as one would a frightened rabbit.

"You poor mite, you look dead tired," she crooned, stroking Stefa's hair, the rasp-like fingers catching at the strands. Stefa recoiled but not so that the woman would notice. "Come by the fire my angel and don't you worry none. There's another man that might still take you across. He's a kinsman of mine and lives in Gorylowka, the next village further down the valley. There now. Warmer? You wait here till my son gets back and he'll take you."

Too terrified to speak, Stefa nodded her head.

While they waited, unsure of the demented creature, she warmed up a jug of milk for them and gave them each a slice of bread. Set on making amends she could not have been nicer. Helena and Stefa could not have eaten the bread even if it hadn't been stale, and both of them surreptitiously slipped chunks of it under the table for Lala. Marian stoically ate his and didn't seem in the least put out by their bizarre reception.

Sipping the milk, Helena let her thoughts wander to the type of people who could live in such a hovel. Most of the peasants' homes she had been to were fresh-smelling and scrupulously clean. Here, this woman alone made the place look slovenly.

Stefa finished her milk and lay her head on her mother's lap. Instantly she was asleep. The woman's eyes closed and soon her head began to nod. Then Marian hunched himself over the table and he too dozed off. Helena looked at her watch. 1.30 a.m. She fought against sleep but her eyes closed. *Well, maybe just for a few minutes...*

They all jumped as a volley of sharp raps rattled the door. It was 4.30.

"That'll be my son," the woman told them, hurrying to unbolt the latch.

He was a big brute of a fellow in his twenties, with an untidy mop of red hair, a round beefy face and massive hands. He froze in the doorway and shot a questioning frown at his mother.

"They've come to be taken -" a meaningful jerk of the head in the general direction of the river completed the sentence.

He slammed the door shut and shambled inside. "Like bloody hell they have!"

"All right Stasiu, don't get het up. I told them we wouldn't do it. Just take them to Woj-"

"For Christ's sake mother!"

"Oh, I forgot. Well, will you take them to him."

She addressed this lout of a son in such a pathetic mixture of diffidence and forlorn authority that Helena could almost feel sorry for her. He grunted something about having just walked a devil of a long way and didn't see why he should trouble himself with strangers.

"Please," Helena said. "I will pay you." His eyes grew cunning.

"How much?" "50 *Zloty,*" she offered.

"100 or nothing."

"50 or nothing," she repeated firmly, standing up to go.

He hastily extended a ham-like hand for the cash, as she knew he would. It was probably more money than he had ever possessed.

Pocketing the notes, he opened the door again and without a word walked out.

Helena hurriedly thanked the old woman for the milk and bread. She made the sign of the cross and murmured a blessing, but whether it was intended for them or for her precious boy, it was hard to tell.

Helena had no idea how far this Gorylowka was, but any distance would have been too great after their long walk and little sleep. They had no choice, and the man set a relentless pace through fields and woods, where the ground was wet and slippery. Clumsy in such unfamiliar surroundings, all three of them stumbled along, often tripping and falling to their hands and knees. To add to their misery, it began to drizzle.

In awe of the big man, Stefa made no protest in support of the tears that streamed down her unhappy little face. Keeping close behind their guide, Marian turned a grim face now and then to make sure his sister was all right. Lala panted close at Helena's heels, with hardly a patch left to show the original color of her coat.

"Next time one of us falls, I'll make the *cham* (Lout. Pronounced 'ham') slow down," Helena muttered, and tripped and fell heavily, the case flying out of her wet grip.

"Hey you!" She called out, furious now. "We can't keep up with you. Slow DOWN will you?!"

He didn't respond but she knew he heard her for he slackened his pace a little and, afraid that he may have inherited his mother's mental instability, she dared not ask for more. He obviously did not want to be seen with them in daylight.

With the first light of dawn, they reached the village. The man stopped at one of the larger cottages. The housewife who opened the door to them this time showed none of the fear the other had done. Her intelligent eyes took in the situation at a glance and without any questions she led them straight inside, saying that they would have to sleep in the attic as both the living room and hallway were occupied by strangers, like themselves.

Helena turned to their guide but there was no sign of him. They followed the woman up a ladder leading to the attic. It was warm and fragrant-smelling from the long heaps of straw piled in neat rows along the floor. Each 'bed' was covered with clean sackcloth and had a folded blanket.

"Give me your coats. I'll have them cleaned up a bit for you," she said, helping Stefa off with hers. "My husband will be here later on in the day, then you can talk to him."

She took a few steps down the ladder, hesitated and came back.

"I suppose your dog could do with a bath," she smiled, scooping Lala up. She gave a whimper of protest at the unexpected threat of separation but a nod from Helena was enough to reassure her and she obediently let herself be carried away.

"We'll find some proper bandages for your feet," Helena said, taking Stefa's shoes off and noticing that the blood had soaked through the strips tied around her heels. "Later," she added in a whisper, adjusting the blanket on the already sleeping form.

It was late afternoon before she woke up. She took a clean blouse and underwear out of the suitcase, left the children sleeping and went in search of whatever washing facilities might be available. Even a bucket of cold water would have been welcome right then. Lala, silky-white again, was waiting for her at the foot of the ladder. Her barks of joy brought the landlady hurrying along. She took Helena to her own room, where there was a zinc bath filled with hot water, a cake of home-made soap, a small brush and a towel neatly laid out.

"When you're finished," she said, "just go straight through to the end room. The rest of the folk are all there."

"Thank you. Oh, and could you let me have a strip of gauze or something. My little girl has some bad blisters on her heels."

"I'll attend to her myself."

"Thank you again." Gratefully Helena touched the woman's arm.

She got into the bath and began to scrub herself. "So this is what they mean by peeling off layers of mud," she said to Lala who was watching her attentively. As she climbed out, she looked up and was startled to see a drawn, hollow-eyed face peering at her through a bush of tangled hair and even more taken aback when she recognized the apparition as her own reflection in an old stained wall mirror. She rummaged in her bag for her comb and gave battle to the knots and the bits of straw in her hair. The result was an improvement but she could do nothing about the mud-caked skirt which she had to put on again.

It felt hard and unpleasant to the touch. She shrugged. "No time to be fastidious. Come on my doggie, let's go find the others."

The room she had been directed to was the parlor. It had that impersonal atmosphere associated with rooms seldom used, but now there must have been a dozen people grouped around the center table. At the head sat a tall, elderly man. He rose to greet her and asked her to take a chair. She had the uncomfortable feeling of being under the surveillance of a dozen pair of eyes and was relieved when the tall man began to address them in the soft, lilting dialect peculiar to this region.

"You must all be aware by now that crossing the San is not an easy matter these days and that the danger lies on both sides."

"Could you explain why that is," a cadaverous-looking woman interjected. "After all, the Germans and the Russians are supposed to be allies now, so why all this vigilance over their precious border?"

"As far as the Russians are concerned, they consider it unpatriotic for anyone to want to leave a country they have 'liberated' and ten years in the salt mines is the minimum sentence awarded for an infringement of this tenet. Providing of course, one is not suspected of espionage. If one does happen to fall into the category of a spy, then twenty to twenty-five years is the usual term."

"Jezus Maria!" The woman gasped, pressing a bony hand to her chest.

"As for the Germans," he went on smoothly, as if he had not heard the many exclamations that echoed the woman's. "I can only assume that they are equally determined not to let anyone through for fear of jeopardizing the good Russo-German relations."

Unlike the general run of peasants, this man was educated and Helena looked at him with renewed interest, deciding he must be a kinsman very far removed from the crazy female in Krakowiec.

With a fleeting smile he continued. "I'm not telling you all this in order to alarm you but so that you know what you are up against and so that those who wish to change their minds might still do so. We've made many successful trips across, but will have to wait for the right opportunity before attempting another one. In the meantime, you are welcome to stay here."

A murmur of disappointment drifted round the table and a peevish voice piped up, "Look here my man, I paid you to take me across and I'm damned if I'm going to spend another night on your blasted floor! What is the point in delaying, anyway?"

The muscles of the fisherman's jaws tensed but he framed his answer carefully. "Because I don't intend to endanger the lives of my passengers or my own for that matter, unnecessarily. I have to take into account the change of guards on both sides and when I am satisfied that the time is right, only then will we make a move. If that doesn't suit you sir, you are perfectly at liberty to swim across as many others have done, and I shall gladly refund your fee."

Waiting for comments, his keen gaze swept the room, but as the reply he gave the dandy seemed to have squashed all further signs of dissention, he went on. "Providing the Germans stick to normal routine, there should be no guard at the spot where we'll be landing, but in case there is a hitch, we'll have to try and pass off as Germans. Is there anyone among you fluent in the language?"

Automatically Helena's hand went up.

"Good." This time his smile was warm. "Then if necessary, will you do the talking?"

She looked at the faces turned towards her and was suddenly struck by the enormity of such a commitment. She felt the familiar sensation of fear and made herself look directly at the fisherman. His smile broadened at her nod. Helena became aware that everyone there was manifesting a common emotion in their own way. They were all frightened but only one or two didn't or couldn't hide it. She guessed she was the youngest in this group, with the dandy a close second; the others were anywhere between forty and sixty. The man sitting next to her had been pulling at his moustache in that absent way grown of habit. Now he left it for a second to give her hand a reassuring pat, as if to say, don't worry my girl, you'll manage all right.

As none of the others had anything more to say, their host got to his feet in a sign of dismissal.

Now, for the first time since leaving Bielsko, Helena paid cash for their food and lodgings. The 200 *Zloty* asked for included the boat trip. As exorbitant as the fee was, she would have gladly given more in return for an escape from the blue uniformed N.K.V.D., the Military Police and the Russian soldiers.

They were divided into smaller groups. Eight remained at the cottage and the others were accommodated with neighbors.

The most trying member in the party was Lady Borowska, a revoltingly obese woman on the wrong side of fifty, still playing the part of a spoilt flapper. Everyone tried to avoid her. Her constant complaints about the unsanitary conditions, the bucket toilets, communal sleeping quarters and above all, her reference to Lala as a potential hazard and an unnecessary menace, created an immediate animosity between her and the Poleks.

Some of the people waiting to be transported across the river San came from this side of the country but rather than face possible deportation to Siberia, they preferred to chance their fate under the Germans.

Helena drifted from one group to another, but with the exception of the painfully thin female who spoke up at the meeting, she could find no common ground with these people. Their fears and useless speculations did nothing for her morale, nor could she take part in their covert grumbling about the amount of money they were being charged. When she did point out that the man was risking his neck for them, she was dismayed to realize that that was an arbitrary that didn't enter into the equation.

That night she discovered that theirs was not the only man in the village engaged in rescue operations. Wrenched awake by the blast of gunfire, loud angry voices and screams, she reached for Stefa.

The hatch to the attic burst open and the people who had been sleeping below were rushed inside.

"Hurry!" The landlady panted. "Pile the straw on top of you. See that no blanket shows and lie still."

"What's happening?" Helena asked, quickly burying Stefa under the straw.

"They've caught a party trying to cross the river. I don't know how many they've shot but they've captured the boatman. The Russians are searching some of the other cottages right now. They may not come here at all, but someone might talk, so for God's sake don't make a sound until I come back."

"Mother of God," sobbed Lady Borowska, burrowing herself under a heap of straw like a frantic hippo. "What if they use bayonets to prod us with? I've heard they do that."

"In that event, dear lady," hissed the dandy maliciously, "you bite your bloody tongue until the prodding stops."

Angry "shshs" silenced them.

Helena's arm around Stefa's shoulders began to heave. Panic stricken, she fumbled to get a finger under the child's nose to stop the sneeze. It came out in a muffled grunt, fortunately not loud enough for anyone else to hear. Stefa relaxed. Helena's heartbeats slowed down to almost normal. They waited.

Then the sound of running boots getting closer, stopping beneath the attic window, moving on. A torrent of obscenities growing softer -- and a rush of controlled exhalations from beneath the straw.

Gun shots could still be heard, but more distant now and probably fired to intimidate the people.

A few minutes later, the landlady returned to announce that the crisis was over.

At home, Helena slept through the morning rush and only woke up after Adam had gone to work and the children had been sent off to school. This was an old habit dating back to her mother's coddling, but one which Adam liked to foster. Most habits die hard, this one expired overnight. Over the first night of September, to be exact. Since then, she had been waking up at dawn.

That morning, dawn in Gorylowka was a sight to make one forget the terrors of the night before. She stood at the little window and gazed at the miracle of the sun edging its way from behind a distant hill and in vivid hues of red, gold and umber, bringing the countryside to life and to another day. The thought of another day of waiting, worrying, listening to other people's worries, was enough to break the spell and blind her to the most spectacular views. She dressed quietly, picked Lala up and went to the washhouse.

The water was bracingly cold. Winter was not far off. Another month or so and the Russians could relax their sentry along the river. Rowing across would be out of the question and the uncertain ice over fast currents would prove an even greater deterrent than their guns.

On the way out of the washhouse she met the fisherman's wife.

"Any more news about last night?" She asked.

"Three people shot, as far as I know. Two dead and one seriously wounded."

"Tell me," Helena asked. "Why does your husband do this? I hardly think he would do it for the love of his passengers -- certainly not the types that are here now. And money alone is no compensation for life."

The woman shot her a swift glance. "No, it isn't, but it's one way of making a living these days."

"And is that all?" Helena persisted.

"No. He's got it into his head this is one way he can still get at the Russians." Her face closed.

It was obvious she didn't want to talk about it. Helena didn't press it.

Later in the afternoon the fisherman assembled his group and told them to be ready to leave that night.

Helena turned down the paraffin lamp and looked up at the tiny gauze-covered window. The stars winked back as steadily as ever, a cloud wafted calmly past, even the frogs enjoyed their symphony. Nature had not changed. Its normalcy merely made their own situation seem so much more unreal. It was hard to believe that a few hours from now they would start out on a trip that might end it all.

Restlessly she turned over. A piece of straw pricked into her side. Lala sensed her uneasiness and moved closer. Helena felt the warm tongue on her hand and tried to project a measure of reassurance into her stroking fingers, forgetting that you can fool yourself before you can fool a dog. Her eyes fell on the sleeping forms of her children and she prayed that they at least would come through safely.

The thought of what the Russians had done to last night's party made her come out in a cold sweat. That, according to the fisherman was supposed to be to their advantage, since the guards would probably not suspect anyone to dare venture across so soon again. She hoped he was right. She wouldn't have thought it possible but she dozed off then and Marian's tug on her arm sent her springing upright.

Tousle-haired, cheeks flushed, he called impatiently, "Come on you two. Everyone's waiting. The cart's ready to go!"

"How many are coming with us Mommy?" Stefa asked in a small voice, fumbling at her coat buttons with stiff fingers.

"Fifteen I think. But don't look so worried love, it'll get us across all right."

Stefa doubted if they would get across all right. Didn't a boat sink under an overload of 17? They said that a lot of people drowned then and the others were shot by the Russians. It's fair enough to ask God to help you but it's not fair to ask for the impossible.

"Shouldn't we go next time?" She pleaded. "When there aren't so many people with us?"

"Look, if the fisherman says we can go, then it's perfectly safe. He knows what he's talking about, so stop worrying. Here, let me help you with those buttons."

They hurried down the ladder with Lala flung across Marian's shoulders in a sack. Not a sound came from her.

With everyone's nerves at breaking point, their clamber onto the back of the cart was nothing short of chaotic. The fisherman, who had done this so many time before, tried to keep the party under control, repeatedly urging them to be quiet.

"Will somebody have the decency to help me up?" Lady Borowska panted, struggling to heave her bulky form up with the others. The fisherman came to her rescue but nothing could stop the incessant whine of her petulant voice. "Oh, the smell of this beastly cart" she moaned, pressing a scented handkerchief to her nose. "It's making me feel positively ill."

"You'll be more than ill if you don't keep your voice down," Helena told her sharply.

The cart did stink of manure. She looked at Stefa and felt a glow of pride that her child was showing a better control of her own phobia than this adult. Then they were off, headed for the river bank.

Helena found herself pressed close to a dark little man whom she had not seen before. Although his face was partly obscured by the coat collar he had pulled up above his ears, the glimpse she had had of his features convinced her that they were Semitic. If the Nazis caught them harboring a Jew, they would all be done for. She knew this but she also felt sure that so far, she was the only one aware of their gate-crasher. He sensed her gaze upon him. Their eyes met and in that moment an understanding passed between them. He gave her a tremulous smile and she could feel some of the tension leave his body.

The cart stopped. The dark stranger lifted Stefa off, then held his hand out to help Helena down.

They were shepherded down a long, sloping river bank. In a harsh whisper the fisherman warned them to stay hidden behind the tree trunks. Silently they darted from tree to tree, until the vast expanse of river could be seen below, glistening silver in the cold light of the moon.

A gunshot broke the silence. One of the party dropped to the ground. More shots came in quick succession. In a wild panic everyone rushed back up the bank, followed by loud commands of *"Wertaj nazad!"* (Come back).

They all made it to the cart. The fisherman dragged the wounded man up next to him and cracked his whip. Crouching on the floor, the rest of them were tossed about unmercifully as the farm horses responded to the unfamiliar lash of the whip.

Helena's arm began to throb and as she touched it, her fingers felt the sticky wetness through the tear in the coat sleeve. She didn't think it was serious and said nothing.

Once they reached the village, the fisherman called out, "Those of you willing to risk it again tonight, come with me." With that he walked off. Nearly all followed him to a dimly lit barn.

He locked the door and stood facing them.

"You were careless," he began grimly. "I hope this has been a lesson to you. When I said keep to the trees, I meant keep to the trees! Now I feel sure the Russians are satisfied that we won't try again tonight, so we'll start off in half an hour's time. In the meantime stay here while I see to the wounded fellow."

Helena stopped him at the door and quietly asked if he would also bring a bandage for her arm. Giving no sign of alarm, he just as quietly told her to accompany him.

Curious to know what they were whispering about, Marian came over but before he could speak, Helena took hold of his arm.

"Listen Marian, go back and look after Stefa. A bullet must have grazed my arm and I'm going to have it attended to. Shan't be long."

As his eyes fell on the dark stain on the coat, he paled.

"It's nothing to worry about, honestly," she reassured him and hurried out after the man.

She expected him to first collect the wounded fellow and then to take them both to his house but these people were better organized than she had imagined. Someone had already moved the patient to a well-concealed outbuilding and when they entered the narrow white-washed room, with its First Aid box and strong smell of antiseptic, she had the impression of stepping into an improvised clinic. Which it was.

The unfortunate victim, whom she recognized as the dandy, was laid out on a low bench. He looked like death. There was a deep wound in his side, on which a clumsy-fingered female was working. It was as well the man was unconscious.

"Will he live?" She asked the woman.

"Don't see why not. I've seen worse cases than this pull through. Ah, here it is!"

Helena shuddered at the size of the bullet the woman triumphantly held up.

Meanwhile the fisherman had gotten water, swab, iodine and bandages ready. He helped Helena off with her coat, rolled up the sleeve of her blouse and gently dabbed at the arm until the exposed wound clearly bore out her first belief that it was no more than a nasty graze. The iodine treatment was pure murder and she had to grit her teeth not to make a fool of herself.

As soon as he finished he told the woman to take Helena back to the barn while he took over her patient. Helena felt the poor man would now stand a better chance. The fisherman's treatment of her wound had been almost professional.

She was pleased to see that Marian had kept their secret, for her return excited no one's interest but his own.

"All right?" He whispered anxiously.

"Yes, fine," she stretched the truth. The weakness and nausea soon passed.

Her Jewish friend had managed to win Stefa's confidence. She joined them on the floor in the darkest corner of the barn. Stefa was badly shaken, but seemed to find the man's gentle, soothing voice comforting.

If anything, Marian appeared more exhilarated than ever for the close shave they'd had.

By now there were eleven left in the party. Someone remarked that Lady Borowska was no longer with them.

"Now perhaps we'll get across the river," someone else put in with a heavy sigh of relief.

Punctual to the minute, the fisherman returned within the half hour and had them all on the cart again in a much more orderly fashion. No one thought to push or grumble this time.

Quietly they wove their way in and out of the trees, the only sound the distant notes of a rollicking song -- the Russian's way of celebrating what they thought to be another successfully foiled escape.

They slithered down to the water's edge and there, hidden among the reeds was the boat.

Expertly the oars cleaved the water, with barely a ripple and at such speed that within seconds they were out in the open.

Fervently Stefa prayed that none of the guards would spot them and open fire. With only eleven passengers on board, the water still came to within a few inches of the gunnels and each swell was enough to make her heart leap.

Marian's eyes roved from one embankment to the other. If there was the slightest movement from the Russian side, he'd be able to alert everyone to duck. He wasn't quite sure what he could do if a German sentry showed up. Maybe they could row further down the river...

A poor swimmer, Helena couldn't see herself being able to save Stefa, especially with one arm that now felt stiff and more painful than she would ever admit. Marian could take care of himself, could even help her with Stefa, that's if the bullets didn't get them first. But what was she thinking of? *We'll make it. We've got to make it. Dear God please, please help us make it.*

They had almost reached the other side when a heavier swell rocked the boat. The fisherman steadied her, letting her coast a while. The silence was accentuated by the gentle lap, lap of the water against the hull. All eyes were on the river bank. It was impossible to penetrate the gloom that surrounded the reeds and bushes but the fisherman seemed to know where he was headed for. He steered the boat into a hidden landing spot and tied her up.

They were about to climb out when a voice called out, *"Halt! Wer ist da?!"*

Silhouetted against the edge of the bank was a German guard, his rifle pointed directly at them.

*

CHAPTER EIGHT

"The First Escape – out of the frying pan..."

"Who goes there?" The German barked again.

A sharp nudge brought Helena back to her senses. She licked her lips and called out, "We are German refugees. We want to get back to our homes in Silesia."

Emboldened by the guard's silence she went on in a steadier and louder voice.

"Have you a torch? There's an awful lot of mud here and we can't see properly."

Still covering them with his rifle, the man took a few steps down the bank and blinded them with a powerful beam of light.

She plucked up more nerve and told him the ground was what they needed the light for. Obediently he lowered his torch and told them to climb up.

He led them to a small clearing and said they would have to wait until the officer in charge arrived as he had no authority to deal with them.

They stood staring at one another in mute dismay. Presently an officer appeared, gun in hand. A torch searched their faces. Once again Helena repeated her story and since they must have heard the shots fired at them, she gave an account of the bestial treatment they had received under the Russians.

The officer didn't reply but snapped an order to his sentry. The man saluted smartly and marched off. The German stepped closer, scanned their faces one by one and when his eyes rested on the dark stranger, he turned to Helena.

"Naturally I don't believe a word you have said." His voice made the night seem colder. "In the first place you cannot tell me that this child," pointing to Stefa, "is anything but Polish. Furthermore, you have a Jew with you." His hand shot out again, this time towards the dark little man who visibly shrank in an effort to hide his face.

She visualized them being shot on the spot, their bodies thrown into the river. And if the Germans didn't do it, the Russians would. She felt a tightening of the chest and a sick hollowness in her stomach. The river would carry them no one knew where. And Adam would never know. *No! It can't end like this!*

"What's in the sack?" The officer was asking. Marian opened the sack and Lala's eyes gazed out at the man. She turned her head sideways in that appealing way of hers and uttered a sound that for all the world sounded like "Me." Helena could have sworn she saw him hide a smile.

"You know very well what I have to do with you, don't you?"

"Yes," she replied, amazed at the strength in her voice. "But all we want is to get back to our homes. We're all civilians here. No threat to you. We aren't spies for heavens' sake." She took a deep breath. "And I can't believe you would treat us the same way as those barbarians across the river."

For a long moment he stood silent, looking at the tense, white-faced group in front of him, liking the woman's courage. He thought of his wife Gertrude, a spunky woman too. His three beautiful little girls. How he loved his family. No, he wasn't a barbarian.

"What I am about to do could cost me my life," he finally said, putting the gun away, "but I'll be frank with you Madame. I am a German, yes, but wear this uniform because I have to. I also have a family, children -- and a dog, like yours." Fleetingly, he let the smile show. "Who knows what lies ahead of any of us?" He paused. "You are free to go." And in a barely audible voice added, "Just say a Hail Mary for me."

Without waiting for an answer he turned on his heel and disappeared into the night.

They stood stupefied, until the full meaning of his action penetrated minds already numbed by resignation. Then, as one, with excited spontaneity, they fell on each other's necks. Helena was made to give a word for word account of her talk with the German. They loved it. They loved her. Even Lala came in for her share of praise for the part she had played in triggering the man's humane instincts.

"Whew!" The fisherman passed the back of his hand over a glistening brow. "I've never come across anything like it. It's a miracle. But the sooner we get away from this place the happier I'll be. My cousin's house isn't far from here and as I told you, she'll put us up for the rest of the night. Let's go!"

In less than fifteen minutes they were outside a fairly large cottage. A sweet-faced, barefoot woman with a baby on her hip ushered them inside. She had spread straw and blankets on the floors in readiness for them. In their exhausted state, no one felt any discomfort that night.

The noise, slight as it was, woke her instantly. Helena opened her eyes to daylight and just in time to see her Jewish friend gingerly placing her shoes on the floor next to her.

"What are you do-" she broke off in embarrassment when she saw how clean the shoes looked.

He spread his hands in a typical gesture. "It's the least I could do."

"There was no need."

"No," he agreed with a smile and quickly left.

This small service moved her as no act of largesse could have done. She sank back into the straw. Thank God things had gone the way they did, she thought, blinking to get rid of the tears, for if they hadn't, this little man would probably have had to bear the blame and the vengeance. She knew they would have sacrificed him if necessary, in order to save themselves. How complex was human nature. You found kindness where you least expected it and evil where there should be goodness. *Should* be? "Don't expect things from people and you'll never be disappointed," her mother had told her and although it wasn't always the easiest thing to put into practice, she'd never forgotten it. As she thought about it now, she realized that since they'd left home, she had not taken anything or anyone for granted and all the help along the way had been so much more wonderful for being unexpected. It made her feel... she groped for the right word, humble, she supposed. She smiled, surprised at this revelation.

She shook her head and sat up. Most of the 'beds' were already empty, including Marian's. She glanced at her watch and saw that it was almost 7. She woke Stefa and together they went to wash their faces in the basin of fresh cold water that had been provided. The delicious smell of coffee led them in the direction of the kitchen. Seeing only a handful of the party there, Helena asked about the others and was told that they had already left.

The young woman brought in freshly baked bread and a bowl of cottage cheese. The fisherman walked in behind her.

"Good morning," he beamed. "My name is Wojcik, by the way, and this is my cousin Marysia." He went on to explain that it had been agreed between the villagers not to disclose the names of the boatmen to any of the guests before they were safely across the river.

"Why, Mr. Wojcik?" Marian asked.

"Because when we first started taking people across, one of the party was caught and he gave away his boatman's name. They hunted him down and that was the last we heard of him. Not that anybody could blame the informant. Poor devil, they gave him a rough time.

"This senseless war," his voice harshened with emotion. "It has brought about so much tragedy and unhappiness. Marysia here lost her son on the river. He had helped more than a hundred refugees across. Such a good lad he was, no more than a boy."

The woman's face crumbled. She turned away and began stoking the fire. She had also lost her husband in the war as well as their only means of livelihood, as neither the Germans nor the Russians allowed fishing any more.

Helena could find no words of comfort and her offer of payment for the night and the food was met with flat refusal.

"No my lady. The Lord knows you'll need all you've got to get you and the children home." She pushed the money back. "Wojcik here helps us out."

Helena felt oddly relieved to hear her say that. This then, was where some of the proceeds of his earnings went to.

When the rest of the party began to leave, Wojcik motioned Helena back to her seat. He saw the others off and came back saying, "They should be all right now. It's you I'm a bit worried about. Silesia is a long way off."

Didn't she know it.

"And there are the children," he went on. "I can take you as far as Jaroslaw, but you'll have to apply to the Magistrate's Office there for permits to go on by train."

"The only thing that bothered me was getting to the nearest station. It's more than kind of you to offer to take us. The permits will be no problem."

He regarded her for a moment. "No, I don't think they will be, for you," he remarked. "Not often one finds a woman of your caliber. How is the arm?"

"Fine," she said, somewhat disconcerted by a compliment which she felt to be quite undeserved.

"Let's have another look at it."

He unwound the bandage. "Yes, it looks fine. Doesn't even need a fresh dressing. I don't think you should have any trouble with it."

"Thanks to your able doctoring. I was very impressed with your clinic you know. Where did you learn all the first aid?"

"He studied medicine," his cousin proudly explained. "But there wasn't enough money for him to carry on with it."

"What a pity."

"Oh I don't know, there's a lot to be said for a fisherman's life," he replied with a rueful smile. "More coffee?"

"No. No thanks, I've had two cups already." "Then shall we be off?"

"I'm ready when you are."

She was about to climb onto the cart after Stefa, when their Jewish friend came up to her and, under cover of saying good-bye pressed a wad of notes into her hand.

"What's this for?" She whispered.

"For recognizing another human being," he said with wry humor. "You'll need it. Take it. "

He must have known, as well as she did, that he would have been better off under the Russians.

"What made you come with us?" She asked him.

"My family is on this side. They will need me."

"In that case, you had better hang on to the money. It's the only thing that might still help you," she told him bluntly.

"No Madame. If God cannot help me, this certainly won't."

Reluctantly, and because she didn't know what else to do, she accepted the cash. "God's speed then," she murmured, squeezing his hand.

Marian helped her up. She turned to wave but the man was gone.

"Poor bugger," Wojcik muttered, flicking the horse with his rein. The cart squeaked into motion. "By the way," he said. "There's been another raid on the other side of the river. We heard shots in the early hours of the morning."

"Will you be able to get back?"

"It won't be so difficult on my own," he said. "And, I'll time it for when our trigger-happy Comrades are celebrating again."

Helena sat back, thankful that they had left all that behind them, the bloodshed and terror that represented the so-called liberated part of Poland. Right now she didn't want to think of what lay ahead of them. Enough that they were together and out of Russian hands. They drove slowly on, passing signs of immeasurable damage. Burnt out villages, where emaciated dogs still searched for scraps. Wrecked tanks, trucks, cars and overturned carts, all gave their mute testimony to the battle that must have raged here. A dip in the road brought them to the grimmest part of all. As far as the eye could see stood grave mounds with crude crosses perched on them, some bearing a soldier's helmet. Helena turned away with a shudder. It was Stefa's nerves that snapped. "I can't stand looking at all those graves. I can't! I can't!" Hysterical with grief she threw herself against her mother. "Please don't let Daddy be there!" Having to comfort her child forced Helena out of her own despair.

"Don't get so worked up silly," Marian said testily, unaffected by his sister's outburst. "Dad's alive I tell you."

Wojcik kept his eyes on the road. He hoped the boy was right. Despite his policy of non-involvement with his passengers, this little family had gotten to him. They had made this last trip that much more worthwhile.

Now, only the squeak and rattle of the cart and the rhythmic clip-clop of the hooves broke the stillness that surrounded them. Not a living soul passed them all the way to Jaroslaw. Not a bird hovered in the sky.

Wojcik stopped the cart on the outskirts of the small town. "This is as far as I dare go," he explained. "One has to have legitimate reasons for coming into town these days."

Stiffly Helena climbed out. Marian and Stefa had already jumped off and were pulling the straw out of Lala's hair. Unaccountably, she had dug her heels in again and had to be forced to leave the cart.

Wojcik thrust his hand out. "The first large building on the main street is the Magistrate's Office. You can't miss it. Good luck and, God bless."

"Thank you-- for everything," Helena said with feeling.

She watched him drive off, the last link in the long chain of helpers. From now on, she would have to fend for herself and as much as she felt at home with the Germans, there was the fearful uncertainty of a new order. She reasoned that she had always gotten on well with them, at least before the war. Her best friend Olga was of German extraction, Olga's husband was German born. She wondered what had happened to her friend. Nothing much probably. She would have had more sense than to go wandering off all over the country. And if they hadn't, none of this would have happened to them either. She stopped herself. Wallowing in recriminations for God's sake, when she had an interview to think of. Squaring her shoulders, she began to walk faster.

……...

A long line of people stood outside the Magistrate's Office. She learned that most of them were refugees, waiting for papers to give them the right to return to their homes. Many of the faces looked distinctly Polish and those, she noticed, were hustled back almost as soon as their turn came. The Germans were dealt with first. It was something worth knowing and she immediately made Marian and Stefa sit down on the pavement, away from probing eyes. Next, she delved into her bag for mirror and comb. Scathing glances met this public display of vanity, but she guessed appearances still played their part in the right quarters, and she added a touch of red to her lips.

She managed to get through the officials before closing time and was shown into a cheerless tobacco-filled office. The fat man behind the desk ignored her. He had a directory in front of him and with great precision was running a stained finger down a column of names. He flicked the page and started from the top again. On the wall above his head was a blown-up photograph of the Fuhrer. Helena decided on the offensive. She walked right up to his desk and helped herself to a chair opposite him, scraping it loudly on the floor to attract attention. He looked up with hooded eyes.

"I am German," she announced boldly. "And should like to be provided with whatever papers are necessary to enable me and my children to return to Bielsko."

"Where are your children?"

"Sitting outside. Probably asleep by now. They're tired out."

"I'll have to see them," he insisted.

"Then take a look out of your window," she said, with just a hint of impatience. "There they are, on the filthy pavement."

He got up to see better. Huddled together in a sorry heap were Marian and Stefa, their backs to the window.

"All right, Frau...?" He asked, picked up his pen. She let her breath out and said, "Von Heise."

"Any identification documents?"

"None." Her tone was bitter. "The Poles saw to that!"

He nodded and with more courtesy now, handed her a document stating that as a refugee she and her children were entitled to a free train passage as far as their home town.

The 'Von' had evidently impressed him, for he even opened the door to let her out, before stepping back to give the stiff-armed *Heil Hitler* salute.

On the way to the station she congratulated herself on the success of her first encounter with the enemy. *I can handle them,* she told herself triumphantly, *providing I keep my nerve and the children out of sight.* At Bielsko it would be a different story, because there they were known and more particularly, people knew of Adam's anti-Nazi activities. She felt the fear pricking at her again and resolutely determined to cross her bridges when she came to them.

And the first bridge was to get on the train, which was already crowded to capacity. They fought their way on board but there was no hope of securing seats and they were forced to stand in the carriageway throughout the night. Helena envied some of the people's ability to doze on their feet. Marian was one of them. After a while Stefa's knees buckled under her and she slipped to the floor. Safely wedged between her mother's legs, she too was able to doze on and off. Morning brought a vacant seat. Helena snapped it up from under the noses of two equally determined German *Fraus*. Too tired to worry about their black looks and offensive language, she sat Stefa on her lap and promptly fell asleep. Lala's main concern had been to avoid being trodden on. Now she was safe under the seat, but still restive and strangely woebegone.

The long journey home was broken at Krakow, where they had to change trains. For some reason the waiting rooms were out of bounds to the public and they were made to sit on the cold platform, together with a multitude of fellow travelers and wait for their connection. The train for Bielsko was due within the hour. This, Helena learned, could mean anything up to five hours.

There had been no time to look for food before they left Jaroslaw and apart from one or two dry *Pierniki* (gingerbread biscuits) they had had nothing to eat in over twenty-four hours. The Restaurant was closed but the Kiosk sold German literature and coffee. They got in line eagerly, expecting the coffee to be hot if not palatable. It was neither.

An officer strolled past them several times. Helena was soon to learn that the swastika armlet meant he was a member of the Gestapo. He showed more than a passing interest in Lala and on one occasion warned them to watch their dog or she might get lost in the crowd.

They had been waiting for over two hours when Stefa said she could hold out no longer. Helena took her to the toilet, leaving Marian to keep an eye on Lala. Here too, there were long lines and when they finally returned, they found Marian fast asleep and no sign of their pet.

It was impossible. Lala had never left their side before. Almost frantic, they searched and called until their train was due to leave and they could do nothing else but go on without her.

All three boarded the train in tears. "She knew something would happen to her," Helena's voice was hoarse with grief. "That Gestapo pig stole her. And he had the gall to warn us about it too." It was small comfort but she hoped that if the man fancied Lala enough to steal her then he would surely take good care of her.

Stefa could not forgive Marian for falling asleep. His own grief and remorse stopped his mother from adding her own reproaches.

By the time they stepped off the train at Bielsko, all were utterly dejected, numbed with cold and desperately hungry. The station was no longer familiar. A large portion of it had been blown up, leaving dark, gaping cavities where the Kiosk and Restaurant had been. Helena looked up to see the time on the clock above the main entrance -- that too was gone. Her watch said 11.45 p.m.

Outside, the snow came down in large flakes.

A solitary car stood at the Taxi Rank. She rapped on the window to wake the man behind the wheel.

"Could you please take us to Zielna Street."

The cabbie blinked once and sat up. "Sure lady, if you've got the money."

"How much?" "25 *Zloty*"

She tried to bargain with him over the ridiculously stiff fare but he knew he had a captive passenger and would not budge. Dispassionately she counted out the notes.

As they drove closer to the house, Marian spotted lights in the upstairs windows.

"I don't like it," Helena muttered, telling the driver to stop. "Marian, go and take a look."

He came back with the news that there was a German nameplate on the front door.

They'd lost their home. Beyond surprise, resentment or grief, Helena accepted the fact, thankful that they still had somewhere to go. She asked the cabbie to take them to her mother-in-law's country home at Lesno, some fifteen miles out of town. After much haggling, he agreed to take them.

The roads were made treacherous by ice and snow and the Taxi kept skidding and stalling. Twelve miles later they came to a decisive stop.

"This is as far as she'll go lady," the man announced nonchalantly.

She had no choice but to pay the rogue his full fare and walk the rest of the way. The snow was still coming down, swirling and whipping at their faces. It was thick on the ground and in places came well above the ankles. It took them the best part of an hour to cover the last two miles. Teresa Polek's property was at the very top of the steep hill, commanding majestic views which only made the climb that much more difficult.

They could see the house now, isolated from all the others. A solid structure of whitewashed brick, with steps leading up to the mahogany doors and a broad verandah stretching along the entire front of the house. The snow-capped conical tops of the firs that jutted from behind the sloping roof and the wooden outbuildings gave the place a Swiss poster-like appearance. As they approached the house, a dog began to bark. The moment he recognized them, the Alsatian was beside himself with joy. He yelped and jumped on them in an ecstasy of excitement.

The noise brought Teresa Polek to the door, a stout stick clutched in her hand. She took one look at the panting stragglers on her doorstep and the stick dropped to the ground.

"The Lord be thanked," she cried, enfolding them in a huge embrace. "We'd given you up for dead."

"Have you heard from Adam?" Were Helena's first words. The older woman's shake of the head was like a blow.

"We'll talk about that later," she went on hurriedly. "The first thing is to thaw you out and get you to bed."

She helped them inside and put on the light. A wave of compassion swept over her as she saw the utter weariness in the three faces.

Her own face also betrayed weariness, sleepless nights and worry. There were lines on her forehead and at the side of her mouth that Helena had not seen there before. Her hair, streaked with gray, was parted in the middle and pulled back into a bun at the back of her head. A large woman, handsome to the point of masculinity, she had given her son not only a strong family resemblance, but also the proud lineage of great land owners and the deep patriotic convictions that ruled his life. Helena had always admired her for her strength as well as her intellect but they were never very close and the first three months of her marriage under her mother-in-law's roof had certainly not been the easiest. Now, looking into the striking brown eyes, softened with compassion and tears, she knew things would be a lot different between them. She too, had changed.

Eager as she was to hear their story, Teresa asked no questions. She woke the maid to prepare the beds and busied herself with warming up a pot of soup.

'Patches' came hurrying in as fast as her old legs would carry her, her face alight with a wide, toothless smile of welcome. She curtseyed to Helena and Stefa in the old tradition and then, unable to contain herself, went to embrace Marian. To her he represented a second edition of her beloved Adam.

Adam's pet name for his old nanny could not have been more descriptive. The heavily lined face might have been a patchwork in leather and it had been like that for as long as Helena could remember. She never did find out what her real name was.

"I won't be a minute with the beds," she said, making for the door. "Little Marian will have Master Adam's room?"

"Yes," Teresa smiled at the other's eagerness. "And Mrs. Polek and Stefa can share the front bedroom."

They literally pounced on the thick vegetable soup and slices of brown bread but a few mouthfuls were all that their tired bodies could cope with.

By the time Patches came back, Stefa had already fallen asleep in her chair. Clucking with sympathy she carried her to the bedroom.

"Now, what about Adam?" Helena asked.

"We don't know where he is, but I'm sure he's alive." "That's what I keep telling them," Marian put in.

"Let's talk tomorrow," Teresa said, taking Marian by the shoulders and steering him towards the door. "You're all done in."

Helena nodded. There was nothing left to talk about.

She peeled off the grimy clothes she had worn for so long and left them lying where they fell. She washed in the warm water Patches had poured into a huge basin and put on the tent-like cotton nightdress she had laid out. Already half asleep, she threw her aching body next to Stefa on the high, old-fashioned double bed.

When she opened her eyes again it was broad daylight. She snuggled deeper into the soft down, luxuriated in its warmth, in the fresh country smell of the sheets. She listened to the regular thud-thud of a wood chopper outside, finding the sound intensely reassuring. For the first time in months, she felt a measure of security. Little did she suspect how short-lived that feeling was to be.

Stefa was still asleep. One hand rested on the pillow and out of the clenched fist hung the beads of her rosary. Helena leaned forward to kiss the smooth forehead. Instantly she was awake.

"Is it time to go Mommy?"

"No my darling. We're not going any more. We've arrived."

Teresa came in with steaming cups of coffee and Marian followed with rolls and a raisin loaf.

Between mouthfuls Helena briefly recounted the events since they left Bielsko. When she came to the hardest part of all, to Alex and Wanda, the bread choked in her throat. Teresa's eyes turned bleak.

"We'll have a Mass said for them," was all she said.

Afterwards she filled them in on the happenings at home. These were enough to make Helena grow cold. Adam's name and photograph appeared on the dreaded "Black List" wanted for pre-war anti-Nazi operations. This meant that as his family, they were equally suspect.

Their home in Zielna street had been ransacked and subsequently occupied by a German official and his family. Fortunately, before the enemy moved in, Teresa had managed to salvage some of their clothes and valuables, among which was a life size oil portrait of Adam in his full Cavalry uniform.

"It's a pity you couldn't get there before that bitch Rozia walked off with my jewelry."

"Don't worry, I suspected her and traced her to her own village. Purely on the off-chance I demanded the return of your silver and jewelry under threat of the Police. She was so scared she admitted she had already sold some pieces but handed over what was left of it, including several cartons of cigarettes. I've hidden it all away."

"That's wonderful Mother. Better than I dared hope for."

"Yes. The only bit of good news there is, I'm afraid. The Gestapo have already been here looking for Adam and we can expect another call soon. Those devils don't give up easily."

"God, I wish I knew what has happened to him," Helena burst out, the tension under which she'd lived for so long finally catching up with her. Losing all control she flung herself at her mother-in-law and sobbed like a child. In a moment they were all in tears.

Above all a practical woman, Teresa was first to recover. "It certainly won't help anyone if we sit here bawling." She took a handkerchief out of her apron pocket and blew her nose hard. Putting her arm around Helena's shoulders she said more gently, "You musn't lose faith dear. God has protected you so far, he won't desert you now."

Caught up in their own emotions, no one noticed Stefa turn pale until she suddenly leapt out of bed with her hand over her mouth and ran towards the pail under the washstand. Before she could reach it, her body pitched forward and her head hit the edge of the stand.

Helena was out of bed and bending over the still form, before she realized what had happened. She turned the glassy-eyed blood-stained face up and panicked. "Stefa! Oh my God!"

"Mind Helena," Teresa pushed her aside, a glass of water already in her hand. "Fetch a clean cloth Marian." She sprinkled some of the water on Stefa's face, lifted her head and forced a little into her mouth. Stefa spluttered and her eyes focused. Teresa took the cloth from Marian's trembling fingers and dabbed at the cut. They saw then that it was not very deep and just over an inch long over the left eyebrow.

"Nervous exhaustion, that's what it is." Teresa picked her up and laid her back on the bed. "What she needs is a good rest and she'll be fine, won't you Stefciu?"

"I'm all right now. Honest I am, " Stefa protested. "I don't need to stay in bed. I don't even feel sick any more, truly."

"That's good my angel. You just rest a moment then. There's my baby." As she spoke she stroked Stefa's forehead up and over the hairline. The soothing voice, the gentle touch was all Stefa needed to put her back to sleep.

The next day she was as well as ever and Helena had a hard time getting the child to stay at home while she took a train into Bielsko.

She would never forget that day. It was a Friday. She wanted to see her brother who had somehow managed to hold onto his grocery store in town, despite the crippling shortage of stocks and no assistance.

When she walked into the shop Tadek flung his arms wide and bounded towards her.

"Helena! For the love of God where have you been all this time? There were all sorts of rumors about your car being smashed up, the lot of you killed..."

"Well, it certainly wasn't us," she told him, returning his embrace. "But how has it been with you? Mother told me you still have the business."

"Huh, if you can call it that. They confiscated my apartment though and I'm living here at the back of the store." He held her at arms' length. "You've lost weight. Gives your face that interesting Greta Garbo look."

Helena laughed. "Always the diplomat."

"No, it suits you. But this calls for a celebration! Wait a bit while I shut up shop. The trade's lousy anyway."

A bachelor at 40, Tadek was a peculiar blend of joviality and moody sensitivity. Not much taller than his sister, there was a marked resemblance between them, the full lips, the easy smile and he was also the only other member of the family with the same deep blue eyes. His single state had provoked a great deal of speculation until it was discovered that he kept a mistress more than 20 years his junior. However, the affair fizzled out shortly before the war.

He had made a neat job of converting part of the store into living quarters. The partitioned-off room was dark and the tiny recess a poor apology for a kitchen, but it was comfortable and homely looking. From under a pile of socks he produced a half bottle of Vodka.

Oblivious of the passing time, they chatted on until Tadek looked at his watch with a guilty start.

"Half past 8."

"We'd better hurry then. I'll see you to the station."

"No, really, I'll be all right on my own."

"If you insist. I'll try and get out to see you and the kids soon."

At the station she learned that the services had been changed and that she had missed the last train to Lesno. No problem, she told herself, Olga's apartment was just around the corner. She had spent many a night with her friend when Adam had been away on his political campaigns. It would be good to see her again. Mother would think she had stayed over with Tadek.

She knocked on the door, fully expecting to be met with shrieks of delight at her safe return. Instead, Olga's eyes rounded in alarm, her face turned ashen and her first words of greeting stabbed her like a knife.

"Helena! Oh Jesus, did anyone see you come in here?" The expression on Helena's face stopped her for a moment. But she did not move and still wedged in the doorway, she stammered, "Please don't be angry but you know there's a price on Adam's head and if I'm seen associating with you, they, they may have us arrested. Please, you've got to understand, Helena...!"

With a bitterness she'd never before experienced, Helena turned away. What made it worse was that Olga was safer than most.

She walked back to Tadek's shop along the now dark and deserted streets. She saw the pavement through a blur of tears and it didn't occur to her that she was out without the necessary *'Passierschein'* to justify her disregard of the curfew. It was hard to accept that the loyalty of one's best friend could be so fragile a thing. Times had changed, people had changed. Perhaps this time, she had expected too much.

With the experience gained in the short time with the Kowals, they were now able to make themselves useful on the farm. Marian fetched and chopped the firewood. Stefa was eager to try her hand at milking the cow but after one swish of the smelly tail into her face, left the job to Patches. Helena helped with the cooking, separated the cream from the milk and made the butter. It was satisfying work and she was glad to be able to keep herself occupied.

The change in Helena had not gone unnoticed. Often Teresa would watch her at work and think to herself that some good inevitably came out of the worst disaster. It was hard to imagine that this was the same young woman she'd known before the war. Vain, spoilt and headstrong, as beautiful as she was, Helena was the last girl she would have picked for Adam. He must have seen deeper, for he loved her and now she was beginning to think of her as her own daughter.

......

Two weeks after their return, Helena went to register at the Town Board for their food coupons. Teresa had been against it. She didn't think it wise to advertise their presence so soon and maintained that they could manage well enough on whatever the estate could still yield. Knowing the extent of her estate, Helena could not agree. One cow out of a large herd, a small, worthless patch of wood out of vast forest lands, the house and vegetable garden -- that was the sum total of the assets which had been left to her by the Germans, with old Patches the only remaining servant. So far, the authorities had made no demands on the garden produce, but she knew it was only a matter of time before they would.

Helena's hopes that the farm might prove to be a safe retreat were shattered when she was called to report to the Magistrates Office, Room 24.

She presented herself before the plain-clothed *Gruppenfuhrer,* a tall man in his fifties, with an irritating air of impatience. During the interview he sat down and stood up at least half a dozen times. His hands were never still. If they did not jingle loose change in his pocket, they would fiddle with his fob watch. Whether by intent or not, he gave the impression that he was a very busy man and that you were wasting his time.

He waved her to a chair, sat well back into his, checked the time again and with an abrupt movement leaned across the desk towards her.

"How did you manage to return from Soviet occupied territories?"

He was guessing but since he guessed right, she told him, omitting the part played by the German frontier officer. If he was impressed he did not show it. He leaned back, regarding her coldly. She was ready for his next question.

"You are, of course, aware of your husband's whereabouts?" "I wish."

"Hmm. We will leave that for the moment. Now, since you were born and bred in Silesia, you understand that you are, in effect, a German citizen and you must enroll on the *Volksdeutsch* list and send your children to a German school. Your son will, naturally, be accepted into our *Hitlerjugend* movement."

In support of this preposterous statement he went on to 'remind' her that Silesia was part of Germany and only at intervals had been unfortunate enough to fall under Polish rule.

For one disbelieving moment Helena could do nothing but stare at him. *Why?* It just didn't make any sense and was a situation she had not reckoned with. Realizing that he was waiting for a reply, she dropped her eyes to the immaculately shod foot perched insolently near her on the desk and said, "I understand."

"Good. The matter will be dealt with, as well as your, eh application for food coupons. You will be hearing from us shortly."

He dismissed her with a *Heil Hitler* and she left him absorbed again in his lovely gold watch.

*

CHAPTER NINE

"Daring the Berlin Gestapo Headquarters"

"I don't care what the reason behind it is, I'll never register as a German!" Helena stormed. "And I'll never allow my children to become denationalized!"

"No, of course not," Teresa said, adding a stitch to the socks she was knitting for Stefa.

"How can you be so calm about it all?" Helena burst out.

"Well, we certainly won't solve anything by getting mad about it. My main concern is that they should want to include you on their *Volksdeutch* list, when they've made no attempt to convert the other thousands of Poles born in Silesia. Maybe...oh never mind."

"What?"

"I just thought it might be their way of getting Adam out of hiding."

"Except that they can't even be sure that he's still alive."

"No. Well, we'll soon find out and by the time they're through with all their formalities and their paper work, we will have thought of a way out."

Helena looked at her mother-in-law. No doubt about it, she meant what she said. More than anything, Helena wished she could share in the optimism that seemed to be inborn in the Polek clan. She hadn't done too badly up to now but this time there was too much at stake and all the cards were stacked against her. She felt her composure slipping and turned to go.

"Wait," the quiet voice stopped her. "I know how you feel Helena, and I know it's difficult to have faith against all logic. But come, say a prayer with me."

She put aside her knitting and knelt before an effigy of the Holy Mary of Czestochowa that she kept on a specially built pedestal against the wall. It was a particularly life-like image of the dark-faced Virgin, the scarred cheek a reminder of the wanton destruction of past invaders. Legend has it that the blow was inflicted in frustrated anger because the soldier could not remove the jewels embedded in the crown.

After that, no one dared to rob the Holy Mary of Chestochowa, for the blow had caused blood to spill from the wound. And the warriors fled in terror.

Helena knelt beside the older woman.

"Our blessed Mary," Teresa began, "we know we are not worthy of your great compassion and so we ask only that you intercede for the children. Please, do not let them lose the freedom that you yourself helped to preserve." She bowed her head. "Let us pray: Hail Mary, full of grace..."

As Helena joined in the prayer, a sudden wind whipped at the trees outside the window and just as suddenly died down. Helena felt goose pimples crawl up her arms. The women stared at one another.

"I think we've been heard," Teresa's voice was filled with awe. Helena wished her own faith could be as strong.

It looked as though her mother-in-law was right about the local administration at any rate. It was three days since her visit to their Offices and not a word from them.

Helena threw a sweater over her shoulders and went out onto the verandah. She wondered how long she would be afforded this comparatively mild treatment -- and, more importantly, why. The question cast a shadow of fear and she knew she would have to act soon. The idea occurred to her to move to Krakow, where the name Polek would have no special significance, but she knew that if they wanted to, the Gestapo could run them down no matter where. If nothing else, their system was thorough, that she knew. It would only be a matter of stalling for time. And once time ran out?

She pushed herself up from the low wicker chair and went to stand against the balcony, a troubled figure. Her eyes followed the distant hills to the white and purple mountains beyond, as if searching there for the answer to her problem.

The shot and Stefa's scream caught her completely off guard. Heart pounding, she rushed down the steps, almost colliding with Marian. Together they ran for the back of the house from where the shot had come.

Stefa was standing unharmed but crying hysterically, her eyes on the inert body of the Alsatian. Next to her was a blond German officer, in the act of replacing his gun into the holster.

"What did you do that for!" Helena screamed at him in German.

"This will teach you to keep savage hounds about the place."

It was only then that she noticed the tear in the man's trouser leg.

"He would never have touched you if you hadn't given him good cause."

"That's enough of your impertinence woman!" He yelled back, the good-looking features distorting with rage. "I don't have to account to you for my actions!" With that he marched off.

Both Teresa and Patches had appeared on the scene. The dressing down that Helena expected for her uncontrolled tongue did not come. In her undemonstrative way, Teresa had been as attached to her Alsatian as they had been to their Lala.

Marian had also loved the dog and now, with tears running down his cheeks, mouthing curses under his breath, he set about digging a grave for the animal.

At that moment the Postman arrived with a registered letter. Too agitated to look at the postmark, Helena tore open the envelope, certain that this was her final notice. Stupidly she stared at the contents, unable to grasp the fact that this was no formal notification for enrollment on the *Volksdeutch* list, but a letter, a letter from Wieliczka and in a handwriting she did not recognize. "Enclosed is a note which had been left with me. I do hope it reaches you," it read.

The signature looked like the name of Alex' neighbor in Wieliczka. She ripped open the smaller envelope and had no trouble recognizing the writing this time. Only a few words, but from Adam. He had signed himself *Mazur,* a nickname from his Army days. The message was short but blissfully clear. He was well.

Reading over Helena's shoulder, Teresa cried out, "Praised be Our Lady. At least we know he survived the battle. But wait a minute, this is dated October and it's December now."

Helena's momentary elation turned to utter despair. "Something must have happened if he couldn't send word in all this time," she reasoned, biting her lip until it hurt.

"Let's see the letter." Marian took it out of her fingers, scanned it quickly and, incredibly, beamed. "Didn't I tell you? Dad's all right. What are you so upset about?"

"Can't you *understand!* Dad wrote this over two months ago and we haven't heard a word from him since."

"So what. Do you expect him to walk right into the Nazis' hands? They're looking for him don't forget. He'd be crazy if he came back here. The main thing is that he survived the battles. I'm telling you, Dad's over the borders by now."

"You know Helena," Teresa put in thoughtfully. "That son of yours shows more sense than either of us. He's probably right."

Helena looked at her son's eager young face, and once again was struck by the boy's confidence and faith in his father. If he was right, then it was time she made a move as well.

A plan began to take shape in her mind. Nothing very definite but it was something to work on. She decided not to say anything about it until she had made all her arrangements.

The first step was to make contact with the Underground, which she knew operated throughout the country.

Hoping that Tadek would be able to put her onto them, she went to see him. As she had expected, her brother's timid nature recoiled from her daring plan but she was determined that none of his objections would sway her.

"Damn it Helena, do you know what you're up against? Are you aware of the consequences?"

"Perfectly."

She was sitting back in his only easy chair, legs crossed, foot swinging. She'd always been the headstrong one. He looked down at the pointed boot, reminded of the time he had found her on a Sunday morning, freezing in the courtyard, determined that she wouldn't go to Church in the inelegantly broad walking shoes her mother had made her put on. How old could she have been then -- 14, 15? It had been funny at the time. He had even admired her stubbornness and her audacity. Now he felt cross and realized his anger was a manifestation of his own fears.

"All right," he said. "If you're quite sure you want to go through with this, I'll arrange for you to see Mark. He's the only one I know in Bielsko who could do it for you."

Two days later they were on their way to the hideout of the Underground, the embryo of what was later to be known as the "A.K." or *Armja Krajowa* (Land Army)

She had become used to the quiet streets, plunged into a murky darkness immediately after dusk. Nor had this ever bothered her. What did bother her was the way Tadek kept looking over his shoulder as he led the way in a confusing labyrinth of streets. His uneasiness began to communicate itself and soon had her jumping at the slightest noise.

"Look," she finally said. "Perhaps it would be better if you gave me the man's address. There's no point in involving you in this as well."

"Don't be silly," he snapped. "Just keep your eyes peeled in case someone follows us. It's unlikely, but better to be on the safe side."

She did as she was told but no one seemed to be interested in their movements and on arrival, they were led into the basement of a pile of ruins.

The name of the contact had been given to her merely as Mark. She did not expect to be introduced to a man whom she recognized as one of Adam's old colleagues. He grinned when he saw her surprise.

"Welcome to the Underground. And what can we do for you Mrs. Polek?"

She told him, watching closely for his reaction. It came -- astonishment, doubt and then a kind of curiosity.

"I realize it isn't an altogether brilliant plan, but don't you think it's worth a try?" She pleaded.

"Might be at that. What name would you like on your new documents?"

She heaved a sigh of relief. He was prepared to help.

They discussed a few more details and then Mark stood up.

"Leave it to me. Everything will be ready for you by tomorrow. No reason for you to come back here. I'll send the papers over to your brothers and you can collect them from there."

He searched her face and held her eyes for a long moment before making up his mind to make the approach he was reluctant to make. He pulled her aside.

"Do you know anything about the work your husband did in the Army?

"Yes, I think so. Flushing out the Nazis."

He smiled at her choice of words. "Well, that's one way of putting it, but of course there was much more to it than that. He was in fact attached to our Intelligence."

That didn't surprise her.

"I don't mean to be pessimistic, but *in case* your mission proves unsuccessful, would you consider carrying on from where he left off? We need people like you," he added simply.

His proposition was so unexpected that she had no answer for him.

"Think about it, if the occasion ever arises. In the meantime, I wish you luck."

She walked out of there with her mind in turmoil and at the same time feeling oddly elated. The elation was only partly due to her success in winning their help. "We need people like you," he had said. *Me, who had done nothing but stand in Adam's way,* she thought, but she also could not help thinking how proud he would be of her if he could see the change that had come about in the wife he had known. It suddenly dawned on her how much he must have loved her and once again she was swept by a feeling of humility. She took out a handkerchief, wiped her eyes and blew her nose, hoping that Tadek had not noticed the tears.

As for the actual work in the Underground, this was now out of the question.

They walked back to the store in silence.

He knew it was an extravagance since there was precious little to celebrate but he opened his last bottle of Zubrowka.

"I've put out an extra blanket for you," he said, half filling their glasses, the stick of buffalo grass inside the bottle giving the Vodka its distinctive aroma.

"Thanks," she accepted the drink. "Never drank so much in my life," she laughed.

He raised his glass. "Success," he said and downed the strong liquor in one go. This was his favorite drink. A pity the Germans seemed to share his taste in Vodka, for it had become impossible to find anywhere in town. Not that he had ever been a heavy drinker either, but somehow the 'special occasions' were coming around with greater frequency these days.

"Success," Helena echoed her brother's toast.

"So, what did Mark have to say to you that made you so thoughtful?" Tadek searched her face. "Or shouldn't I ask?"

"You shouldn't ask."

"Sorry." Stiffly he refilled his glass. "War can have the strangest effect on family relationships."

"Oh come on Tadziu, don't be so touchy. If Mark had wanted you to be involved he would have spoken in front of you. There's no point in jeopardizing your safety unnecessarily now, is there?"

"Does nothing for my ego either."

"Will it make you feel better if I tell you that what Mark spoke about is now irrelevant and of no consequence whatsoever?"

"Thanks. I am relieved to hear it. One drama at a time is about all I can take." He smiled, relaxing. "Now, do you want to wait here for your papers or should I bring them out to you?"

"No. I think it's best if I wait."

"Right. Another Vodka?"

"No thanks, I'm ready for bed. And Tadek, thanks eh?"

"What on earth for?"

"For taking me to Mark against your better judgment."

"Hm. You want to use the bathroom first?"

She walked over to him and kissed him on both cheeks. "Yes thanks."

Just after 1 o'clock the next day a messenger delivered the papers and half an hour later Helena was on the train back to Lesno.

It was a long time since she felt this kind of excitement and if it had not been for the steepness of the hill, she would have run all the way home from the station.

She burst upon the family in the living room. "Meet the new Frau Konig!" she announced, striking a pose and waving a set of perfectly forged documents in front of them.

"What are you going to do with those?" Teresa demanded.

"I'm off to Gestapo Headquarters in Berlin, dear people, to request a visa for Hungary. It's as simple as that."

"Good Lord Helena! You don't think you can get away with it do you? The Germans are no fools you know."

"And neither am I, I hope. There's no harm in trying and even if they refuse me the visa, at least I'll have seen Berlin. Always wanted to." And she stopped all further protests by starting to pack her things.

She knew the store the Germans placed on fashion and good appearance and took pains to look her best. She put on her black Persian Lamb fur coat with matching hat and sling muff, high black fur-trimmed boots and some good pieces of jewelry, all salvaged by Teresa. She picked up the new red leather case Tadek had given her and shot a last critical glance in the mirror.

"It needs something," she said. "Your red paisley scarf Mother, can I borrow it?"

"It's yours," she said, going into her bedroom to get it. "Perfect." Teresa's voice was full of admiration. "No one would guess you have two big children."

"Hmm, quite stunning," Marian added.

Not do be outdone, Stefa clung to her mother. "And I think you're the most beautiful lady in all the world."

And so it was with a buoyant step and a great deal of confidence that Helena left home, with a promise to be back within a week at most.

......

"Your papers please." The man's tone of authority was far beyond that of a conductor.

She'd had no difficulty in buying a train ticket, but to secure a private compartment had been something of a problem, despite the fact that there were very few travelers on board. It took a substantial bribe to persuade the conductor that she preferred her own company to that of a group of leering German soldiers.

Once in her own coupe she tried to relax and had herself almost believing that her papers would pass the most rigorous scrutiny, when the door was pushed open and all her confidence escaped.

Attempting to match the man's manner, Helena handed over her papers. He went through them with such meticulous care that she was rendered speechless with apprehension and could not respond when he returned them to her with a polite *"Danke"*.

She felt disgusted with herself. *If a stupid conductor can do this to you what are you going to be like in front of the real thing?* More experienced, she answered herself and shrugged with impatience at the ridiculousness of this one on one conversation. She pulled down the coarse blanket from the overhead rack, wrapped it around herself and lay down on the bunk.

She fell asleep easily and alighted at Berlin station early on the following morning with much of her confidence regained.

Berlin and its citizens seemed vastly different from all previous descriptions. The people, poorly dressed, trudged the streets looking no happier than the Poles back home. The bitterly cold weather and brooding skies added to the general impression of misery.

Helena pulled up the collar of her coat and closed the last button. She stopped an elderly man to ask for directions to the Gestapo Headquarters. He gave them to her very precisely but not before she caught the startled look that crossed his face at the question. This was something she had not expected. If the Germans here squirmed under the yolk they themselves had fashioned, then there was some excuse for Olga's attitude. But now she herself began to feel tremors of uneasiness as she made her way along Prinz Albrecht Strasse towards the building which could instill fear into millions.

A smart young clerk presided over the reception desk. He studied her papers and informed her respectfully enough, that she should address her enquiry to the Hungarian Consulate. He even offered directions on how to get there.

She walked out of the lion's den on burning feet. She'd been over-confident. Stupid to think that the Germans would co-operate. Perhaps she should go back before she got herself into real trouble. Her mind was objecting, but her feet were taking her there.

At the Hungarian Consulate she was brought before a senior official. Briefly she stated her business and handed him her papers. He gestured her to a chair. Once again she tried to appear unconcerned while her documents were carefully looked over. The man's distinctive accent and arrogant air at once identified him as a Berliner. He used after-shave powder and scented lotion on the close-cropped hair. The half-mooned fingernails showed regular manicuring. But there was nothing in the slate gray eyes to suggest weakness.

One particular paper seemed to hold more interest for him than the rest. She tried to make out which one it could be but could not see without bending forward and appearing anxious.

Without a word he stood up, swept the documents together and left the office.

Her heart began to thud. The palm of her left hand felt damp against the fleece of the glove she'd forgotten to take off. She pulled it off quickly, searching her mind for possible arguments to support her claim. And realized she was hopelessly unprepared for any type of contingency, let alone an emergency. She willed herself to remain calm by reminding herself that that was a bridge which had not yet presented itself so there was no point in worrying about crossing it.

The Berliner returned in a few moments, took his seat and began to sort out the papers on his desk with maddening precision. He had not said a word.

At last he looked up. "I do regret delaying you like this Frau Konig, but you understand -- regulations..." he trailed off with an expression which she could only assume was meant to convey some sort of apology. She nodded and he went on glibly, "You say you are a teacher and would like to instruct the Hungarians in our mother tongue. A most worthy sentiment *Gnedige Frau,* most worthy. Unfortunately however, owing to the present unsettled state of affairs, it is quite impossible to issue visas for anywhere outside the country."

Handing back her papers he treated her to a fleeting smile. "If you would care to re-apply in the next few months, we shall most probably have, ah, persuaded Hungary into our territories and there should be no difficulty after that."

She was careful to show just the right amount of disappointment, thanked him and with a brisk *"Heil Hitler"* left.

As soon as the building was out of sight she dived into the nearest Cafe. The goose-pimpled waitress who eventually sauntered up to her table fitted in with the cheerless decor and atmosphere of the place. She eyed Helena's fur coat sourly and took her time in bringing the order. The coffee tasted foul but its warmth helped to relax her a little. Slowly strength returned to her knees.

She knew she should be thankful that the failure of her mission had nothing to do with the forgery job so excellently executed by her friends in the Underground, otherwise she would no longer be a free woman, but the longer she sat there the more frustrated she became. Success had been so *close* dammit.

She paid her bill and went out to find the Unter den Linden. She couldn't leave Berlin without at least seeing the famous Brandenburg Gate. She stood under the massive structure. It was imposing enough, but the mighty pillars looked starkly somber against the snow-laden sky and remembering the ruthlessness with which Poland's own architecture had been demolished, she found she was in no mood to appreciate Berlin's aspirations to culture.

She ambled through a city littered with statues and monuments to national heroes, and everywhere the image of Adolf Hitler to strengthen the German megalomania or to jolt any would-be flagging spirit back to its true ambitions. As always, the glitter of a jeweler's window caught her eye. She stopped for a better look and was amazed to see the low prices on all the watches. Obviously rolled gold at these prices but as authentic looking as the genuine article.

Adam had often laughed at what he described as her Jewish acumen for business. *Well,* she thought, *this is where my business sense might yet serve me.*

She had sufficient money for a week's stay in Berlin but as there was now no point in staying on, she could buy a good number of watches and hopefully sell them at home at a profit. Polish jewelers had been raided in the first days of the invasion and there were thousands of Germans there now with money to spend and little to spend it on. It was a gamble but she felt it was one worth taking. She made up her mind quickly and walked into the shop.

"You want *all* these watches Madame?" The man asked in surprise. "Yes, all," she repeated. "Providing I get a good discount."

She got it. And that left her with enough money for one night in Berlin. She booked in at a modest looking Hotel and wasted the evening in a futile attempt to engage the guests in conversation. Everywhere it seemed, there was this reluctance to talk to a stranger, even on perfectly innocent topics.

Early the next morning she was on the train back to Poland.

As soon as she arrived in Bielsko she went to see Paul Hellermann, an old friend and one of the finest jewelers in the city. To her intense relief he pounced on the watches and offered her a price far beyond her expectations. The gamble had paid off, she made a profit of 60% on her money and the trip to Berlin not a total failure.

Having entertained no optimistic illusions about her daughter-in-law's visit to Berlin, Teresa was overjoyed at her safe return and positively amazed to see the extra money.

"What a remarkable woman you are Helena," she laughed. "Fancy thinking of business deals at a time like this. Wait till Adam hears about it."

"What chance is there of that now? I didn't get a visa, remember."

"No, but Hitler won't last long now that we've got the Allies on our side."

"AND," Marian added excitedly. "Did you hear that the Polish forces are rearming themselves in France?"

Helena said nothing. She'd heard the news, but she had also seen the power of the German armies and could not foresee an easy victory for the Allies.

"Talking about watches," Marian said casually. "I've sure missed mine. Hope it never worked for the Russian pig that swiped it." "There might be one here."

"Really?" Marian rushed over to give her a hug. "Where is it?"

She took the watch out of her handbag. "Not an Omega exactly but goes well."

"Oh by the way," Teresa said, "that officer who shot our dog came looking for you."

"Oh? What did he want?" "You," she replied evenly.

Helena felt herself go scarlet. "Let him come. I'll deal with the lout."

"Careful Helena. That one looks like a particularly nasty character."

"Don't worry. I'll be diplomacy itself."

The officer appeared the very next evening, immaculately shod and wearing a black leather coat over the well-pressed uniform.

"I have come to apologize for my behavior," he began, lifting Helena's hand to his lips. "I'm afraid I lost my temper the other day. Can you forgive my bad manners?" He begged with a smile that made nonsense of his words.

She thought of her brave words to Mother and of the older woman's warning. How did one cope with such a situation?

Extricating her hand as casually as she could, she said, "The incident is forgotten but thank you for coming," and began to steer him towards the door.

Adroitly he intercepted her maneuvers. "I brought a bottle of wine with me -- a peace offering if you like. Will you do me the honor of sharing it with me?"

She could not refuse and excused herself to fetch the glasses.

Teresa was waiting in the kitchen, her face pale and drawn. As Helena walked in, she shot her a questioning look.

"He's brought some wine with him," Helena chuckled. "Let's give him a party shall we? Take your apron off." She took down three glasses and the two of them went to join their visitor.

His face fell when he saw the older woman following Helena into the living room, but short of displaying the bad manners he had so recently regretted, there was nothing he could do about it. He left early but not too soon and asked Teresa's permission to call again.

Helena went to the window, her eyes following the jeep until it was out of sight. It had began to snow again. She watched the flakes falling obliquely against the fading light -- and decided to work for Mark.

*

CHAPTER TEN

"Helena joins the Underground"

The draught whistled through the badly fitting window, joined forces with the draught from under the carriage door and in concert, whipped at the solitary passenger. Helena hugged herself closer, huddling deeper into the seat.

She had caught the late afternoon train into town, telling Teresa that she would be spending the night over with Tadek. Strange how detached she felt from it all. It was as though she was an on-looker, untouched by the enormity of her decision. Nor had she given very much thought to it. She just knew it was the right thing to do.

She stared out of the grimy window, only half aware of the broken gray-white mist that flashed past. The lights came on and she was looking at the reflection of her face. She studied it with distant interest. Hollow-eyed still, but yet attractive she supposed. She smiled at her own assessment and patted a stray lock of hair into place, wondering if Adam would notice the slight intrusion of gray.

The train began to slow down. She reached for her overnight bag.

Mark had been expecting her.

"I was hoping you would come Helena - may I call you Helena? Sorry you didn't have better luck in Berlin," he added.

She hid her surprise and shrugged. "If I'd had more luck, you wouldn't be getting my services -- for what they're worth."

"That is so."

"Before you go any further, I must tell you that I expect to be pestered by a German officer." And she told him about her blond suitor. "I might be able to deal with him myself, but if he becomes a nuisance it may interfere with my work for you."

Mark looker her straight in the eyes. "On the contrary," he said carefully. "He could prove an invaluable source of information to us."

She didn't like it and said so.

"I'm not asking you to prostitute yourself. See how far you can go, that's all."

"All right. What shall I tell Mother? She's bound to become curious about my trips into town."

"That you're helping your brother in the shop, perhaps?"

She laughed. "He needs help there like I need my German. Though it could be a useful cover. The old lady's shrewd enough to arrive at her own conclusions anyway."

"A typical Polek, I understand." "Yes, only more so."

"All right, this is what I have in mind for you." He briefed her on her part in the operations and to start off with left her with a pile of notes to translate into German.

Her duties would eventually include substituting these translations for original orders from the Reich. This, hopefully, would cause enough confusion for the Underground's own plans to go into effect.

Helena suspected that her admirer had had the house watched, since his next visit coincided with Teresa's weekly trip to the village. She had also taken the children with her.

This time he did not beat about the bush. He came up close and said, "I love a woman with spirit. You look superb when you're angry, did you know that? Especially when she has your kind of eyes. How they sparkled! Like blue sapphires. But angry or not, you are a most beautiful woman." With that he made a lunge for her.

She couldn't see herself being able to hold this clod off for very long. "You are in a hurry, aren't you?" She laughed at him, turning her face to avoid his kiss. His lips worked down her neck in hungry sucking noises, while his hand explored her body. She could feel her anger rising and pulled away from him.

This brought a scowl to his flushed face. "I could be useful to you, you know," he said, trying another tactic.

"And I have no intentions of selling myself for any favors."

His eyes narrowed. "We will see about that."

"Why go to all the trouble? Is it so difficult for you to find a more willing paramour?"

She'd done it again and could have bitten her tongue.

She thought he was going to strike her. The moment passed. Abruptly he turned on his heel. "You will regret this!" He threw over his shoulder.

She had failed in her first assignment even before it began. She did not think Mark would be very pleased with her.

She tried to be away from the house as much as possible after that, but as the days passed without a word from him, Helena initiated her own discreet enquiries. When she learned that her admirer had been transferred, she couldn't wait to rush home with the news.

"Looks as though my luck's still holding out," she told Teresa.

Her mother-in-law shook her head. "There's no such thing as luck," she said. "I believe we shape our own destinies by our actions and the Lord alone makes judgment of them."

Helena did not want to argue the point but at that moment in time it certainly didn't seem as though one's own actions had any bearing on one's fate. And this was made even more real to her when the very next day the S.S. (Secret Service) came to escort her to the Police Station.

She had lived in Bielsko all her life but had, until that day, never set foot in the Station. Her escort walked slightly ahead, his footsteps sharp and clear on the wooden tiles. He rounded a corner and she saw that a whole section of the building had been allocated to the Gestapo.

The same impatient, money-jingling *Gruppenfuhrer* who had interviewed her before at the Magistrates Office, now asked her why she had delayed enrolling the children.

"But I understood I had to wait for my registration to go through first," she hedged.

"Nonsense. Your registration has nothing to do with the children's schooling."

"All right then, I shall do something about it in the new year."

"And I think you are stalling for time. What is there to think over? Why the delay? We have a remedy for people like you, but I am sure our friend will be happy to tell you more about that." His smile turned her stomach.

He nodded to the escort who had been standing stiffly at attention. The man went out for a moment, to return with the 'friend'.

The pink face was vaguely familiar but she could not immediately place it. He filled the doorway and could have been impressive had his suit fitted him better and his body not looked soft and overfed. As he walked in, he very politely asked the *Gruppenfuhrer* if he would mind leaving them alone.

No sooner had the door closed behind the two men, than the pink face underwent an unbelievable change. The lips thinned to a cruel line, the nose flared until the nostrils showed white. But it was the eyes that held her the most. They flashed a venom she had not imagined possible to see. Fear charged through her. He took three measured steps towards her, raised his hand and swiftly brought it down on her cheek. Hard.

Shock, outrage and then the taste of blood in her mouth gave her the courage to voice her admiration for his bravery and breeding.

This incensed the man into a fit of madness. His face turned purple and he slapped both sides of her face in rapid succession. Helena had no idea how she managed to swallow the cries that sprang to her throat, she was aware only of going for his face with her nails. He stepped back with astonishing speed and gripped her hands in a bone-crushing hold, slowly adding pressure until he saw her wince.

"That was a debt I owed your husband, Mrs. Polek," he hissed. "When next you see him, do tell him that Heinrich Eckhart, you will remember the name won't you? Tell him that Eckhart always pays his debts with handsome dividends. The dividends are still to be awarded of course. A smart *Hitlerjugend* uniform for the son of the great Polish patriot and the privilege of *Volksdeutch* nationality for his charming young wife."

Nothing could have wounded Adam as deeply as the ingenious method of revenge devised by this twisted creature, whom she now recognized as a member of the Nazi Party in Bielsko.

"May I let go now?" He asked genially, his eyes on her numbed hands. She nodded.

"And if I decline the honor?" She was aware of the foolishness of her bravado yet felt quite unable to hold her tongue. She wished her lips had not began to swell already. The words did not sound as crisp as she wanted them to.

"Oh that would be most unfortunate, for you that is. Naturally there is an alternative. You might be invited to take a trip to Germany. Dachau to be exact. You might have heard of our Camp there. I see you know about it," he smiled at her involuntary start. "In which case you will no doubt be persuaded to fall in with my arrangements for you. So much easier don't you agree?"

She knew his victory would be so much greater if she could be made to agree to his plans voluntarily. She also realized why they had been treated with such leniency until now. They were this high ranking official's special pawns with whom he could deal as and when he chose to. He was probably a very patient man, when not provoked.

He clicked his heels smartly and left. She was allowed to go home.

This interview with Eckhart produced the strangest effect on Helena. Far from leaving her cowed, it evoked a kind of abandon, an unconcern to the possibility of danger. She'd been there and she'd come out clean. There had been no compromise in her mind. Elated, she now felt almost free to carry out any assignment Mark might have for her. And much, much more than that, it had brought Adam closer to her. She finally understood his uncompromising attitude, for she now shared it.

She debated whether to show her red and swollen face to Tadek or at home and decided it would be easier to convince the children that she had met with a slight accident rather than have her brother worry over her. Her mother-in-law would understand. And God how she needed someone to talk to!

Teresa took one look at Helena and quickly pulled her into her own bedroom. She dipped her face cloth into the jug of cold water she had standing on the washstand and gently pressed it against the one cheek then the other. "Looks as though you might have a couple of black eyes from this as well. The lips should go down soon though."

She had assisted the local Doctor in more cases than she could remember and this type of battering was nothing new to her. But that it should have happened to her family!

"Who did this to you?" She asked, her voice tight with fury.

Suddenly Helena knew she could not add another burden to the older woman's problems and said, "Just some petty Nazi official exerting his authority to encourage me to sign up."

"We might have to find a hiding place for you soon." "Where?"

"We'll think of somewhere. In the meantime, I could do with a cigarette. How about you?"

"Why not?"

Time after time, Helena was able to gain access to the Departments important to the Underground, with messages to and from planted members of the staff. She reasoned that if anyone accosted her, she could fall back on the excuse that she was making enquiries about her *Volksdeutche* nationality, a pretext she only once had to resort to.

The more successful she became in her outside work, the less tolerable life became at home. The Gestapo persisted in their unexpected visits at any hour of day or night. The loud banging on the door and the barked *"Aufmachen!"* became a command no less dreaded for its familiarity. They searched every conceivable corner of the house, until one day they came across Adam's portrait.

"A very good likeness to the photograph we have of him," one of the men remarked. Then, with wanton satisfaction he threw the picture on the floor and stamped on it.

Neither Teresa nor Helena gave him the added satisfaction of showing the slightest reaction.

"Well?" The man turned to the older woman. "Do you admit that is your son?"

"Yes, that *was* my son," she whispered. "He was all I had."

Oh that was superb! Helena shot her an admiring glance. She had no idea that acting was one of her mother-in-law's accomplishments.

The man hesitated. "Don't lie woman!" He barked. "You know very well where he's hiding out and unless you tell us, we'll smash everything in this house."

"Go ahead, smash everything!" She flared at them. "Do you think he would endanger me, his mother, by telling me where he is, even if he *was* alive? But I know you've butchered him. Along with all the others."

Her performance was so convincing that after one more half-hearted attempt they gave up the search and left, causing no more damage.

Teresa bolted the door, waited for the sound of their footsteps to fade and almost giggled with delight. "You see, even an old woman like me can outwit the omnipotent Gestapo."

"Hm. I can see now where Adam gets his talent from. He could always worm himself out of a situation." She picked up the portrait. "Let's hope he's been able to do it this time," she murmured, her eyes filling up.

Shortly before Christmas Helena was instructed to collect her food coupons. These would be allocated providing she 'co-operated with the authorities'.

She didn't think the lack of food coupons would affect them too badly for a while, but she could not go on accepting the small packages of groceries that Tadek sometimes slipped her, nor could she continue to consume their share of milk and butter which ought to have been sold. With very careful rationing, their pantry might see them through the winter. And then? And because these were not the kind of thoughts she could share with anyone, they assumed a worrying quality impossible to shake off. Eckhart's appearance on the scene aggravated matters to the point where it became almost natural to come awake each morning to the sinking feeling that something was terribly wrong.

Then came the day most revered in the Polish calendar. *Wigilia* -Christmas Eve, with nothing but the snow-capped firs outside to remind them of its arrival.

All day Stefa had been waiting for 6 o'clock, when the appearance of the first star would be a sign to begin Supper. Traditional in its basic course of *Barszcz* (clear beetroot soup), fish, stewed fruit, nuts and above all, Communion Bread, broken and shared along with good wishes between each member of the family, the meal, ostensibly a fast, usually turned out to be a feast, culminating in a rush for the glittering ceiling-high Christmas tree, under which each one would find a gift. After that, the plaintive or gay, but always sweetly melodious voices of the Carol singers would be heard well into the night.

On that Christmas Eve of 1939, there was no Christmas tree and, with the exception of the thin slivers of Communion Bread and some local hazel nuts, the table, undecorated, was laid as usual, only this time for eight. They were expecting Tadek and two of Adam's cousins from Lesno, Zygmunt and Jerzy.

Teresa placed Adam's damaged portrait on the mantlepiece overlooking the table. No one spoke. With so little preparation to be done, they sat in front of the fire, glumly awaiting the arrival of their guests.

Tadek was the first to arrive. He came in covered in snow and blue with cold but as pleased with himself as Santa Clause. He rummaged into the deep inside pockets of his overcoat and produced sweets for the children and a full bottle of Vodka.

"Thanks to my unparalleled cunning, we still have something to warm our bellies with," he said with a lightness that did not deceive his sister.

"What do you mean?"

"Oh, I had a deputation at my shop just before I left this evening."

"What sort of deputation?" She pressed.

"Goodness knows. Board of Trade probably -- they didn't say. Anyway, they didn't find any black market stuff but that didn't stop them from restricting my permit even further. At this rate they'll compel me to hand over to some bloody German."

The look on their faces made him feel a heel. Why couldn't he have kept his mouth shut. "Come on everybody, don't look as if this was the end of the world. I'm still better off than most. So, out with the glasses!"

The door flew open and in swept Zygmunt and Jerzy, their presence igniting the place to life. Both a few years younger than Adam, they shared a strong family resemblance and exuded the same strength and vitality as their cousin. Their contribution to the *Wigilia* was a kingsize trout.

Patches lost no time in scaling and frying the fish and they all sat down to a far better meal than anyone had expected.

Towards the end of the evening Zygmunt announced that he and Jerzy had decided to escape to Hungary over the mountains.

"I know it's not an easy route," he said, turning to Helena, "but you ski pretty well. Why don't you come with us?"

She shook her head. "And the children?"

"They'll be all right here. It's your position that I'm not happy about. I've heard that the Gestapo Administration in town is being replaced with new men from Germany. They've been lousing things up here apparently and they've found several of the local officials too sympathetic towards the Poles. Adam is a wanted man and believe me, they won't spare his wife."

Or exercise patience in a personal vendetta like my friend Heinrich Eckhart, she thought.

Stefa's eyes brimmed with tears. Marian's face was set. They both waited for their mother to speak.

"No Zygmunt, I could never leave them."

With an audible sigh Marian reached for a nut, his hand not quite steady. Stefa gave her a look that would have melted stone. She smiled at them. Did they really think she could have gone without them? Things were bad enough without the added insecurity that they obviously felt within the family itself. *I must spend more time with them,* she told herself.

The boys left early. With worried eyes Helena watched the two figures disappear almost instantly behind a thick screen of snow. They would have to be more than lucky to get across the mountains in this weather.

Was there no way out?

*

CHAPTER ELEVEN

"The parting"

Boxing Day had an almost pre-war feel about it. The day was incredibly lovely, with the azure sky and dazzling sun turning the landscape into its fabulous Swiss-like travel poster. Breathing in the pure air, Helena stood on the verandah and wondered why Poland's Department of Tourism could not have promoted the country's beauty spots as Switzerland had done. Zakopane for instance, a resort in the splendid Tatry mountains was every bit as alluring as any winter playground in Europe. *We've been too damned independent,* she mused, *and too involved in our own political squabbles to open our doors to the outside world.*

In the distance she spotted one of their neighbors puffing up the hill towards the house. A frequent visitor, fat Maria Debnicka never ceased to amaze her by the speed with which she manipulated that steep hill. Still some distance from the gate she called and waved a piece of paper.

"Pani Polek! *Pani* Polek! There's a postcard for you!"

Helena ran down to meet her, her heart thudding at the prospect of good news. On a day like this, it *had* to be good news.

The card was addressed to Mrs. Debnicka and bore a Hungarian postmark. It read:

"Just to let you know that I am well and looking forward
to being reunited here with my family as soon as possible."

And it was signed *Mazur,* Adam's Lwowian nickname.

"Mother! Marian! Stefa! Come and look quickly!" Helena yelled, almost choking with excitement. "He's alive, he's safe."

They tore the card out of her hand and each read it in turn. The only one who didn't seem to share in their near-hysteria was Teresa.

"So, he's safe," she said. "But then I never doubted that. What I want to know is what he means by glibly talking about a reunion as soon as possible and in Hungary, of all places."

"He wants us to get out of Poland and join him of course!" Helena cried, surprised at the woman's sudden obtuseness.

"That part of it is clear enough. What I'd like to know is how exactly does he think you're going to do it?" She retorted dryly.

"I'll find a way, don't you worry," Helena laughed with reckless assurance. This card was all the encouragement she needed. She would now find a means of escape come hell or high water.

"The food's ready. Let's go and eat." Teresa took Stefa's hand. "We can talk about this inside."

They sat down to a hash of beans and mushrooms, all talking at the same time. No one heard the knock on the door and for a while no one noticed the slight form that stood there. Then Helena looked up. The fork fell from her hand and she ran towards her sister, wrapping her arms about the thin shoulders. Eva's sobs came in harsh gasps. Helena took the bag out of her hand and led her to a chair.

Eva turned stricken, dark-rimmed eyes on her. "They've killed Henry."

Marian chocked and rushed out of the room. It was a while before Helena could speak. "How did it happen? When? I saw you on the train at Lwow but couldn't get to you."

Yes, she said, Henry had been with her then. They never got beyond Lwow at the outbreak of the war but spent the weeks hiding in some dreadful rat-infested basement with a number of other people. Hunger and Henry's deteriorating health had driven them out. They had, as Helena had guessed at the time, managed to pass for Germans and were transported all the way into the Reich. It was while they were trying to return to Krakow that the Gestapo became suspicious. Henry was arrested but for some reason they let her go. She was staying with friends in Krakow when she developed a fever so high that they had to move her to a hospital. While still in hospital, and a few days before Christmas, she received a parcel. In it were Henry's suit and his Concentration Camp number - no longer needed.

Eva stopped talking. Helena reached for her hand.

"They discharged me from hospital soon after that -- I can't quite remember how long I was there -- and I decided to come to you Helena. Those new tenants at Zielna Street wouldn't even let me in the door and so I went to Tadek."

Tadek had already told her something of Helena's experiences but Eva wanted to know all the details.

"Not until you've eaten," Teresa said. "You look as if you could do with some fattening up Eva. I've never seen you look so thin."

With tears in her eyes, Helena watched her sister struggle with the food, her tiny fingers trembling under the weight of the fork. She left most of it untouched. No one had any appetite left. Marian had not come back to the table. Helena knew how he felt and thought it best to leave him alone. Henry had always held a special place in his heart. Their natures had been very much alike; both good-tempered, somewhat phlegmatic and wholly lovable. Why, Why did they have to pick on the innocent and the harmless?

Henry, her eldest brother. She saw the gentle eyes smiling at her. He was helping her with her homework, trying to be stern. He was there, glowing with pride when she won first prize at school. And he stood by her when her father had objected to her marriage. It just didn't seem possible that she would never, ever see him again. Her eyes focused back on her sister and a great empty sadness engulfed her.

She waited until they moved to sit before the fireplace before telling Eva of her decision to leave Poland.

"Are you crazy? There's no way out!" Was Eva's shocked reaction.

"We'll make it. I don't know how yet, but we will. The Underground will help us. Hurry up and get your strength back and we'll make it together."

"No Helena. I couldn't," she said. "But you don't have to worry about me. Tadek has already asked me to stay on with him. He said he could easily extend his living quarters and make a partition for me. I've left some things with my friends in Krakow though, so I'll have to go back there first."

She had made up her mind to leave the next day and neither Teresa nor Helena could persuade her to stay any longer. She was like a badly operated marionette. All her actions were accelerated by nervous bouts of energy and it seemed impossible for her to sit still for any length of time. It was heartbreaking just to look at her. Eva, who had always been the most composed, the most stable of them all.

Early the next morning Helena took her into town. She made Eva put on her three-quarter length sealskin coat which came below her knees and hid her hands completely. It made her look even more pathetic but was warmer than the coat she had worn. At the station they learned that the train for Krakow was not due until late that afternoon.

After the episode with Olga, Helena had been avoiding all her friends, although Janina Puchalska had been on her mind a great deal. A blue-eyed blond, her old classmate's sweet nature and doll-like prettiness had made up for any lack of intellect. This would probably be her last chance to see her friend. On an impulse she turned to her sister.

"Let's go and see if Janina is still here. Do you mind?"

Eva was quite happy to go along, if only to escape the draughty station.

They took the tram out to the Mickiewicz Gardens, a newly established suburb where Szymon and Janina had built their ultra-contemporary home.

Janina's welcome could not have been more different from Olga's.

"Jesus, it's you Helena!" She cried, kissing her full on the mouth. "Where have you been? I've been so worried about you. And Eva! What on earth have you been doing to yourself?"

Before Helena would answer any of her questions she asked about Szymon.

"Haven't heard from him since the beginning of the war," Janina replied with averted eyes. "Have you seen Olga?" She asked in a voice grown over loud.

Helena got the impression that the mention of her husband's name caused Janina as much embarrassment as pain and wondered why she was so quick to change the subject.

"Have I," Helena snorted and described her last meeting with Olga.

"The cow. She doesn't know me on the street any more either. But I really didn't think she'd have gone that far. I mean you two were inseparable."

"You're quite right," Helena murmured. *"Were* is the word. Ah, forget her. What about you? How come you've been allowed to stay on in this large house of yours?"

In a voice filled with bitterness Janina explained that she was no more than a glorified housekeeper, having to look after four German officers who billeted with her. Helena noticed the work-worn hands over which her friend had once taken such fastidious care, the strain in the face that, though still pretty, looked ten years older and could only guess at the kind of life the girl must be leading.

Janina met her look of sympathy and all at once the toughness went out of her. She buried her face in her hands. "Oh Helena," she sobbed. "You've no idea what it's like to be molested by four sex starved swines"

"Then why stay on here, for God's sake?"

"What else can I do? Can you imagine what they'd do to me if I left? I've been *ordered* by the Gestapo itself, to take in boarders."

And, Helena thought with pity, *you lack the courage to disobey them.*

Having resigned herself to martyrdom, she would not listen to any suggestions for breaking away from a life that was clearly destroying her. It was small wonder that the very mention of Szymon's name was enough to give her a guilt complex. Helena tried again.

"What about moving to Warsaw. You've got family there haven't you?"

"You think they wouldn't find me there? Those bastards will trace anybody anywhere. And why put the rest of my family at risk."

Instinct prevented Helena from mentioning her own plans. As much as she liked her, she felt the girl was too weak to be trusted. Janina broke down again when they parted and Helena could find no words of comfort. She held her close for a moment. "Stay with God," she whispered.

On the way back to the station, Eva was very quiet. The visit to Janina had made her feel more depressed than ever. She had lived a comparatively sheltered life and it wasn't easy for her to accept the baser side of human nature, especially when demonstrated by those whom she had always loved and admired. Most of her contemporaries were of German origin. She had gone to school with them and frankly preferred them to her Polish friends. The closeness had been too strong for her not to feel a sense of betrayal.

No sooner had they entered the waiting room than Eva tugged at her sister's arm. "Let's wait on the platform," she said, recoiling from the stench of stale tobacco smoke and urine.

Helena could not agree more but she had noticed Eva's uncontrollable shivering and was worried about her lowered resistance to the cold. "All right, as long as we keep walking."

Helena set a brisk pace down the length of the platform. As they drew nearer to the wired-off goods terminal on the far side of the station, they heard the chilling chorus of voices raised in lamentation.

They stopped and looked at one another. "Jews," said Eva.

"Sounds like it. Let's go and see."

Eva held back. "Do you think it's safe?"

Without answering her Helena walked on. She came to the end of the building and peered around the corner, there to be met by a sight she would never be able to forget.

Huddled together in their hundreds behind the wire fence were the Jews; men, women and children. Many of the men had long beards and side ringlets and wore the orthodox black gowns and hats or a Yarmulke. White-faced women shivered in their flimsy dresses -- not a coat between them. Children stared at their praying parents out of great dark eyes, dulled with confusion and too many tears. Unconcerned German guards marched up and down before this wretched spectacle.

Eva came to stand beside her. "Merciful Jesus," she whispered, crossing herself.

They both knew the fate that awaited those people and they walked back in silence. There were no words that could describe their feelings.

When the train arrived Eva held on to her sister fiercely, with a final plea that she forget her mad scheme. Helena bent to kiss the tear-streaked face. She felt mean about leaving her but the plight of these people only added fire to her determination and now more than ever she knew that she must think of her own safety and that of her children.

Concentration Camps were not restricted to Jews alone. Hitler's loathing of the Poles came very close to his anti-Semitic psychosis. In most of his ravings over the radio he made some reference to the *"Polnische schwein."* The hopeless but valiant defense of Warsaw had been more than this madman could take. Poland should have capitulated with negligible losses to his Master Armies. As for the Jews, they had for too long capitalized on their inherent abilities and commercial enterprise at the expense of his own country and people, and yielding to this glaring admission of inferiority, he had to have them exterminated.

With the ruin of Eva's face before her, and the chant of despair still ringing in her ears, Helena once again turned her steps towards the Underground Headquarters.

And once again, Mark knew what she had come for even before she'd opened her mouth to speak. He left the table where he had been talking with a small group of men and came over to greet her.

He pulled out a chair for her and gave her a searching look. "Where to this time?"

"I was hoping you'd be able to tell me."

"I take it you wouldn't consider the mountain route? Without the children of course. No. Well, there is another possibility. It's one that I haven't mentioned before because I didn't and still don't think it's something that you should attempt."

"If there *is* a way out, for the love of God tell me!" She almost shouted at him.

"I know you don't lack courage Helena, but honestly, I could not see you throw your life away, as well as your children's."

"Would you rather see us interned then? And gassed?"

He perched himself on the edge of a desk, facing her and with deft fingers proceeded to roll a cigarette.

"I suppose that is the alternative, sooner or later." He stood placing the unlit cigarette in an ashtray. "Alright, I'll tell you all I know, and that isn't very much, I'm afraid."

"Here is the name and address of a Priest in Vienna," he said. "One of the few still alive and willing, to risk helping us. He'll put you in touch with someone in Klingenbach, close to the Hungarian border which, I can tell you, is heavily guarded. And that's as far as I can help you," he finished with a worried frown.

She knew Vienna fairly well and had no difficulty in memorizing the address. As soon as she did so he put a lighted match to the transcript, then lit his cigarette.

"Bless you Mark. Sorry I can't go on with my work here."

"You've done more than your share, and I don't have to tell you what that means, to all of us. Oh yes, you'll be pleased to know that we managed to destroy that ammunition store."

"I love good news," she grinned at him.

A final handshake, a guarded all-clear call and she was scrambling over the debris and out onto the street.

Mark went to rejoin the group at the table.

"Think she'll make it?" One of the men asked him.

Mark shrugged his shoulders. "There are no guarantees. It will take a special brand of courage. That she has."

Before going to catch her train for Lesno, Helena called to say good-bye to Tadek. She could now also tell him about Eckchart.

For all his previous resistance to her contact with the Underground, he now agreed with her decision to make a bid for the border. When she taxed him on this change of tune, he gave a mock shrug.

"I've known you long enough to realize that you are totally unresponsive to your brother's sound influence. But seriously Helena, in your case I see no other course open. If I'm not mistaken Eckhart's the fellow they kicked out of the Ministry after Adam exposed him. The more I think of his proposal the more convinced I am that he'll put pressure on you to sign on the dotted line and then have you sent to Dachau anyway. Especially now that he's expecting a transfer."

"That's what I thought" she admitted.

He put his hand on her shoulder. "And for what it's worth little sister, I think if anyone can get out of the country, you can."

"Thanks, big brother. Wish Eva shared your confidence."

"Yes. Eva," he sighed.

"Think she'll be all right?"

"Yes, I think so. As far as I can see, her main problem is malnutrition and I've got the cure for that. I'll soon get her right, don't worry. Oh by the way, there's something I want you to have."

He opened his safe and took out his gold fob watch and chain.

"Don't be ridiculous," Helena protested. "What am I going to do with that?"

"You'll swop it for German, Hungarian, or any other currency you may have to trade it for."

"You'll need..."

"For Christ's sake don't argue Helena. You always have to bloody well argue!"

She looked at him. There were tears in his eyes. Meekly she put the watch into her handbag. For a moment they clung to each other then he opened the door for her. Neither of them could say good-bye.

Teresa didn't like it. She could foresee the difficulties that a woman with two children could come up against in a strange country, to say nothing of the circumstances in which they would be traveling and their purpose for doing so. Since Helena intended traveling under the name of Konig again, her first objection was that the children would give the game away. They did not speak German. Helena reminded her that they had managed pretty well posing as a German family all the way from Lwow.

"I don't see how you can make the comparison Helena," Teresa objected. "And what about the actual crossing of the border?"

"Well, I don't know much about that yet," Helena admitted, "but the contact Mark gave me will fix all that up for us."

"It's not just that." Helena put her hand on her mother-in law's arm and told her about Eckhart.

"Yes. I see." She patted the firm, slender hand, her brown eyes showing an understanding of Helena's reason for having kept her secret until now.

"When are you thinking of leaving then?"

"The sooner the better. Tomorrow. I've arranged for a Taxi to pick us up here at 9 o'clock. There's a train at 9.30."

"In that case, I must take Stefa for her First Communion. The child can't go without that at least."

Since Hitler shared Stalin's obsession about the nullification of all religious beliefs, Teresa came to dress Stefa for Church before daybreak, before there was any danger of being caught in the act of worship.

Her final instructions to Stefa made it clear why her son and those like him fought and died so readily for their country.

"Now listen carefully Stefciu," she said earnestly. "When the Priest puts the Communion into your mouth, the very first thing you are to pray for is the freedom of Poland. Do you understand?"

Bright-eyed, Stefa nodded, thrilled at having her First Communion, despite the fact that there was no white dress for her, no garland or veil, nor any of the fine gifts usually bestowed by members of the family.

"After that," her grandmother went on, "you can pray for your mother and father and those you love and lastly, for yourself. Oh, and make sure you don't bite the Communion Bread."

Marian came in with the small white Missal he had been given on his First Communion.

"Here," he said gruffly. "You've always wanted this."

Helena stooped to kiss her, promising to buy her anything she wanted as soon as they were free. An easy enough promise to keep, she thought, with an undemanding child like this one. For a moment she was shaken with emotion. Pity and sorrow and a hopeless regret for the way it should have been. Quickly she turned away.

As they were leaving, Patches hobbled in all out of breath. In her hand she held a posy of snowdrops for Stefa. Ready now to take her first step towards that oneness with the Universal Being sought after in so many different ways, Stefa walked out tall as a queen.

Helena began to sort out the things they would need most for the journey. A change of underwear, extra socks. Better leave the shoes, they'd be too heavy to carry and they'd be wearing boots anyway. But what if they got wet in the snow. Stefa's feet were always cold. Well, perhaps an extra pair for her. And they could both go in their ski suits. She'd wear her black barathea suit under the Persian Lamp coat, and boots. She was trying to make up her mind about the pajamas when Teresa and Stefa came back.

"How was it?" She asked.

"Oh Mommy, it was wonderful! But I was so scared I'd bite into the Communion that I just swallowed it, even before I could finish all my prayers."

"Go and ask Patches to make us some coffee darling," Teresa shooed her out and closed the door behind her.

Helena looked up and saw that there were tears in her eyes.

"Helena —" she began and stopped.

"What is it Mother?"

"I've been thinking. Perhaps it's just as well that you've decided to go, not only because of Eckhart but, before they find out what you're doing."

"What do you mean?"

She shook her head reproachfully. "You don't really take me for a fool do you? I've long suspected this work of yours in town had nothing to do with Tadek's business. But we'll say no more about that. What I have in mind is, well, couldn't you leave Stefa with me? No, don't interrupt until you've heard me out. Listen, the child is so small. It's winter now. Whichever way you go, you'll be faced with frost, perhaps hunger, or God forbid, worse. She'll not only hamper your and Marian's chances but I doubt if she could stand up to whatever lies ahead of you, which is something even you don't know. As a mother, can you honestly take a gamble like that?"

"And as a mother," Helena said gently, "do you think I could leave my child, Adam's child, to the mercies of the Germans? Don't think I haven't weighed all the risks, all that you've said, because God knows I have, night after night. No Mother, Adam expects not only me. He expects me to bring the children with me and you know that as well as I do. You yourself told me not to lose faith. Please," she begged, reaching for the older woman, "help me strengthen that faith now."

"Oh Helenko."

They held on to one another, conscious of a bond that had not been there before.

Patches brought in the coffee and a bag of food for the road. She had been crying but now as she came to kiss Helena's hand her eyes were dry and a brave smile broke through the clutter of lines. Helena withdrew her hand and hugged her. The tears came back to the old woman as she put her arms around Stefa and Marian.

The Taxi came and Teresa walked to the gate with them. For a long moment she held the children to her before turning to Helena. Their parting was made more painful by a shared feeling that this was their final good-bye.

*

147

CHAPTER TWELVE

"In bleak Vienna"

The journey to Vienna was a grim, silent ordeal. She had instructed Marian and Stefa that, whatever happened, they were to keep their mouths shut.

As before, the Railway official could find no fault with her papers. A family man himself, he gave the children a fatherly look and in a tone of voice that Helena feared might turn into a prolonged friendly chat, said, "Very quiet, aren't they?"

"They're tired," she replied shortly, stifling a yawn. He took the hint and wished them a good night.

This time she had taken a second-class compartment where the heating system was out of order and bedding facilities could scarcely have been worse. The blankets were so threadbare that she had to pile all three on top of Marian, while she and Stefa huddled together, fully dressed, under the fur coat. Not even their ski suits and caps were proof against the icy air currents that swept the compartment.

Next day they arrived in Vienna a little after four in the afternoon, made straight for the Buffet and ordered coffee.

"Ugh!" Helena spluttered. "And I thought Berlin's ersatz brew was the world's worst."

What a change from the delicious coffee she'd once enjoyed in this city, even when served at the station. The heyday of the Vienna *Kaffeehaus* was decidedly over.

"Well, you can't say it isn't hot," Marian pointed out and finished his to the last drop.

Stefa used her cup to warm her hands. "Really Marian, you'd eat and drink anything that was put in front of you."

"That's because I know how to survive. You'll learn," he added.

Helena helped herself to a conveniently displayed map of the city. The Parish at Kahlenberg lay some distance from the station but was simple enough to find.

Marian picked up their small case. Helena took the bag with their food, slung her handbag over her arm and out they walked into a shimmering vista of white. The crooked streets inside the Ringstrasse had all but lost their look of familiarity for her under their heavy blanket of snow. Here and there she could still make out the baroque facades on the buildings and there stood the spire of St. Stephen's Cathedral, as majestic as ever. A fiacre stopped hopefully for them. Helena was tempted to take the ride. Good sense prevailed and they walked on.

Once outside the hub of the city, the streets became more densely covered in snow. Helena chanced a cab drive some way up the hill, from where they pushed on as fast as Stefa's short legs could move and an hour later stood outside the Parish house.

A wizened and very bent old caretaker answered the chiming gong.

"Could I see Father Hirst please?"

"I'm afraid Father is not in," he said, adding, "and won't be back for another three to four days."

"Oh no!" Helena cried out.

The look of concern on his face encouraged her to play on the old man's sympathies. "Look, she said desperately, drawing Stefa forward. "This child is frozen stiff -- couldn't you please put us up here until the Priest gets back?"

His mouth flew open. "Oh dear me, but that's, that's quite impossible *Gnedige Frau,*" he stammered. His eyes shifted nervously. "You are, I mean in case you are, from Poland, I can give you an address of a Polish family in town. They might help you."

The people he sent them to lived on the other side of town and it was close on 7 o'clock before they found the semi-detached bungalow. A short, broad-hipped young woman came to the door. She greeted them pleasantly enough until Helena explained the purpose of their visit. Instantly her manner became strained and fearful. With a swift glance up and down the street she pulled them inside.

Her husband, in striking contrast to his wife, was tall and almost scrawny looking. The placid face seemed out of keeping with so thin a form. He sat with his hands clasped tightly together and left his wife to do all the talking. Not surprising, since the woman only stopped long enough to take breath for the next barrage of words.

Helena learned a lot in the short time they spent with the couple. Everything, she said, had changed from the time of the *Anshluss* (annexation of Austria to Germany) The widely acclaimed charm of the House of Habsburg, the easy-going ostrich policy of Francis Joseph, had all made way for a Vienna whose walls had ears and whose neighbors reported on one another to the Gestapo. There were those who had become open followers of Hitler, while others again were being arrested and sent off, no one knew where. Gone were the days when Vienna was a carefree, happy town, brimming with fun and laughter.

Once only did the man interrupt the woman's rapid flow of words.

"I'm sure our visitors would like something to eat," he suggested mildly.

"No, no thank you," Helena declined. "We must be on our way."

Lavishly showered with every kind of good wish, they found themselves out on the streets again. There was nothing for it but to take the chance and book into an Hotel. Finding one in this poorly lit residential suburb was another story. After a while they gave up peering at every likely building until they reached a better illuminated part of the city.

Turning into Fasangasse, they came upon the Hotel Sonnenaufgang. Helena virtually breezed inside, striding straight up to the man at the reception desk.

"Please let me have a double room with three beds and send up hot tea as soon as possible. We have just arrived from Hamburg, frozen to the bone and dead tired. The name is Konig but," she hurried on, "could we please attend to the formalities tomorrow."

Dumbfounded by the rush of words, the little man didn't know what to do first. Chubby hands waving about like butterflies he trotted out from behind the counter, handed a key to the porter, bowed as far as his pot belly would permit him to and gave short nods of understanding.

"But of course, Frau Konig," he agreed in a melodious Austrian twang. "Please follow the porter up to your room and I'll have the tea sent up directly, and an extra bed."

"Danke schon."

"Bitte schon, bitte schon," he replied, still bowing.

That night Helena lay awake for hours, worrying. Were they safe to stay in this Hotel? Would the Priest ever return, or had he already been caught? And, above all, would the crossing into Hungary indeed prove too much for them. She tried to recapture the resolve once made: To cross her bridges when she came to them, but what if there was no bridge that could span this chasm? The sound of Stefa's labored breathing prayed on her mind as well. All three of them had been sneezing and blowing their noses but she knew how a cold could affect the child and could only hope that the sniffles would not develop into a serious bout of 'flu.

The next day, the snow came down in a blinding blizzard. Helena thought it best to stay in their room and have the meals sent up, making their chills a valid excuse for not showing themselves in public. The room was ideally ventilated for summer conditions. But it was large with three comfortable beds and an adjoining bathroom. Their biggest problem was the sinking temperature. Two thin blankets per bed were not enough to stop the cold from penetrating right into the marrow of the bones and one fur coat could not cover all three of them.

The same little man who had met them at the reception desk answered Helena's ring for service. She learned that he was also the proprietor. He could let them have only one additional blanket but also brought some magazines, a pack of cards and dominoes.

It was during this period of close confinement that Helena learned what the children really thought and felt about a great number of things, things adults normally consider to be beyond the scope of a child's understanding or interest. Their views on Nazism for one, were a revelation to her. Here, Marian showed a surprising insight.

"I can see why Hitler has so many followers," he said. "If you listen to the way he talks on the radio, a German's bound to be, what's the word..."

"Stirred?" Helena suggested.

"Yes, that's it, stirred but good. Now they really believe they're better than anyone else and so naturally no other matters to them, so they can kill them."

"That's because they are bad Christians," said Stefa the zealot. "Jesus taught that you must be humble. He said that no one was any better than anybody else."

"In that case, the Russians must be the finest Christians out because that's what they preach."

"Oh don't talk to me about the Russians. What they preach has absolutely nothing to do with religion. They're pagans, that's what they are. And as you have obviously never read the Bible, let me explain that what Jesus meant was that you must *love* everybody in the same way."

"Thanks for the scripture lesson. Now, are you by any chance telling me that, being the good Catholic and Christian that you are, you love Stalin and Hitler as much as you love Mom here, or Dad?"

"Well..."

"There you are!" He gloated. "You've defeated your own argument."

"No I haven't. I never said I was all that good, but I don't hate anybody. At least I don't think I do."

"I know Stefciu, forget it. You're trying." He could afford to be patronizing.

No less interesting were their speculations on how long the war would last. With his usual weakness for taking bets, Marian was willing to put his shirt on it that Germany would be vanquished before the year was out. For once Stefa took him up on it. She made a diary note of this together with an estimate of her own, that shook Helena. Even she thought the year 1945 was rather an immoderately long prediction at the time.

When he could not persuade either of them to go on playing cards or dominoes with him, Marian would take to scribbling on the back of the menus. At first Helena paid no attention to it but when she saw the extent of the boy's concentration on his 'doodling' she asked him what he was doing.

"Just working out some sums."

"Let's see?"

She took the paper from him and was amazed to see mathematical calculations advanced beyond her understanding.

"You *like* doing this?" "Mm. It's fun."

"But how do you know if your answers are correct?" "Well you work them out backwards, like this, see?"

She shook her head. No she could not see but she was sure he knew what he was doing. She studied him with renewed interest. None of them had suspected that the boy had a bent for Maths. She pictured Adam's delight and as she did so she became aware of the positive trend that her thoughts had taken. She put her hand on his shoulder. "Dad will be so proud of you," she told him.

But with each passing day it became harder to sustain the mood of optimism. The snow gave way to sleet, reducing what had been left of the winter daylight, while the wind howled through the corridors and tugged at the shutters. Room lights could be switched on from a little before dinner time until 9 o'clock. Beyond that there was candlelight. Power rationing extended to hot water and that too was available only for a couple of hours a day which, the maid told Helena, was a luxury they were very lucky to be afforded.

It wasn't until the fourth day that the sun came out and they went to pay another visit to the Parish at Kahlenberg.

Father Hirst had returned. He was a frail, soft-spoken man with the unnaturally high color of a consumptive. Inviting them in, he said the caretaker had already spoken to him about them.

"Forgive me that I cannot speak to you in your own language, but although I am of Polish origin, I have lived here all my life and, well-" he broke off with a gesture of resignation.

"What does the language matter as long as we understand each other, *nicht wahr?*" Helena said meaningfully, adding that his name had been given to her by the Polish Underground.

"Ah, then there is certainly no need for further explanations. We do understand one another." He stopped, putting his hand up to his mouth to muffle the two short dry barks that shook his shoulders. "But surely you do not propose to venture on this, er, 'expedition' with those small children?"

She had anticipated that he might not want to give her the Klingenbach contact because of the children and was equal to the well-meant arguments that followed. The bouts of coughing increased with his agitation but she finally managed to convince him that under no circumstances could they remain in this country or go back to Poland.

Thirty minutes later they left the Parish house with a map, the name and address of another Priest in Klingenbach and a warm blessing.

That evening Helena told the proprietor that they would be leaving and asked for her account. He came personally with the bill.

"Frau Konig," he began, avoiding her eyes. "You ought to be more careful. I overheard you speaking in Polish."

The blood drained from her face.

*

CHAPTER THIRTEEN

"The Second Escape- into jail"

God Almighty we've been caught. Caught before we've even made a start!
She *had* to get them out of this. Helena's mind raced. What could she
tell the man? That they were repatriated Germans who'd been living in
Poland - of course!

"There's a perfectly good reason why-" she began but he cut her
short.

"No, don't try to explain, please. I shall certainly not give you away.
To tell you the truth," he went on softly, "I am ashamed of the way we
Germans are treating you people. Whatever your plans may be, I wish
you the very best of luck."

She took his hand in both of hers, not trusting herself to speak.

......

The night was starless, the moon all but obscured by heavy clouds. They
stood on the railway siding on the outskirts of Klingenbach, three dots
in a desert of snow. The train had pulled away almost immediately,
giving Helena no chance to ask or look for directions.

The journey from Vienna had been a nightmare. The guards and the
Gestapo had obviously been looking for someone. Thank God it had
not been for them. And now this utter bleakness of the little siding in
an unknown country, the uncertainty of the location of the town and

the air so cold it hurt to breathe. Having nothing better to rely on than Marian's sense of direction, Helena asked him which way he thought they should go.

Drawing himself up to his full height he said, "Let's try to the right. I think I see a speck of light over there. Damn, it's gone. No, there it is again, see it?"

It took her several moments to find the tiny flicker of light in the distance. With no other sign of life in that desolate frozen plain, they started out towards the light.

It was hard going through the snow and after a while Stefa's strides began to drag. She was exhausted and kept complaining of her aching hands and feet.

"Let's go back and wait for another train to Poland," she moaned. "We'll never make it."

The pathetic weariness in the voice as much as its hoarseness, made Helena wince. "We'll stop for a minute to get our breath," she said.

This was worse than she had expected and they were barely on the verge of the so-called 'expedition'. Tears stung her eyes as she looked at the two muffled forms. Mother's fears were fast materializing. Already Stefa's hands and feet were showing signs of frost-bite and she had developed a persistent cough. Had she been wrong to bring the child along after all?

"For Pete's sake don't be such a ninny!" Marian yelled at her. "You know we can't go back and the Priest said this was our only chance. Of course we'll make it. Now, stamp your feet and beat your hands across your chest like this, before you freeze to death, you silly."

"Silly yourself," she muttered but did as she was told.

He said nothing about his own frost-bitten ears. It wasn't so bad now that they were quite numb but he didn't like that warm feeling either. He knew that was the danger sign. Seized by sudden panic he pulled his cap further down over his ears. He couldn't bear to have his ears fall off.

With an effort Helena pulled herself together, aware that what they needed most at that moment was someone stronger than themselves, they needed a leader. "Right you two, let's step on it," she said briskly. "Can't be too far now."

On and on they struggled, legs sinking at times into two feet of snow, through uneven country, through ditches that only revealed themselves when they stumbled into them, until, almost unexpectedly, the dim outlines of a large building loomed ahead. "I'm not going in there!" Stefa cried.

"There she goes again," Marian groaned. "We're almost there and *now* she has to start performing."

Helena looked closely at her daughter's ashen face and fear-dilated eyes and concluded, emotionally at least, that something was very wrong here. But what?

"No Marian," she said slowly. "I don't think Stefa is performing. She must have some sort of premonition."

In her own state of indecision she was ready to grasp at straws. Moreover, whether it was Stefa's attitude or the eerie, completely still atmosphere of their surroundings, she couldn't say, but all at once she too felt strangely uneasy.

"Please Mommy, let's turn back. I don't like it here," Stefa shivered.

"It's evil."

By this time even Marian realized that there might be something to his sister's peculiar behavior and the three of them stood motionless, listening.

From a long way off, somewhere to their left, came the faint sound of a dog barking.

Helena felt the tingling sensation as the hair rose on her scalp. "That's where the town must be," she exclaimed. "Where there are dogs there must be people."

Stefa gave a shuddering sigh of relief.

"Wonder what this place is then." Marian looked up at the building.

"I don't know and I don't care," Stefa hissed. "Let's just get out of here." She held onto his arm, terrified that he might be tempted to explore the place.

Certain that they were on the right track this time, they turned away from the silent, depressing walls. With only the occasional bark to guide them, they had to make periodic stops and wait for the sound of the dogs to reach them again before moving on.

Finally, a short steep rise and they were looking down onto a cluster of dark outlines that was Klingenbach. Here and there, tiny shafts of light showed through drawn window curtains. The town was small enough for the Church spire to stand out clearly from the other buildings.

Helena rapped on the door of the adjoining Parish house. A slender plain-faced woman in her mid forties opened the door.

"Ja?" She said in a friendly tone.

"I have come to see the Priest", Helena said.

Without another word she ushered them inside, placing a warning finger to her lips. They understood that they were not to interrupt the Fuhrer's speech blaring at them from a radio in the living room. She pulled out chairs for them and they sat facing an enormously fat man whose entire form seemed hunched in concentration. There were deep furrows between his eyebrows and his eyes were riveted on the set as though Hitler himself stood behind the round speaker. He made no sign of having heard them come in. The woman gestured towards their coats, which they took off and with a last resounding yell, Hitler finished his speech. The usual frenzied *"Sieg Heil, Sieg Heil, Sieg Heil"* that followed was cut short by a turn of the knob.

Devoid of any expression, the man looked at Helena for the first time.

She felt compelled to answer his unasked question. "I have come to see the Priest," she repeated. "Eh, on a private matter."

"Father Emil is away at the moment, but should be back within an hour or so. Would you like to wait for him, or-"

"Yes, if you don't mind," she cut in gratefully.

"In that case," the woman said, "I'll go and make some coffee. It should warm you all up a bit. You poor dears look frozen stiff." And she left them to the disconcertingly frank scrutiny of the giant. He chose not to speak and for the life of her, Helena could think of nothing to say either. The arrival of coffee was a blessed deliverance.

The woman introduced herself as *Frau* Ziegler, the Priest's sister and although she was kindness itself, her artless questions made Helena grow uncomfortable and even more so when she began addressing herself to the children.

Marian did well with his most winning smile and a *"bite"*

when she asked if he would also like to soak his hands in cold water, for she had already attended to Stefa's lifeless fingers, but when her conversation became too involved for him to follow, he became mute.

Not discouraged, she turned to Stefa. "And what about you my dear. Come, don't be shy. Wouldn't you like a slice of bread? I might even be able to find some nice gooseberry preserve to put on it."

It became impossible to ignore their agonizing silence, or the imploring looks they shot her and Helena decided to put her cards on the table.

"They cannot understand you, *Frau* Ziegler. They can only speak their own language, which is Polish."

The sentence hung suspended in the silence between them. Helena felt two pairs of eyes boring into hers in shocked amazement.

"Then, then what on earth are you doing here?" The woman gasped. "Did anyone see you come in?"

"No. No one could have seen us. It's very dark outside." Another long silence.

"Would you mind answering my wife's first question. What *are* you doing here?" The man spoke again, his voice still neutral.

Very deliberately she said, "We have come to ask the Priest to help us escape to Hungary."

He stood up, lit a cigar, walked over to throw the match into the fireplace and came back to tower over her with his immense bulk.

"I think you ought to know that I am the *Burgermeister* of Klingenbach and have orders to co-operate with the authorities in matters such as these," he said slowly. "As for my brother-in-law, I know nothing of his activities, nor do I wish to."

Moved by her stricken expression, he added, "But if you decide to be sensible and go back to wherever you came from, we will say no more about it."

"I understand your position *Herr* Ziegler and I wouldn't want to implicate you in any way, but to go back is positively out of the question," she rushed on, "You see, my husband's name is on the 'Black List' and to go back now would mean to walk straight into a Concentration Camp. I'd risk anything rather than commit my children to such a fate."

There was another long silence, broken by the steady tick of the mantelpiece clock and the crackling of firewood. The whole situation had acquired a curiously unreal sense of melodrama. In contrast to the frost outside, it was stiflingly hot in the room. The air grew laden with humidity, cigar smoke and suspense. Helena struggled to marshal her thoughts into coherence, to hear what the man was saying, although her eyes had never left his.

"I know what I *ought* to do, but I also know that I have never seen such courage, and frankness, in a woman and for this I admire you." He paused. "Very well, you may go to the Priest's room and wait for him there." He placed the cigar between his teeth then withdrew it without inhaling. "I have not seen or heard anything tonight."

His wife gave a choking little sound of relief. Whether or not she had been aware of her brother's none-ecclesiastical function was of no importance. All that mattered was that her husband had demonstrated the humanity she always knew he had in him. Overcome with joy she hugged them all, before leading the three fugitives out through a courtyard and into the Priest's quarters. She brought them more coffee and added a log to the barely glowing embers in the minute fireplace.

In the far corner of the room a candle burned at the foot of a statue of the Virgin Mary. Her tiredness forgotten for the moment, Stefa walked over to it and knelt on the prie-dieu. Under the candle light, the honey colored hair glowed and shimmered, creating an almost halo-like effect that made Helena catch her breath. She was still on her knees when Father Emil arrived.

He was a year or two younger than his sister, square-jawed, tall and muscular and the cassock sat awkwardly on him, but there was the glow of the dedicated in his eyes.

"Sorry to keep you waiting," he began. "I have been expecting you. Father Hirst told me-" he broke off with a look of dismay when his gaze fell on Stefa. "I had no idea the children were so small! You couldn't possibly-"

"Please," Helena interrupted, knowing what was coming. "You *must* help us Father."

Once again she explained their position. He sat for a long while looking thoughtfully at his large fists held tightly on his lap. Then he raised troubled eyes to meet hers and nodded.

"In that case, as much as I am reluctant to do so, I must help you."
"Thank you Father," she breathed.

He produced a sheet of paper and pencil and drew his chair closer. Swiftly he scribbled a rough sketch of the surrounding district.

"Now this is what you must do. First of all, to avoid causing *any* suspicions here, you will take the first train back as far as Wienerneustadt -- it's a couple of stations away -- and from there buy your tickets for Neckenmarkt. Your train will cover about eighty kilometers of Hungarian territory before it makes its circuitous route back into Austria further south and reaches Neckenmarkt. The train makes one stop while passing through Hungary, this is at Sopron. Are you with me so far?"

Helena nodded, wondering how they would disembark at Sopron.

"Naturally it will be impossible for you to get off the train with the other passengers as there are German and Hungarian guards at the station and you would be required to produce your Visa. This then is your alternative." He paused and looked at her intently.

"As soon as the train pulls out of the station at Sopron and while it is still moving fairly slowly, you will have to jump off."

She swallowed hard, trying to hide the shock his words had given her. "We - jump off the train?"

"It may not be quite as bad as it sounds," he went on. "You see, the train runs on a high embankment and you will roll into deep snow."

At this she breathed a little more easily but his voice took on a warning note.

"There are serious snags however, and these you will have to bear in mind at all times."

He then proceeded to drill them in the method of jumping out of a train: He stressed that they must leap out with the momentum of the train. In other words, throw their bodies in the direction the train would be traveling, to ease the impact of the fall: That they would have to gauge the distances between the treacherous mile-stones that may be covered by snow: That they would have to watch out for telegraph poles.

He made Marian and Stefa repeat the instructions over and over again. Finally he took Helena aside.

"Look, you may have to throw the little one out yourself," he said. "It's a lot to expect of a child."

Jesus, he thought, looking into the great blue eyes, *and isn't it too much to expect of her?* She didn't look more than a girl herself. Anything could happen. It was not easy to gauge the distances between milestones and telegraph poles out of a moving train, especially if they're covered by snow. Strong men had baulked at the last moment to take the plunge. And there would be no one to help them once they reached Sopron, a town teeming with Nazi personnel.

"Listen," his voice took on an urgent note, "my sister might be able to find a safe home for you somewhere in this district. Won't you reconsider?"

"No," she shook her head. "My husband is waiting for us."

"He is a lucky man. All right, let's go through it again."

When he was satisfied that they knew exactly what to do, he suggested they snatch a little sleep as the train was not due for another hour or more and they would be catching it from the nearby Klingenbach station this time.

"Not the siding across the hill," he smiled. "I'll fetch blankets for you. You will find that couch quite comfortable."

"Just one more thing," Helena stopped him at the door. "What's that large building to the right of the siding? We almost went in there by mistake."

He regarded her wonderingly. "That," he said, "is the Border Guard House. Anyone seen approaching it within so many meters is shot! You can thank Our Lady for her merciful intercession."

"And our Stefa," she whispered, gathering her daughter to her.

......

Ra-ta-ta-ta; Ra-ta-ta-ta; you-may-be-killed; you-may-be-killed, taunted the rhythmic clatter of the wheels. Stefa's mouth felt so dry she kept wanting to lick her lips. How *can* Marian doze? She was agonizingly sleepy but too scared to let herself drift off. In any case her whole body kept shivering and she wished her knees would stop knocking together. She wished she could have stayed behind with *Babcia,* her grandmother. Maybe they could still turn back without having to kill themselves jumping out.

Ra-ta-to-ta; will-not-be-killed; can-not-be-killed.

As she looked down at the frightened little face resting on her shoulder, Helena began to pray as she had never prayed before. She tried not to think of what they were about to do. Time for that when the actual moment came, yet the most awesome pictures kept presenting themselves in vivid detail. There was Stefa's body smashed against a telegraph pole. Around Marian the snow melted in a dark pool of red. Who gave her the right to tempt fate with their very lives? Dear God, what was she *doing* here? If by some miracle they should land unharmed, how would they be able to enter Sopron? Father Emil had said there were guards at the station. It seemed logical to suppose that no part of this border town would be left unguarded. She could feel her heart speeding up, feel the sweat breaking out, running down between her breasts.

She looked at her watch for the third time in 20 minutes. It felt as though they had been traveling for hours. Helena was certain they must be approaching Sopron when the train began to brake and slowly came to a stop. Doors slammed.

To her horror, two officers of the Gestapo entered their compartment. They could have been twins, cheeks pink from the cold, clear blue eyes, smart in their uniforms. Helena watched in morbid fascination as they politely clicked their heels and took the seats opposite them. *The whole bloody train is almost empty and they have to come and sit opposite us!* She felt Stefa shudder against her and for a moment her mind went blank. This sort of thing had not featured in their well-rehearsed plan.

The swastikas on the men's sleeves reminded her of the brutal killing of Alex and Wanda, of the innocent Nuns and children shot down like some toy targets, the Jews at Bielsko station. And a cold anger swept over her. When and how did Germany spawn this race of maniacs? *Well, they're not going to destroy **us**!* The anger cleared her wits and all at once she knew what to do.

Loudly enough for the Germans to hear, she said to Stefa, "It won't be long now darling. We can't go to the toilet until the train starts moving again." At the same time she was squeezing Stefa's hand in a frantic effort to make her understand that she was to keep quiet. She understood all right.

Quick to grasp the situation, Marian leaned towards his mother and whispered in her ear. Aloud she said, "Yes, all right, you can come as well."

With a shrill whistle the train began to move off. Helena got up, making her movements seem unhurried while every fiber in her body strove to rush out before the train gathered too much speed. She picked up her bag, leaving the rest of their luggage on top of the rack and carefully closed the door behind them. She ushered the children ahead of her through to the open platform between the wagons.

A cold wind whipped at her face as she stood on the narrow landing. By this time the train had gathered speed and the snow below shot by at what seemed to be a fantastic pace.

"I can't Mommy. I just can't!" Stefa cried.

Helena forced the small clawing hands away from her and physically heaved her off the train. She watched as Stefa tumbled, rolled and lay still. Her heart stopped. Above the singing in her ears she heard herself shout, "Hurry Marian! Jump! *What are* you waiting for!"

With slow, maddening nonchalance he turned round. "Hang on, I'm looking out for the telegraph poles." Then he too was gone.

Barely conscious, Helena was aware of pushing herself off the step, a jarring impact and nothing more.

She came to almost at once for the first thing she heard was the sound of the train puffing by. Lifting her head, she saw two wonderfully alive silhouettes running towards her. She tried to move but could not. Her right arm and shoulder were completely numb and her head was ready to explode.

"Mommy, Mommy!" Stefa was shrieking. "Oh Marian, why is she lying like that? She's dead. Oh God, she's dead!"

"Come on, run!" Marian shouted, fear cracking his voice. As he came nearer, Helena heard him repeating over and over, "Why couldn't it have happened to me."

Her throat tightened at these words so that she could do not more than whisper a reassurance. "Don't worry. I'm alive -- it's just that I can't seem to move my right side. Are you both all right?"

They were kneeling beside her, sobbing, telling her they were fine. Stefa had broken a tooth and had actually seen stars, she said, but otherwise both were unhurt.

The pain that followed the numbness in her arm was excruciating and she had to fight against losing consciousness again.

"You must have hit one of those damned mile-stones," Marian croaked. "Come on Stefa, let's help Mom up."

Slowly they got her to her feet. The ground sprang up to meet her and she had to be helped up again. They stood there with bated breath, waiting for the train to disappear from view, still fearful that someone may have seen them and would pull the emergency cord. Then there were the two Gestapo men -- but the train continued on its way until it was no more than a dark speck in the distance. It rounded a bend and was out of sight.

They'd made it!

The pain forgotten in a moment of unbelievable joy, she began to laugh. "We're free! Do you realize that we're free!"

That set them off. Released suddenly from all the pent-up tensions and long-suppressed fears, they burst into a deafening chorus of exultant shrieks and laughter. Helena waited for them to get it out of their system before reminding them that they still had to make their way back to Sopron, an unknown town, whose lights now blinked at them from a long way off.

Supported on either side, she stumbled along the railway lines. They kept to the lines for as long as they thought they would not be spotted and then branched off onto a country road to avoid the station.

The town clock struck 3 a.m. when they finally reached Sopron. Turning into a narrow street, they came upon a night watchman warming his hands before a brazier. "Could you direct us to the nearest hospital?" Helena asked in German.

With an incredulous look he pointed to a building directly in front of them.

The nurse on duty quickly called a Doctor. Engulfed in a sea of pain, Helena barely noticed the nurse's departure, nor did it seem in any way unusual at the time that the Doctor should dismiss the girl and help her onto the theater table himself. All that she was aware of were his firm fingers on her shoulder. Before she knew what had happened he gave a jerk. A moment of searing agony and the pain was gone. She could not believe it. The relief was so great that for the first time she allowed the tears to come unchecked.

The Doctor warned her that he had merely manipulated the bone back into place but that her shoulder blade was smashed and would have to be set without delay.

"I take it you are not staying in Sopron?" He asked discreetly, his eyes flickering momentarily as they rested on the deeply embedded snow in the curls of her fur coat. She had not thought to shake it off. It came to her suddenly that there had been no sign of a recent snowfall in the town. She felt the blood drain from her face, a moment of giddiness.

"Eh- no. We're on our way to Budapest," she murmured, willing him not to ask any more questions. He walked over to a chest of drawers, picked out a sling made of strong black cotton and as he tied the knot at the back of her neck, told her that she should go to a hospital as soon as they reached Budapest.

It occurred to her then that she would have to pay him. Nothing could have been designed to give them away more surely than the German Marks which was the only currency she had on her. Hesitantly she opened her bag and asked how much she owed.

"Not a *Mark,*" he replied with a smile and an unmistakable emphasis on the last word.

They looked at one another. He held her gaze with a frankness she knew to be completely trustworthy. Before she could thank him, he said, "Come, your children are waiting." He took her good arm to escort her to the waiting room and left. She had not realized until then, how worried they had been about her. It was painful to see Marian biting his nails again, a habit he had triumphed over some months before. Stefa's ashen face was contorted with the effort not to cry. She came running to meet her mother.

Marian nudged her to keep quiet. "And stop jumping about like that. You'll bump Mom's arm. So they gave you a sling eh? It was obvious the arm was broken," he said knowingly.

She had to recount the consultation in every detail. Satisfied, they decided they could now leave the Hospital. Their mother had become their patient and their responsibility and they, her self-appointed guardians. She was weary enough to accept the new role without protest, even with some relief.

The streets of Sopron looked featureless in the dark. An occasional street lamp vaguely outlined the walls of a building, as though reluctant to bring its shabbiness into full view.

"We'll have to see if we can exchange some of my jewelry for Hungarian Pengo," Helena told Marian. "We need enough money to pay for tonight's lodgings somewhere and buy our tickets for Budapest."

"Here's an open Bar," Marian pointed across the road. "I'll go in and see what I can do."

She gave him Tadek's gold watch and chain. He came out beaming and handed her some Hungarian money. It was only later that they discovered to what extent they had been robbed, but for the moment they had cash and that was all that mattered.

The next problem was to find accommodation. They turned into what seemed to be the main street and almost at once spotted a small Private Hotel. After repeated knocking, the door was opened by a disgruntled looking woman in a tattered robe. When Helena asked for a room she said she had none. It required no great perception to see that she was lying.

"Please, just for the night. We'll pay cash and won't trouble you for food."

"Well, in that case-" The woman opened the door wider and grudgingly told them to enter. Her searching looks darted from one to the other, taking in every detail. Helena did not like her or her attitude but right then nothing seemed as important as a bed to sleep in.

The room they were shown into was as bare of warmth as its owner. It smelled of mildew. There were two iron-posted, iron-hard beds, an unstable upright chair and an old-fashioned stand with an enamel basin and water jug. A once-white towel hung limply from a nail in the wall. There was no soap.

Making the best of it, they splashed their hands and faces with ice-cold water. This time all three knew the agony of pins and needles as life coursed back into numbed fingers. Marian helped his mother out of her coat and skirt but when he and Stefa tried to take off her blouse she cried out in pain.

"Leave it. I'll sleep as I am," she panted.

"In that case I can leave my socks on. My feet are-" Stefa began when Marian held up his hand for silence. He tiptoed towards the door, eased it open a fraction, looked up and down the passage and came back frowning.

"I thought so. That woman's been spying on us. I've just seen her sneaking down the steps."

"Jesus, if you're right and if she had been listening, then she must have heard me cry out," Helena groaned. "Let's pray you're mistaken Marian."

He wasn't. No sooner had they climbed into their beds than they heard the knock on the door. Helena struggled back into her skirt. She opened the door and was confronted by the woman in the same tattered robe.

"The Police want to see you," she announced with undisguised glee.

Two Policemen were standing in the passage behind her. Helena asked them in German what they wanted of her and although the embarrassed, almost apologetic expressions on their faces clearly indicated that they understood her, they nevertheless used the woman as an interpreter. She was quick to let Helena know that they must accompany the men to the Police Station.

"But whatever for?" Helena demanded. "We aren't criminals." "Then why don't you prove it and show them your documents?"

Helena ignored her. She asked the men to wait outside and closed the door.

"Put your clothes on again. We'll have to go with them," she said. "That *Hexa* (witch) has betrayed us."

"I bet she's German," Marian spat.

The Policemen were waiting for them at the front entrance. The woman had the door open as soon as she saw the family coming down the stairs. Helena's look of loathing was wasted on her, as she stared back with a mixture of righteousness and triumph. The door slammed behind them.

At the Police Station, Helena was taken before a Sergeant who asked her in German to produce her visa.

"I don't have one," she said. "But please let me speak to the Commissioner."

"Unfortunately the Commissioner is away for a few days. We shall have to detain you until his return."

Stricken she stood before the man. A death sentence could not have been more devastating.

*

CHAPTER FOURTEEN

"Reunion in Budapest"

She looked down to find Marian pulling at her sleeve.

"What did he *say?*" He was asking, partly understanding, hoping he was wrong.

She told him. Her voice was flat and unemotional. After the initial shock, Helena had become devoid of all thought, all feeling. The situation was too abhorrent to confront, and she wasn't ready to face it.

Stefa's hands flew to her mouth. She began to sob quietly. Marian's face had gone white. "Stay *here?*" The Sergeant found himself turning away from the boy's look of bewilderment.

Helana's bag and everything in it was confiscated. She and Stefa were taken to a private cell and Marian was escorted to the men's quarters.

Divorced from reality, Helena stood and gazed at the narrow, concrete cell, the two wooden bunks and bare table, unable to take any of it in. It was the sight of the small barred window, high up near the ceiling that finally brought her out of her stupefaction. She sank onto the bunk.

"My God, so this is what we've come to!" She cried, covering her face with her hands and dissolving into tears.

The Guard made as if to speak, shook his head in despair and turned the key to their cell.

He was back in a few moments with a couple of blankets and a tray of food.

"Here we are," he said in his broken German, the homely face creasing into a reassuring smile. "Hot milk, rolls and you will be better. After that you sleep."

The buttered rolls, freshly baked, made them aware of their hunger. Watching them eat, the man nodded with satisfaction.

Convinced that she would never be able to close an eye in this dreadful place, Stefa lay down and immediately fell asleep.

Helena lay suffering. No matter which way she turned, the boards triggered shooting pains in her shoulder and arm. Finally she rolled up her blanket and placed it in a position to alleviate some of the pressure. She covered herself with her fur coat. At least they had not taken that away from her. But sleep would not come. The more she tried not to think about it the more absorbed she became in running a post-mortem on the events. If she hadn't lost her head over Stefa's stumble she may have spotted the mile stone. On the other hand, it had been embedded pretty deeply. She should have thought of the snow in her fur though -- that was an unforgivable blunder. Say the Doctor had been someone like that bitch at the Hotel. The woman's venomous face haunted her now. How could anyone be so callous? The children had meant nothing to her. The train! That's what was bothering her. It was the train. She sat up, covered in sweat. The two Gestapo men had expected them back in the carriage. Their luggage was still on top of the rack. If an alert had been sent out it wouldn't take them long to trace the fugitives. What would, or could, the Hungarian authorities do about it?

It was still dark outside when the lights came on and she heard the rattle of keys in the lock.

"I have fixed for your son to sit with you to eat," said the Guard, beaming.

"Come on Stefa, we're going for breakfast." "Can't he just bring us some more of those lovely rolls and butter? Please ask him Mom, please."

"No. He's just done us a favor to have Marian with us. We musn't chance our luck too far. Go on, put your shoes on."

He led them down a long, nakedly lit corridor, at the end of which was the communal eating hall.

"There," said the Guard, pointing to where Marian was sitting.

Pushing Stefa ahead of her and avoiding the curious stares of the men who sat in rows along the narrow benches, Helena weaved her way towards Marian's table. Incredibly, he seemed to be enjoying this experience and lost no time in reciting the offenses of his cellmates. Helena learned that they were in the company of a classic assortment of hoodlums.

Drunks, swindlers, petty thieves and even a murderer was said to be amongst them.

"How do you know all this?" She asked him.

"You'd be surprised how many of these chaps speak German and some of them even know a bit of Polish. See that man sitting over by the window? The one with the broken nose?"

"Yes." The man met her gaze boldly and smiled. Helena quickly dropped her eyes.

"He's in for wife beating."

"Really Marian! Do you have to take such a morbid interest in these people?"

"Well all right, if you don't want to hear about them just say so and I'll shut up."

"You do that."

Not in the least put out, he transferred his attention to the business of eating. Helena made an effort to eat the foul-looking gruel pushed in front of her on a tin plate but a couple of mouthfuls was enough to make her want to retch. Doubled up in a fit of coughing, Stefa made no attempt to sample the dish. The company did nothing to make their ordeal any more bearable. As the only females present, they were subjected to a great deal of speculation, smirks and stage whispers. Helena had had enough of it. She signaled their Guard who was standing with two others at the entrance. He came forward immediately.

"Please," she asked "Could we leave now? I don't feel too well and the child can't stop coughing."

He nodded and took them straight back to their cell, soon to reappear with more milk and bread rolls.

"Your son he say your arm is very bad. I am bringing pills to take pain away." And he handed her a bottle of pain relievers.

Helena's thanks were drowned by another bout of coughing from Stefa. The chills that Stefa and Marian had caught in Vienna had, in both cases developed into hacking coughs. Stefa's more persistent.

"I have put honey in the child's milk," the Guard said gruffly. "Very bad cough."

Helena noticed that the central heating in their cell had been raised a good few degrees as well.

"What is your name?" She asked the man

"Janos."

"I shall never forget your kindness Janos," she said to him. "I also have a family," he replied simply.

After that, they were never again taken to the communal diner but ate whatever food the man could bring from his home or his own prison rations. Sometimes there was goulash, hot and spicy, or a leg of chicken with noodles -- even though they would have been content with the milk and those delicious rolls of his.

Once, he managed to sneak Marian in for a quick chat. This apparently was against the rules and, finger to lips, he cautioned them to keep their voices down.

Marian's nervous attitude, as much as the strange glow in the green eyes, told Helena that there was something terribly important on her son's mind. As soon as Janos was out of earshot, he whispered, "Listen Mom, a couple of the chaps in my cell are planning a break. They said I could go with them if I wanted to."

"Not on your life!" She exploded.

"Don't get excited. Wait till you hear what the idea is."

"Go on."

"It will all be done at night. After supper, as we're filing back into our cell and just before the Guard locks us in, we'll overpower him, grab his keys and run for it."

"What about the outside Guards?"

"There's only one on duty then and he'll be taken care of."

The matter-of-fact way in which he dismissed this obstacle was so out of character that she stared at him, unable to reconcile this new tough youth with the mild boy she was used to.

"And," he went on, "as soon as we reach Budapest, I can get in touch with the Polish Consulate and they will make the Commissioner here set you and Stefa free!"

It was almost a shame to spoil the triumphant finale to which his voice had risen.

"Forget it," she told him flatly.

"But Mom!"

"Now you listen to me. In the first place, I doubt whether they would ever get any further than the front gate, but even if they did, they'd be caught long before they reached Budapest."

"How can you be so sure of that?"

"All right then, let's say, for argument's sake, that you do get to Budapest. Do you think the Polish Consulate has the authority to release Hungarian prisoners? No Marian, our only hope is the Commissioner, believe me."

He could not hide his disappointment but saw the sense behind the argument and said nothing more about the 'break'. And after a couple of days it became evident that his cellmates had also given up the idea of escape.

The pain, the heat in the confined space, Stefa's coughing, the sleepless nights and above all, the uncertainty, all tore at her resources and Helena watched the days change into nights outside the little grid, with a deepening sense of futility. It had all been for nothing. Freedom was a pipedream. Even the thought of the struggle for survival seemed to be too much effort. She tossed on her cot and knew she had a fever. She took extra pills to try and bring it down.

On the fourth day she felt well enough to ask Janos if there was any news of the Commissioner's return.

"He maybe coming tomorrow," he told her and added, "If not, I get a Doctor, good?"

"No. I'm much better. Thank you."

The next morning their friend flung the door to the cell wide open and announced with a broad smile, "The Commissioner want to see you!" As she walked past him he whispered, "Good luck."

Marian was already waiting outside the door marked 'Private' and the three of them entered a simply but well furnished office. A hint of leather and Stefa's eyes instinctively went to the three studded chairs in

173

front of an immense desk. Then to the dark-complexioned man sitting behind it. He was in his fifties, gray at the temples, the horn-rimmed spectacles adding severity to finely chiseled features. He stood up and asked them to be seated, gesturing to the leather chairs on the other side of his desk.

"Now, tell me your story," he said in excellent German. "I want to know everything."

Without disclosing names, Helena began with her first contact in Vienna.

"No," he interrupted. "If you don't mind, I should like you to go back to the beginning. To the reason why you felt compelled to leave your country. Go to the outbreak of the war."

And so she told him of their experiences under the Russians, how they crossed the river San, their return to Bielsko, her trip to Berlin and finally the escape across the second frontier. He listened intently, his eyes resting occasionally on Stefa, moving on to Marian and back again to the ravaged yet beautiful face of the woman. A wave of compassion swept over him. The poor kids, dragged about the country, always on the run, and always the fear of capture and death. Betrayed at the end. And this splendid young woman. It took a special brand of courage to do what she had done.

When she finished, he removed his spectacles, polished them vigorously with his handkerchief, replaced them, stood up and went over to look out of the window, hands tightly clenched behind his back.

"You put me in a very difficult position," he said, slowly turning round to face her. "I have orders to return any escapees that cross our borders back into the hands of the Nazis. Hungary, as you are aware, is a neutral country and we dare not violate our agreements, certainly not at this stage."

Her heart gave a sickening lurch. She heard herself speak in an alien voice. "Oh you *couldn't* send us back now! And, and since it is a neutral country, could you not get in touch with the Polish Consulate in Budapest and hand us over to them?" She pleaded.

"That is a solution I have already considered, provided your escape has gone unnoticed. You had medical attention though and this would have been recorded, would it not?"

The very fact that he had already thought of the Polish Consulate was more than encouraging and she leaned forward excitedly, her eyes alive again, shaking her head in answer to his question.

"No. I'm almost positive it has not been recorded. As a matter of fact the Doctor asked his nurse to leave the room while he examined me and he didn't even take my name nor would he accept a fee."

"Hmm. In that case, perhaps we may be lucky. Let me check with the hospital."

He picked up the telephone receiver and asked to be put through to Outpatients. A few words in Hungarian sufficed to relax the tightness about his mouth.

"You were right," he said. "They have no record of attending to a casualty in the last few days."

She fought with the temptation not to say anything about the Gestapo on the train. Surely they would have traced them by now had they wanted to find them. So why mention it? *Because if they do come after we've gone, he'll be forewarned and be able to handle it somehow. And if I do tell him he may not release us.* That's *a chance you'll have to take, and if you don't give him a chance, you're no better than the Gestapo.* Well, she had taken other chances....

As he began to dial again she stopped him. "There is something you should know." And she told him.

He heard her out and shook his head in a kind of wonder.

"I don't know many people who would have the courage and the decency to do what you have just done. Thank you." He paused. "I am now more determined than ever, to help you."

"There shouldn't be any difficulty at that end, should there?" She asked unsteadily.

"I hope not," he said, "but things are moving so rapidly these days that I am not even certain whether the Polish office is still operational in Budapest. I dare not hand you over to anyone else."

Marian had lost it from the moment he saw the tears in his mother's eyes. As soon as the Commissioner stopped talking he asked what was going on.

"It's all right. He's on our side. We're waiting to hear from the Polish Consulate in Budapest. Just pray that there's still someone there."

Stefa got up from her chair and went to stand next to her mother. Helena took her hand and held it tightly. The tension in that room was almost palpable. They all jumped when the 'phone rang.

The conversation lasted longer this time, but when he replaced the receiver, the Commissioner's face lit up.

"They will be expecting you in Budapest," he smiled. "As soon as I make the arrangements for your journey you will be escorted to the station."

Choked up with gratitude, Helena struggled for the right words with which to thank him.

He held her hand in a warm grip. "Believe me, Mrs. Polek, it makes me equally happy to be able to set you free."

Janos was waiting for them outside the office. One look at their faces was enough to reassure him. Beaming, he showed them into a small room where Helena's handbag was restored to her and where they waited until their escort arrived.

With a Policeman at their side, no one questioned their right to travel. Lightheartedly they boarded the train. Their fares had been paid for and they were traveling under their own names. There was no longer any need for subterfuge, or fear.

Late that afternoon they presented themselves before a busy official at the Polish Consulate. When he heard who they were, he dropped his pen and jumped to his feet.

"It is true then! Frankly I was a bit skeptical when this Commissioner fellow 'phoned up about you. By Jesus, do you mean to say you really crossed that border with those children? But please forgive my bad manners. Do, do sit down."

He pulled out chairs for them, introduced himself, kissed Helena's hand with belated courtesy and asked to be told all about it.

"Not until you tell me where I can find my husband."

"Oh dear. Well, I made some enquiries as soon as the Sopron call came through. Captain Polek has been posted to France. But don't worry, we'll get word to him straight away."

She hid her disappointment and beginning firmly with Vienna, made her story as short as she possibly could.

"It's a miracle, a bloody miracle!" He repeated, buzzing on the intercom to share the news with his colleagues and telling her that she was the first woman to have crossed this, the most closely guarded frontier since the war.

Soon, the entire staff was milling around. They kept them in the office long past closing hours, but they did arrange accommodation, appointed one of the men to take them there and gave Helena some money to go on with.

As she stepped out of the office, Helena was surrounded by press reporters and cameramen. They clambered around, plying her with endless questions and worrying them for photographs. She stood her ground and refused to say anything. She'd had enough!

Crowds of Polish refugees began to gather about and someone said sharply, "Stop trying to make a sensation of these people -- your articles and photos may endanger their families still in Poland!" At that the pressmen stood back, made their apologies and left.

Helena turned gratefully to the owner of the sharp voice and discovered it belonged to their escort. He grinned at her and, taking her by her good arm steered her quickly along the passage, down a flight of stairs and out. She looked back but need not have worried, Marian and Stefa were right behind them.

"Whew! Now I know what celebrities must feel like," she said with a shaky laugh. She had certainly found the experience harrowing.

Still holding her arm, the man slowed his pace to suit hers.

"This place I'm taking you to," he said, "it's only temporary until we find something better for you."

She nodded. "Can't be worse than the Sopron jail."

He looked at her, relieved to see the smile. No need to worry about this one, he thought.

The shabby Boarding House only strengthened the first unfavorable impression Helena had formed of Budapest. Still, it was a roof over their heads and there was plenty of hot water.

A number of Adam's friends came to visit them at the Boarding House but of Adam there was no sign, neither could Helena get anything out of the local Polish authorities. There was something decidedly peculiar about the whole situation. The last time she pressed for information she was told guardedly that she would be hearing from him shortly.

His postcard had said he would be meeting them here in Hungary. Why all the evasiveness? Why the delay? No one could or would tell her and she wished she were in a position to tell them all to go to hell. She realized she wasn't the easiest person for them to have to deal with either, but she did not seem to have much control over her increasing irritability. And on top of everything else she was sorely missing the use of her right arm.

She had still not gone to have her shoulder attended to. It was no longer all that painful, the sling took care of the useless arm and so she kept putting it off, until the day that Doctor Leon Sadowski, their friend from Bielsko popped in to see them. She put out her left hand in greeting but he insisted on her right and when he saw that she could not move it, he frowned with undisguised annoyance.

"Do you realize that you can lose the use of your arm altogether if you leave it like this? Please undress, I want to have a look at it. The children too, they don't look at all well to me."

It didn't take him long to confirm that her shoulder blade was smashed. From the internal hemorrhage, the arm had turned black and blue down to the elbow.

He shook his head in resignation at the stupidity of people and his friends in particular, and went on to examine Marian and Stefa.

"You three must have gone through something," he exclaimed. "They're both suffering from scabies for Christ's sake, as well as bronchitis!"

And she had been foolish enough to dismiss their itches as nothing more than flea bites.

"I'm taking the lot of you into Hospital," Doctor Sadowski said briskly.

"When?"

"Now, so get ready. I'll call a taxi."

At the Hospital Helena was immediately put under anesthetic and her shoulder was set in place.

The next day they moved her to the children's ward. She was unprepared for the shock that awaited her there. Marian and Stefa lay bound and covered from head to toe in a dark, sulfur smelling paste. As she closed the door behind her their eyes opened and she was bombarded by a rush of loud complaints.

"The smell of this thing is making me sick," Stefa began, to be cut short by Marian.

"Smell nothing. I'm itchy all over and can't scratch. Please Mom, loosen these bandages will you? I've got an excruciating itch on my stomach."

"That's all he can talk about, his beastly itches!"

"Oh yes, and what about you. 'If they don't get this stink away from under my nose, I'll vomit all over their lousy bandages' ." Marian mimicked.

"Children, for heaven's *sake!* The Doctors are trying to help you get well and all you can do is complain. Can't you at least show them that Polish kids behave better than this?"

Shamefaced, Marian looked away. Stefa sulked. They made such a comical pair of mummies that Helena burst out laughing. In a moment both joined in.

"Never mind," she told them. "The Sister said your treatment will take no more than five days. That's not such a long time to wait and then we can go out and explore Budapest together. In the meantime I'm coming in here to keep you company. How's that?"

This cheered them up, but a couple of hours of the smell of sulfur and it was their mother's turn to show fortitude.

Later in the afternoon a nurse came in and placed an enormous bottle on Helena's bedside table. "Tonic," she said, indicating that they should all take it three times a day.

The stuff proved to be so effective that soon Helena was able to cope almost cheerfully with the people who came to see her during visiting hours. There were some casual acquaintances whom she hardly remembered, as well as people altogether unknown to her. But the most welcome visitor of all was Piotr, a young lawyer from Silesia and Adam's one-time skiing partner. He could tell them more than anyone else, as it was with him that Adam had eventually made his escape into Hungary.

They listened spellbound as he recounted some of the exploits they had shared. Piotr never tired of Marian's questions, for it was obvious that he had the highest regard for the man whom he described as 'indestructible'.

"You were the last to see him in Budapest then?" Helena asked.
"Yes."

"In that case, can't you tell me what's happening? Everyone here is being so cagey, it's driving me mad. Why did he have to leave anyway?"

"Look, whatever he's doing must be pretty important, or it wouldn't be so hush-hush," Piotr pointed out, as though that answered her questions. "But don't you worry. He'll have been told of your arrival and will move heaven and earth to get here." He said this with so much conviction that she could not help but believe him.

"Won't you be sent to France as well?" She asked him.

"Not right away I'm afraid. I'm to stay here as a link in the ski parties organizing escapes from Poland through the Tatry Mountains."

True to promise, on the fifth day they were discharged from the Hospital. Helena was told to return in three weeks to have the plaster removed.

Outside, the air was crisp and the day bright and clear. The buildings no longer looked gloomy but full of history and character. They made for the Polish Consulate.

They had been promised new lodgings but the last thing Helena expected was that these would be in a first class Private Hotel on Honvet Utca. She thanked the official profusely and assured him that they could find their own way this time. Half an hour later they were shown into a beautifully sunny room with a partition between the beds and their own private bathroom.

"That's better," said Marian going over to the window. "A view of the street instead of those filthy gutters of that lousy courtyard. Jees I hated that place."

"And somewhere to hang out the washing," Stefa added, opening the door to a tiny balcony.

Stefa had surprised everyone by showing what a capable little housewife she could be. Since Helena's accident she quite naturally took over the duties of washing and ironing their clothes. She even took it upon herself to cut up the food on her mother's plate, to the delight of the other residents. All her actions had become brisk and business-like. At first Helena was quite happy to let her have her game but how long can a child play the same game without it becoming reality? Stefa was growing up too fast. It was unfair to lay such a burden on such young shoulders. But Stefa was enjoying herself and she adamantly refused to allow her mother to perform any chores until the arm was out of plaster. Her only concession was to allow Marian to help her with the beds.

Once the plaster was removed, Stefa and Marian took turns to massage and help exercise the arm. The idea was to shake the arm vigorously for a while each day, to bring back the circulation. It also brought beads of perspiration to Helena's brow but the agony was well worth suffering as day by day she was able to lift her arm a fraction higher.

One morning they were visited by two strange ladies. The one was tiny with a beak-like nose and lively eyes and the other, more solemn, stood a good foot taller. Helena took them for door-to-door evangelists because they looked like door-to-door evangelists and in her best Hungarian said, *"Nem bezelek Magyarul"* (I don't speak Hungarian)

"No need to my dear, no need to," said the little woman in German. "We represent the Hungarian Red Cross and your name and address was given to us at the Consulate. We wondered how you people fared for clothing."

Helena admitted that they had nothing but the clothes they stood in. With gasps of sympathy they promised to return the next day. And return they did, laden with parcels. There were coats, suits, dresses, underwear and shoes for all three and still they asked if there was anything else they might need. Helena had a job convincing them that what they brought was more than enough.

Stefa immediately dressed herself in a three-quarter length suede coat with the label 'War relief Fund - Canada' stitched into the hem, a pair of boots two sizes too large for her and a turban meant for Helena.

"Come on Mom, put on that blue suit there and stick to your promise to take us sightseeing," she ordered, her fingers busy undoing the buttons of her mother's blouse.

The suit she selected looked much too small to Helena and she was surprised that it fitted so well.

"Perfect," Stefa approved. She went back to the parcels.

"Now you Marian. Try this on." She handed him a camelhair jacket from Switzerland.

"Hm," she regarded him critically, head to one side, lips pursed. "Could be a size smaller I suppose but you'll grow into it. What do you think Mom?"

"Looks fine to me," she said, unable to keep the smile off her face.

"What's funny?" Stefa wanted to know.

"Nothing my angel." She stooped to give her a kiss. "Are we all set? Let's go then."

Helena bought tickets on a tourist coach which took them around both Buda on the right bank of the Danube and Pest on the left. They sat back, eager to enjoy all that the city could offer.

"To think that I hated this place when we first arrived," Helena said, admiring the ancient beauty of a bygone age. "Those domes are magnificent."

"Yes," Marian agreed. "Everything looks better now somehow."

A stop for ice cream and soft drinks completed a perfect day and they returned to their Hotel in high spirits. In the foyer they found Leon Sadowski waiting for them with a box of chocolates and a bunch of flowers. Not five minutes later the Postman brought a telegram to say that Adam would be arriving within the next few days. Infected by their jubilance, Dr. Sadowski went out to buy a bottle of Port, the only liquor he allowed himself. His popularity with Marian increased tenfold when he poured out glasses for them all, maintaining that a little Port couldn't do anyone any harm.

"Remember those long talks we used to have, Leon?" Helena asked, sinking into an easy chair.

"Yes. Seems like years ago."

"They helped me, you know, more than once." "I'm glad. You've been a help to me too."

"Me? How?"

"You've given me hope. You've shown me that a woman with children can cope under the most adverse conditions. I've been worrying about Jaga you know, and my little Basia. Thank God they don't have my name on the Black List."

"Jaga will be fine," Helena said with conviction.

Leon's wife had been a nurse before they married and Helena had always thought of her as a strong, capable person.

"I heard she took Basia to the country."

"Yes, I told her to do that right at the beginning."

"Safest place for them. They'll be all right," she repeated. He nodded. "I know," he said, smiling at her.

Now that he knew his father was definitely coming, Marian made regular trips to the station. He already knew his way around Budapest well enough to act as guide to the many Polish refugees, conducting them to the Consulate or the institutions for the needy. Quite often, he availed himself of the 'Hungry Kitchen' as it was called, when he directed his 'clients' there. For his services he often earned himself a few Hungarian coins. These he would bring to his mother with as much pride and pleasure as though he was presenting her with a fortune. And because he did not spend the money on himself, it meant more than a fortune to her.

By Wednesday Stefa could stand the suspense no longer and began to accompany her brother to the station, determined to be the first to see Dad.

Helena's own impatience grew and with it a lurking uneasiness. Had he changed? She knew that she had and now it bothered her. There were gray streaks in her hair that had not been there before. The mirror still reflected a gauntness about the face. She had lost a great deal of weight and Adam had always preferred her on the fuller side. Common sense told her that these were silly fears. Didn't she know him well enough to realize that outward appearances were not important to him? Ten to one he wouldn't even notice any change in her. But that wasn't all. There was still the uneasy memory of the friction that had sprang up between them just before the war. And, there was this guilty feeling about Bronek. She hadn't given him a thought since Buczacz and felt annoyed that he should now come to mind. She told herself there was damn all to feel guilty about, yet could not deny that the desire had been there. Well, she had not acted upon it and the last thing she wanted to do was talk to Adam about it.

......

It was Friday evening, the week almost up and still no sign of Adam.

Marian refused to be discouraged. "There's still tomorrow I tell you, so-" he broke off at the sound of a knock.

They tried not to show their disappointment when Piotr's cheerful face peered around the door.

"May I come in? Sorry I'm a bit late, but I had to come to say good bye."

"Good-bye?" Helena didn't mind showing her disappointment this time.

"Yes," he said excitedly. "They're sending me to France at last. It's getting a bit tough here and apparently someone more senior is being sent to replace me, " he said with candor.

"I don't envy him his job, whoever he is," Helena remarked.

"It's not the job I'm pleased to get away from," he quickly explained. "But there's a lot to be done in re-arming our troops in France."

"I know Piotr. You just want to be in there getting the victims ready for the next slaughter."

He gaped at her. "How can you say that Helena! With the French army and Britain to help us, we'll walk over the Nazis!"

"I'm sorry, I didn't mean to sound bitter. It's just that, well, I suppose I've lost faith in our allies. Oh, let's talk about something else. Have a chocolate. Expect I could do with a bit of sweetening right now," she added, unwrapping a nougat.

They chatted on until he glanced at his watch. "Lord, 10.30 already. No wonder poor Stefa looks half asleep." He stood up to go. "Give my best to Adam when he comes. We'll probably see each other again in France."

She saw him out and went into the bathroom to prepare for bed. Donning the burgundy velvet gown no longer presented a problem; the right arm slipped easily into the sleeve. This was her favorite article of clothing brought by the two ladies. It complemented her dark coloring and she suspected that it was brand new. She tied the sash about her waist and thrusting her firm breasts out, stood for a moment to admire the youthful lines in the full-length mirror. Laughing at her own conceit she went back into the room. Stefa and Marian were turning down the bedspreads when a loud and urgent volley of knocks shook the door. Marian sprang to open it and in rushed Adam. She had not expected to see him out of uniform.

Stefa gave a screech and dived into her father's arms. He dumped the small valise on the floor and swooped her off her feet.

His eyes met and held Helena's and the glow from their brown depth made her legs go weak. She stood back, waiting for Stefa and Marian to release their hold. He kissed and hugged them, then came towards her and in that moment all her fears were forgotten.

*

CHAPTER FIFTEEN

"Adam completes some undercover *business*"

"Oh Helenko, my Helenko," he breathed into her hair, clutching her so tightly against him that she winced. His hold immediately became tender.

"Sorry my darling. I didn't realize I was holding you so hard."

"No, no. It's not that," she laughed shakily.

"It's Mom's arm."

Marian's solemn announcement led to a thousand and one questions and a full recital of all their experiences. They talked and talked. There was so much to say, it seemed that they had to cover an eternity since their parting. Every so often the two of them would simply gaze at one another, still unable to believe that their separate paths, each fraught with so many narrow escapes, had finally brought them together.

Helena pressed Adam for more details about his own escape.

"It was September 20th," he began, "when General Piskow called the officers together and announced his decision to surrender. When he ordered us to lay down arms and disperse the army, he might just as well have asked us to commit suicide." Adam looked down. "Many of them did."

Helena could see that he was no longer with them. He was back there in the forest outside Zielona.

"I went back to my boys and told them that I didn't intend to be taken captive and when I asked who wanted to come with me, the whole Company stepped forward. My objective was to press on for Lwow, where General Ander's Cavalry Division was heading. They were wedged between the Germans and the advancing Russian armies and I figured that if we could only get through the forest, we could join the fighting forces and who knew what turn the war might take. And if we did have to flee, we would be closer to the Hungarian and French borders where the new Polish Army was being formed."

By September 24th they had reached Rawa Ruska, surrounded on all sides by the German Infantry and on the broad Rawa-Lublin highway the patrol spotted long columns of German motorized forces. Adam decided to lead an attack to cut their way through the column in order to reach the forest on the other side of the highway. It was a furious, desperate battle. Many of the men fell, many were wounded, with no First Aid dressings or supplies to help them.

"The Germans staged two more attacks which we managed to crush but by 6 o'clock that evening we had run out of ammunition and I called the men together. We used our shirts to dress the wounded and shot the wounded horses. I buried my pistol and one of the boys brought me a uniform taken off a dead soldier and I became Corporal Jozef Sliwinski from Wilno."

"You didn't have to shoot your Chestnut did you?"

"No Marian, she fell, defending me."

"How?"

"She spotted a German raising his rifle to shoot me and reared up to catch the bullet. That horse was trained never to rear" he added thickly.

"So you were taken captive?" Helena prompted him to go on with the story.

"Yes," he got out, "42 of us that were left out of my 120 men."

They were marched day and night, with frequent change of escort, to insure non-stop progress. Near exhaustion, they reached Jozefow where they were divided into smaller groups and Adam and 10 of his men were herded into a temporary P.O.W. Camp. It was a small Church, already packed with prisoners.

Adam and his men settled themselves near the main entrance. Taking off his boots, Adam sat on the steps rubbing his sore and swollen feet his eyes never off their Guard. He saw the man prop his gun up against the wall and waited for the head to droop. It didn't take long. As silently as he could Adam woke his men and moved on tiptoe towards the doorway. Just then his foot caught on one of the planks the Guard had used to sit on. The man asked him where he thought he was going. "To the lavatory," Adam replied. "You're not allowed to leave the Church, do your business here, Polish swine." At that moment he noticed the shoes in Adam's hands and reached for his gun.

Adam stopped talking. How could he describe the events that followed, in front of Stefa. He looked down and saw that she had fallen asleep.

"So what did you do?" Marian was sitting forward, hanging on every word.

"I found myself on top of the German, my hands around his throat. The more he struggled the more I tightened my grip until I could feel the bones crunch beneath my hands and he fell back. One of the boys handed me my boots and we moved on."

They made their way through thick bush, forests, across fields, hid in ravines and shepherds' homes until they separated just outside Krakow, each vowing to meet across the borders.

Unable to find his family in Wieliczka, Adam was about to board a train for Bielsko to look for them when the Germans caught him. He found himself on a train with hundreds of prisoners, taken to work the rich farming lands of Raciborz. Once there he lost no time in organizing an escape party with the help of the local Polish residents and the German Guards missed a good few names at the next roll call. A little more cunning now, he hid with friends in Krakow until his beard could serve as a disguise. And it was there that he met up with Piotr. And it was he who took him to an apartment on the first floor of the Market. This was the temporary Head Quarters of the Commander of the Underground Forces, right under the noses of the Gestapo.

Adam told the Chief of his plans to go to Bielsko but the Colonel had plans of his own for Adam. This involved work in Hungary and France. Characteristically, Adam refused to accept or obey any orders until he had satisfied himself that his wife and children were safely back home.

"That's when he showed me 6 photographs of wanted men," Adam went on, "each with a reward of 10,000 Marks for any information leading to their capture. I was one of them and my list of alleged crimes included the persecution of peaceful, cultured German settlers in Poland, the organization of Polish gangs to break up peaceful meetings and the shooting of several innocent German patriots." He paused with a look of regret. "Pity I never got a chance to be guilty of the last crime. They must have been 5th Columnists and I missed them."

Since the names and photographs of those on the Black List had by then been circulated throughout the country, the Chief, unwilling to risk losing such a valuable link in the Organization, sent a special courier to Bielsko. The man naturally reported Adam's family as missing and was fool enough to repeat the rumor that they were believed to be dead.

With nothing to keep him in the country and desperate enough to welcome any assignment, Adam was ready to cross the mountains into Hungary. He asked for and received permission to take Piotr with him. Their papers, stamped with an official seal from the highest quarters, identified them as Johann Zimmer and Kurt Schwebler and gave them the right to wear Gestapo uniforms.

The sheer effrontery of it made Helena gasp. "But you can't even speak German that well."

He grinned at her. "Piotr and I had three weeks in which to prepare ourselves and believe me, I learned more German in those three weeks than I ever knew before. Anyway, we got away with it." He laughed suddenly. "You should have seen the fuss they made of us at the border station. All I did was tick them off for their inefficiency with a few choice S.S. cliches."

"How did you find out we were back home then?"

"Contacts. I'm still in touch with the Underground."

She looked at him quickly. "Then you knew I was also working for them?"

"Of course. How else do you think I could have been so sure you'd join me here? I figured anyone with enough guts to work for the Underground would have the guts to attempt the border, one way or another."

So casually accepted. What did she expect, medals?

"I'm pleased to see though, that your undercover work left no permanent scars," he added. He thought of the resources she must have had to summon in order to do what she did. He drew her to him, his eyes sparkling. "You should see the expression on your face! My silly, gorgeous, magnificent woman. I'm so proud of you I could burst!"

She could have spared herself a lot of unnecessary worry, for apart from the loss of weight, which he promised he would soon rectify, Adam was blissfully unaware of any other physical changes in her.

But she did see a difference in him. He not only looked older, he seemed more sober, yet more powerful. There was an extra firmness to the well-shaped lips. The lines of his face had hardened, making it even more handsome. But the most notable change was in the eyes. There was another dimension to them that she could only describe as maturity, tempered with a gentleness she had rarely seen before. Yes, Adam had changed.

"You know," she said, "Mother wanted me to leave Stefa behind."

"If you had, I'd have sent you right back to fetch her."

Stefa opened her eyes at the mention of her name. Thrilled by her father's words, she gave a contented sigh, closed her eyes again and was asleep. Adam lifted her up and took her over to her bed.

Marian, who would have listened to them all night long, even though his eyes kept closing on him, was also dispatched to bed.

They sat together for a while longer then Adam got up to turn the light off. She sensed the heat radiating from his body as he moved closer, felt herself being lifted up in strong, urgent arms and reached for his mouth.

He lay staring at the dark shadows of the room. Behind the divider Marian and Stefa slept soundly. He could hear their breathing. Helena was also asleep now. He loved the familiar feel of her leg across his middle, her head on his shoulder. He should be relaxed, content, but he wasn't, quite. Something had been missing. He didn't know what, he just knew that it wasn't there. Her response to his lovemaking had been eager enough but -not spontaneous. That was it. He had felt the restraint behind it. *So what do you want of her you stupid bastard,* he asked himself. *The poor little thing has just gone through the most traumatic time of her life, she's been terrorized, imprisoned, hurt, and you expect spontaneity!* He looked down at the softly outlined sheen of her hair and was torn with a compassion and love so fierce it made his heart ache. She stirred, sensing his emotions.

"Adam?"

"Shsh, I'm here my love," he whispered, kissing the top of her head. She snuggled closer, drawing him with her to sleep.

......

The following morning they were politely summoned to the Office. The Hotel proprietor, a pear shaped little man, blinked at them out of myopic eyes, gold-rimmed spectacles swinging to and fro from nervous fingers.

He cleared his throat and squeaked, "This is most embarrassing," another humph and the voice came back to normal. "What I mean is that I run a respectable establishment and really cannot, that is to say, you understand it is not customary for us to uh, encourage, uh or permit a liaison of-"

Adam threw back his head and roared with laughter.

"I must apologize, it just didn't occur to me when I signed the register that my name would not correspond with my wife's. It must be misleading I know, but wait." He went out and came back with Marian and Stefa.

"Take a look at those children and decide for yourself."

The man put his spectacles on, took a careful look at the four of them and murmured, "It's a fact. Quite incredible. The boy is the image of his father. The little girl looks like the mother, yet also resembles the father.." He spread his hands. "No document could prove more positively that you are indeed all one family. What an old fool I've been not to see this. Please forgive me."

"Of course," Adam smiled. "Let's say present times are responsible for many a misunderstanding and many a *nomes-de-guerre.*"

Full of apologies, the little man showed them to a two-roomed suite, at no extra cost.

Helena waited for the poor fellow to bow himself out before tackling her husband.

"What *is* all this about? Why are you under an assumed name?"

"Don't you think it's more exciting this way?" He asked, putting his arm around her waist. "Imagine, a liaison!"

"Don't be an idiot darling. Answer my question."

"Well, it's because I've had to come here under a Diplomatic Passport. Tell you about that later," and he pulled her towards him.

Since it became physically impossible for her to say anything more at that moment, she had to be content with the vague explanation. What did it matter anyway, she thought, as long as he was with them.

She should have known better of course, for it soon became evident that the only moments she would share with the man whose job she told Piotr she did not envy, would be the short periods snatched between his trips to the Polish, Hungarian and Slovakian borders.

After a while the Hungarian authorities began to take an interest in Adam's activities and the fact that so many Polish soldiers were disappearing from the border detention camps. Adam managed to get out of a number of tricky situations, often made lighter for him by design, but with the appearance of many more Fifth Columnists in the area, he was finding it increasingly more difficult to carry on with his work. On his return from one of his longest trips towards the end of March, he announced that his work was coming to an end.

"Thank God for that," Helena said, noting the tense set of his mouth, the lines of exhaustion around the eyes. "Getting tougher?"

"Yes," he said, sinking into a chair. "The Hungarian Security Police have transferred the helpful officers from the camps and replaced them with either neutral men or men with outright pro-German leanings. These bastards are sticking strictly to the Geneva Convention and there's no way of getting around them!" He lit a cigarette and drew on it furiously.

She went to stand behind him and began to knead his shoulders.

"Aah, that feels good. I shall probably make one more trip and then pack it in."

"Must you go again?"

"Yes. They're depending on me." He turned around and put his hands on her hips. "Before I go, let's see something of the town, shall we?"

"Wonderful idea. Where shall we go?"

"There's a good Gypsy band at one of the night spots near the Fishers' Bastion. How about that?"

"Oh, and how do you know about it? But of course, you spent quite a while in Budapest didn't you? No reason why you shouldn't know some good night spots." "Night spots? No, I went to see a Priest."

"Whatever for?" She asked, surprised, for Adam had never been particularly devout.

"Oh I was plagued by my war crimes."

He had told her a good deal more about his experiences but she had no idea he felt like this about any of them. The burden must have been really overwhelming for him to seek spiritual comfort, despite the elaborately off-handed way in which he now tried to dismiss it.

"Tell me?" She prompted gently.

"Well, you know how it is. You can kill a hundred men in the heat of battle and think nothing of it, but when you have to throttle a chap in cold blood, with your bare hands and in a Church, well, that kind of sticks. I had nightmares for months."

"The P.O.W. Sentry?"

"Yes."

"But surely that was in self defense?"

"Yes I know, but you try and convince a stubborn conscience of that, when it refuses to be convinced."

"And the Priest helped?"

"He was magnificent," he said and went on to describe Father Francis and the many talks they had had together. Helena wanted to meet this Priest who had been successful in justifying such an act in the name of equity and self-preservation, still within the confines of Christ's teachings.

"All right, I'll take you to see him after our outing tomorrow night. You'll like him."

They took a taxi out to the Fishers' Bastion. Using all the Hungarian words he had picked up, Adam was able to make the cabbie understand what he was after.

The Night Club hid one of those intimately dim, character-filled interiors that promised a memorable evening. A waiter in a gay Gypsy costume ushered them to a small table covered with a bright checkered cloth. He took their orders for hot goulash with a smile of approval. Helena was glad he did not stay to see it bring the tears to her eyes. But it was as delicious as it was hot.

The Gypsy band was all that it claimed to be, playing their music with a bravura and fire equal to none she had ever heard before. Their star violinist, a child of no more than twelve, made his instrument echo in turn the smoldering, evocative, melancholy or wildly stirring mood of his race. Helena was spellbound, her evening made complete by a romantic solo, performed at their table for her benefit.

She was amused to see the look of confusion on Adam's face when immediately after the solo, one of the guests from the table next to theirs, came over to pay tribute, so he said, to the most beautiful woman there.

Over a bottle of Tokaj, Adam was expansive, amusing and full of charm. She had almost forgotten what it was like to have an attentive escort across a candlelit table. Only once did he turn serious and that was when he put his hand over hers and searched her face.

"Enjoying it?" He asked. "Mmm, wonderfully."

"I wanted to make this the beginning of a new chapter in our lives, Helena. You know, to sort of cancel out everything that went before, and I mean before the war too."

"Erased as of now." She saw immediately that her frivolous response was out of harmony and turned her hand over to press his.

"No I mean that, with all my heart."

He kissed the palm of her hand, refilled their glasses and, gay again, proposed a toast to their future happiness, commanding that she drink the liquor down in one go to the last drop. Not the simplest thing on Tokaj and her attempts ended in gales of laughter and the ruin of her best Red Cross dress.

It was past 11 o'clock before they decided that the Priest would have to be a saint to appreciate a call any later than that, even though Adam knew him to keep late hours. As it happened, a light still burned at one of the windows when their taxi drew up outside the Rectory.

Brushing aside their apologies for the lateness of their visit, Father Francis welcomed Adam like a long lost son, extending his pleasure and warmth to Helena. Adam had been quite right, she thought, for no one who met this grave-faced man with the unexpectedly twinkling eyes, could do anything but like him.

Father Francis made Helena sit on his one and only easy chair, threw a log of wood onto the dying embers in the fireplace and insisted that they have a glass of wine with him.

"I see Adam has not been exaggerating about you," he smiled. "It's no wonder he was at his wits end to get you out. Perhaps you would satisfy my curiosity and tell me how you *did* manage it?"

Even though she had the story of their escape in concise synopsis form by now, it was well past one o'clock before they finally said their good byes.

Helena reached up to kiss his cheek. "Adam wasn't exaggerating about you either," she said. "Bless you for helping him so much."

"I had guidance from the highest sources," he replied with a smile. He took their hands in both of his and added, "God be with you." The blessing, softly spoken carried so much intensity that Helena no longer wondered how he had managed to help absolve Adam from his guilt.

As neither of them wanted to shorten the evening, they decided to walk home along the elegant Vaczci Utca. Arm linked through his, Helena looked up to tell him what a wonderful evening it had been.

"Shsh," he hissed. The look on his face insured her silence. He steered her into a doorway and whispered, "Stay here."

The gleaming steel of the revolver that had miraculously appeared in his hand made her heart stop. A second later, she too could hear the soft pad of footsteps behind them.

Adam left her, ducking into the shadows of an adjoining doorway. The next moment were was a dull thud, a muffled groan, followed by a second one that had somehow escaped from her own throat. Sick with apprehension she peered out to see Adam bending over the prone figure of a man.

"All right, get up Schmidt!" Adam snapped, prodding him with his foot.

The man stood up groggily. There was a swastika badge on the lapel of his coat.

"Who is this man?" Helena asked, coming up to stand next to Adam.

"That specimen of excreta goes under the name of Schmidt. He's been after my blood for years. I thought I recognized the *morda* (animal face) outside the Rectory. Must have been trailing us for hours, waiting for his opportunity. Much the same as he did that Sunday in the park in Bielsko, eh Schmidt?"

She sucked in her breath. There was just no escape from them. Thank God they would soon be leaving Hungary. Would it be soon enough?

Adam was removing the cartridges from the German's gun. He threw the empty weapon over to him.

"Here, you can take this back with you and tell your masters that you missed eight times."

Dazed still, Schmidt made no move to go.

"Hop it you swine, before I change my mind and let you have some of your own medicine!" Adam barked, cocking his revolver threateningly.

Without a word the man scuttled of.

Adam took Helena's arm again and continued walking as though nothing had happened. But when she looked up at his face she could see the muscles in his jaw working.

"I'd have given anything for that to have been Eckhart," he ground savagely.

She preferred not to say anything. Adam's reaction to her account of the interview she'd had with the Nazi had frightened her. She knew that if it had been Eckhart back there, the man would probably have been dead by now.

They walked on in silence. Finally she said, "So that's why you came as a civilian under an assumed name."

"Right."

"You can't stay on in Budapest now. They know you're here."

"A little disguise will fix that up. I told you how I roamed about Krakow as a doddering old man. It was foolproof. My own mother wouldn't have recognized me." He was composed again, the incident with Schmidt seemingly quite forgotten.

But she did not forget and worried incessantly when he made his final trip to the border in his favorite old man's guise.

It was more than a week later that she heard the familiar footsteps in the passage. She rushed to open the door. He held her tightly, knowing what his absences did to her.

"It's all right my love. This was the last time. No more. You hear?"

Gently he lifted her chin, looking deep into the azure overflowing pools, forgetting his exhaustion.

She blinked away the tears, her eyes roamed his face, seeing beneath the make-up, never wanting to let him go again.

"Oh how I love you," he whispered against her lips. "Where are the children?"

"In the park. I'll go and call them."

"Later."

Still holding her, he closed the door behind them and locked it.

Afterwards, he told her that he had been accosted by a Police Inspector in Budapest and warned to leave Hungary within two days.

"So much for disguises," Helena muttered, as she packed their things.

"Pity we've got to leave Budapest so soon," Marian sighed from his comfortable position on the sofa. He unfolded his arms from behind his head, stood up and went to the window. "I was beginning to like it here."

"I don't think this case is big enough to take all my stuff," Stefa said, jamming her clothes into an overnight bag she had been given by one of their friends. "Especially those oversized boots" Marian put in.

"I'll grow into them the same way as you'll grow into your jacket."

"Here," Helena took them from her. "They'll fit into my case."

Marian looked at his watch. "You two ready? Dad should be back any minute. Let's go downstairs and wait for him there."

Early that morning Adam had gone to the Consulate for Helena's Visa. He was also due two months back pay which he hoped to collect in Franks.

The Inspector was waiting for them in the foyer. He introduced himself and with a friendly smile said, "Thought I'd give you a lift to the station."

"Very kind of you," Helena replied icily. "My husband shouldn't be long. As you can see, we *are* leaving."

He nodded good-naturedly and parked himself in a chair to wait with them. He had no quarrel with these people. Personally he liked the spunky *Lengyels* (Poles).

When Adam walked in and saw the escort, his reaction was much the same as Helena's had been, but for his flushed neck which betrayed a greater annoyance.

"Don't say anything," Helena murmured in Polish. "If nothing else, it will save us a taxi fare."

He looked across at her and nodded reassuringly. She needn't worry. This time he had no intentions of arguing with the authorities.

Their train was running several hours late so they missed the splendid views of the Balaton Lake and since they were traveling through Yugoslavia at night, they also missed the magnificent mountain passes. But above all, they missed the thrill of crossing a border in safety and comfort.

Taking advantage of a brief stop-over in Milan, they stepped out of the station and walked into a city that left them with lasting memories of gay bands of guitar-strumming youngsters with the voices of angels, strolling under a kaleidoscope of bright neon signs.

Two hours later they were on their way to France. Marian produced a mouth organ and entertained them with the then popular Donkey Serenade and some of the Italian tunes he had heard on the streets of Milan.

"You have a good ear Marian," Adam said. "We'll get you another violin when all this is over."

"Oh no," Stefa wailed. "Not those awful scales again."

"It's because you didn't want to play your scales that you didn't get anywhere with your piano lessons," he pointed out.

Helena snuggled up against Adam, her arm through his. "It's hard to believe what we've just left behind us," she said. "There's no sign of war in Italy."

"Not yet," Adam put in grimly. He felt her stiffen and gently squeezed her arm. "Let's enjoy the respite shall we?" He smiled down at her. "Tell me all the places you'd like to visit in Paris."

She fell into the mood and they began choosing their itinerary like a couple of tourists.

They pulled into the Gare de Lyons on a fine April morning. Here too, the station pulsated with the normal busy routine. There was no sign of undue urgency although judging by their luggage, many of the passengers were clearly leaving the country. Helena's eye was caught by the exotic bunches of bananas displayed at one of the stalls. Even before the war, these were an expensive luxury in Poland.

"How much are they Adam?"

"They're cheap here. I'll get you some," he promised.

There was no shortage of accommodation but prices in the heart of the city were heavily inflated and it seemed impossible to find a decent Hotel at a tariff they could afford. Seven Hotels later and Helena was ready to settle for anything but Adam would not give up and the very next Pension offered adjoining rooms with bed and breakfast at the right price.

He went out as soon as he had settled the family in. Although Helena suspected the reason for his disappearance, her surprise and pleasure were very real when she saw the enormous bunch of bananas that he brought them.

Adam's official business at the Polish Headquarters in Paris kept him occupied during the day but the evenings and nights were theirs. Of all the attractions on Helena's list, they decided the Moulin Rouge held priority and Helena went to work on the restoration of her best Red Cross dress.

Adam was back in uniform and the two of them made many a head turn as they walked into the Theater arm in arm.

A cup of coffee after the show seemed like a good idea. They went into a small Cafe and there, alone at one of the tables sat Bronek. He saw them at the same time and jumped to his feet. His face had gone ashen.

"Where the devil have you been hiding yourself, you young scoundrel!" Adam cried, bounding over to give him a bear hug.

Bronek's eyes met Helena's over Adam's shoulder. She shook her head and he looked relieved.

"I heard you had made it, Helena," he said as he kissed her hand, holding on to it until she pulled away.

"Yes. Glad you made it too."

"Which regiment are you with? Sit down, sit down. We can talk over coffee. *Garcon!*"

Adam's enthusiasm helped to put them both a little more at ease and they chatted on. Bronek had escaped with Teodor Gronski. Teodor was somewhere in France.

"Then we'll find him," Adam promised Helena. He looked at his watch, aware that he had been doing most of the talking. "Time we went."

Helena could not help noticing that his leave taking of Bronek was far less warm than his greeting had been, but it was not until they were getting ready for bed that Adam remarked on Bronek's free use of her Christian name.

"So what do you expect?" She turned on him. "We should go through all that we did go through together and he must call me *Pani Polek?*"

"Hey, what is this? What are you getting so riled up about?"

"Nothing."

"There *is* something. It sticks out a mile. And the way he held on to your hand. There's something between you two. What is it, tell me, what is it?"

"Don't shout. The children will hear you. I'm telling you there's nothing."

"Helena, if you don't come clean I swear I will go after him and make the bastard talk."

His eyes snapped and a shiver went through her.

"All right, all right." She dropped her head and murmured, "He, wanted me to go with him."

Adam looked fit to explode. "Oh he did, did he, the little shit. And you no doubt encouraged him!"

"No I did *not* encourage him."

"So that's what's been holding you back from me. I knew there was something. I want to know if you had an affair with him."

"Oh for heaven's sake, no I did *not* have an affair with him. I kissed him once and that's all and I think I owed him that."'

"Jesus Christ! A man asks my wife to commit adultery and she kisses him! You fell for him didn't you?"

"Adam." She forced her voice to stay calm. "In case you have forgotten. I may not have broken my neck for you but I did break my arm to get to you."

That brought him up short. He looked at her for a long moment then took a quick step forward. "Forgive me, my love. What a fool I am."

She felt herself melt in his arms. "That makes two of us," she sobbed, realizing that this *had* been a barrier between them, that you cannot withhold the truth, no matter how well justified, and still hope to keep your relationship untarnished and lasting.

They did not see Bronek again but they did see much of Paris in the idyllic days that followed.

Paris. A city seemingly becoming ever more conscious of the impending threat to her freedom, reached out almost desperately to grasp the last few moments of gaiety. Shops spilled over with Easter delicacies and decorations. Bright lights and music; midnight streets loud with the echoes of laughter and song. Exciting, intoxicating as it was, it was at the same time disquietening enough for Helena to be glad to leave after a week.

And so they packed their belongings and boarded the train for the tranquil South, for Bollene, where Adam's regiment was stationed.

*

CHAPTER SIXTEEN

"France under siege"

At the head of the group of soldiers who met them at the station in Bollene was Georges. He stood out from the rest of the men as much by his outlandish accent and unrestrained pleasure at seeing *Foter* as by his height. What his nickname for his Captain lacked in military protocol, it made up for in affection, for loosely translated, *Foter* stood for 'Pop'. Georges, a French citizen of Polish descent, was Adam's devoted batman. He could not have been more than twenty-eight or nine, but the slight stoop that went with his 6'4" and the prematurely lined face, made him appear much older. Adam had spoken of Georges and now Helena saw for herself that behind this man's perpetual clowning, there was a good deal of intelligence. A miner by circumstance if not by choice, he soon proved himself a superb jack-of-all-trades.

Helena liked Bollene from the moment she stepped onto its sun-baked, cobbled streets. An unpretentious little town bathed in the Provencal somnolence of the South, Bollene's one claim to fame was that Pasteur had discovered a vaccine there in 1882.

The open-heartedness of the local people was demonstrated within an hour of their arrival. Georges had found lodgings for them some two miles out of town with Monsieur and Madame Marius. At first glance, the Mariuses, looked an unsuited old couple. The tall, heavily built body of the husband virtually dwarfed the wife's diminutive figure and his gray walrus moustache and stern features accentuated her own fragility, but they were obviously devoted to one another.

Helena felt an immediate affinity for them and the couple's Alsatian welcomed the children's company with joy.

The Mariuses could not speak a word of Polish and Helena's French was not much better, but they managed to make themselves understood by means of the usual continental gestures. Their house was small but the old couple were only too happy to offer their bedroom to their guests, saying that they preferred to sleep in the living-room.

Georges brought in their luggage and the camp bed he had procured for Marian.

Helena's quest for a bathroom proved disappointing, so she asked Georges to find out the whereabouts of the toilet at least, thinking that she had surely misinterpreted her landlady's indication to the open fields. Hard put to keep a straight face, Georges translated: "there's plenty of space out there."

Her heart sank. The crudest cottage she had ever been to, had a pit toilet. Unaware of the effect that her disclosure had produced on her guests, Mrs. Marius announced that there was coffee on the verandah.

Helena drew Adam aside. "I can't live like this. I'm not going to squat in any field. Tell Georges to find us somewhere else to stay, please."

"This was the only house within miles, that Georges could find for us. But knowing him, he would already have thought of a solution, so don't worry."

Georges' first task was to repair the antiquated radio set which, he was told, had been out of order for more years than the Mariuses could remember. He then produced a zinc bath which he put into the bedroom, and next day further added to their comfort by building a toilet at the back of the house. It took a little while and much persuasion on Georges' part to convince the Mariuses that this wasn't merely an 'unnecessary bit of nonsense', but a useful and convenient device. Eventually, it was Madame Marius who led her husband on the march to progress.

Stationed in town, Adam came up to the house every evening, usually fuming about the lack of arms, supplies and motor transportation.

"How in the hell do they expect us to drill the men with wooden rifles and damned flags!" He stormed. "We'll have to make a move any day now. Holland's finished and so is Belgium and I can't see the Germans being stopped by the Maginot Line."

Evidently neither did the Germans and when Adam came to tell them that France was about to be attacked from the North, he also said his Brigade was being moved to the line of fire.

"We're leaving a small cadre of troops here though, under Lieutenant Szumanski so you won't be all on your own and of course there are some other Polish families in the district. You should get to know them Helena, be company for you."

She knew she was wasting her breath but she had to say it. "Adam, can't *you* stay with the troops in Bollene? Think of your own family for a change."

From what she had heard, France was perhaps in a weaker position to defend herself than Poland had been. In spite of having the advantage of nine additional months after the fall of Poland in which to organize her forces, she was materially and morally unprepared for war. Helena could not help foreseeing the French Campaign as a lost cause.

But basically she knew she was afraid to tempt fate twice in a row. There did not seem to be much sense in all of this. Did she get him back only to lose him? She felt more than justified in making some kind of protest.

"You aren't going to start *that* all over again are you?" He asked, his voice rising in exasperation. "I just don't understand you Helena. The way you talk, anyone would think you couldn't give a damn and yet you were the first to dig your heels in when they wanted you to enlist on the *Volksdeutsche.* You'd have died rather than do that, wouldn't you?"

"Yes, but that was different." "Not to me it isn't."

He pulled her towards him. "Come on sweetheart, you know very well I couldn't stay on here."

"I know, I know," she sighed. "So this is good bye again."

"Only for a while." He ran the back of his hand along her cheek. "Whatever happens, I'll come back for you, so don't go beetling off again as you did in Wieliczka and have me looking for you all over the ruddy country."

She promised.

Stefa clung to her father passionately. He cupped her face in his hands and tried to reason with her.

"Look angel, I must go and fight the Germans otherwise they will capture you again. As soon as we've defeated them I'll come back for you and we can all go back home. Don't you want to go back to Bielsko?"

"No," she sobbed. "I just want you to stay with us."

From the way he had to drag himself from them, it was more than obvious that this parting was harder for Adam than the last one had been. Helena also felt he did not have quite as much certainty about the outcome of this campaign as he pretended to have. She shivered, remembering what she had said to Piotr in Budapest. And here they were — 'victims ready for the next slaughter' -- *Mother of God don't let me think like this.*

He saw the fear in her eyes and drew her to him again. Up to this point he had been too preoccupied to think of their parting. Now he felt it getting to him and he fought for control.

"Hey, where's my brave little woman."

She smiled through her tears. "Go fix the bastards and come back soon."

"You're wonderful! Nothing will stop me from coming back to you, remember that."

Marian asked if he could see the troops off as far as the town. Adam told him to hop on the truck and they shot away in a cloud of dust.

Helena felt Madame Marius' hand pressing her arm. The old lady was saying something, evidently trying to be reassuring. Helena wiped her eyes and forced a smile. Madame Marius nodded happily and said *"Mange?"* To these simple people, food, in its scarcity, was the panacea for everything and Helena allowed herself to be led into the kitchen and watched the old lady prepare a special treat, paper thin pancakes with cinnamon.

The afternoon seemed never ending. Helena felt restless and Stefa was getting on her nerves. Marian should have been back hours ago. By 6 o'clock Monsieur Marius was ready to go and look for him when the Alsatian announced his arrival. Relieved and furious, Helena bowled him out, demanding an explanation.

"I waited until they all left," he said, studiously avoiding his mother's eyes. She thought there was more to it but didn't press him. He seemed upset enough as it was.

The 9 o'clock news was the start to their nightly vigil at the radio. There were repeated references to the unexpected strength of the enemy, that much Helena understood and from Monsieur Marius' expression and shrugging shoulders she assumed the rest of the broadcast to be noncommittal.

It was irritating not to know what was going on and Helena decided to study the Polish-French language book Adam had left with her. She also decided to send the children to the local school.

She mentioned this to Marian later that night when they were getting ready for bed. The idea did not appeal to him over much as it meant sitting in class with six-year-olds but he didn't put up any real argument. In fact, he still seemed preoccupied and unusually subdued. She knew his father's departure had upset him but felt there was something more here. She went to sit next to him on the bed and lifted his chin so that he had to look at her.

"Now, tell me what's troubling you."

He bit his lip and dropped his eyes. "Well he's gone again isn't he?"

"Yes. He's gone," she said softly. "But what else is bothering you?"

He looked up. "You won't be mad?"

"Depends on what it is, but I promise to be reasonable. Fair enough?"

"All right, so I wanted to go off with Dad and hid in one of the trucks and they found me." It all came out in a rush.

"So that's why you were giving me those funny looks before you went."

"Well I didn't really like leaving you, but hell Mom, it's time I got a show in in this war!"

"At thirteen?"

"Dad was only a year older when *he* ran away from home to fight the Russians."

"I suppose you used all those arguments with your father. What did he have to say?"

"He said this wasn't Poland and, well, that I was supposed to know better than to leave you and Stefa all alone."

"So what's upsetting you, the fact that you couldn't go or is it that you feel guilty about wanting to leave us here?"

She got her answer when he buried his head in her shoulder and mumbled, "Sorry Mom."

Stefa had cried herself to sleep hours before. Helena turned down the oil lamp and lay staring into the darkness, trying not to indulge in the pessimism that Adam so despised, trying not to give way to thoughts that reduced her to widowhood with two children to feed on the only commodity that this barren part of the country seemed to abound in -- peas.

Madame Marius was so pleased with Helena's proposal to send the children to the local school that she straight away got herself ready to go with them to act as interpreter, although how she intended to interpret Helena could not imagine.

The school was a humble, white-washed building easy to overlook but for the squeals of laughter that came from the playground. The teacher had a smattering of German which she solemnly promised not to practice on the children. They were signed on, established, as Marian had feared, in the beginners' class and left to battle through their first day as best they could.

Madame Marius then proceeded to initiate Helena in the art of marketing. She pointed to the various vegetables and grocery items and very precisely pronounced their names, making it quite clear which stalls and shops offered the best prices.

Helena estimated that with careful spending she would have enough money to last them two to three months. She could not expect the Mariuses to feed them out of the scant rental money she was paying them, nor could she conceive of her family living on what the Mariuses did. Their staple diet consisted of bread, peas and a salad made from what she at first took to be common grass which the old lady picked in the fields. This was prepared with a dressing of garlic, oil and vinegar and was so tasty that Helena could only guess the grass must be a type of lettuce grown in this part of the world. The meat that she bought was tougher than any steak ought to be and when she remarked on this, she was informed that donkey or horse flesh was rarely tender. She fought down her squeamishness and reminded herself that this was France.

Within three weeks Marian and Stefa had acquired a fairly good grasp of the language. Stefa was particularly quick to pick up the local accent and whatever she said, she said it like a native. Helena was also making progress. With no one to translate for her, there was no alternative but to learn French.

She was pouring over her grammar, saying some words out loud and having either Madame or Monsieur Marius correct her pronunciation, when their mysterious visitor came to pay his first of many unwelcome calls. From the moment he knocked on the door and introduced himself as le Comte de Baer, their new neighbor, Helena felt uneasy about him. She estimated him to be a well-preserved man in his late forties. He was tall and rather attractive in a smooth way, if you could take very pale green eyes. He said he had taken over the Chateau on the hill and was looking for labor and did not seem at all offended when Monsieur Marius laughed in his face.

What would a man of his age be doing out of uniform at a time like this, Helena wondered. And moreover, only a lunatic would dream of taking over a dilapidated estate and look for workers when everyone knew they were non-existent.

He caught her stare of open disbelief and turned to her with a rapid flow of words which meant nothing to her. Monsieur Marius explained that she was Polish.

"Ah, then perhaps we might be able to converse in German, *ja?*" His smile gleamed with a gold filling on each canine.

"Yes, but as my friend has already, eh, intimated, we cannot help you here and I doubt very much whether you will find any labor in these parts. All the able-bodied men are at war, you know."

This barb penetrated no deeper than Monsieur Marius' rude laugh had done. Helena's words merely produced another smile, a little less flashing and tinged with melancholy.

"Ah yes," he said sadly. "To be an able-bodied man, as you so aptly put it Madame, is to some, an unattainable privilege." The vague hand gesture, supposedly designed to express his plight, explained nothing. He looked fit enough to her.

"There are other ways in which one can assist one's country," he pontificated. "The heritage of our land, our noble estates, our culture, ought not to be allowed to deteriorate with the ravages of war. We cannot afford to ignore or postpone restoration or it may be too late." Abruptly he stopped. "Forgive me Madame, I have been boring you with a subject that could not possibly have the same interest for you as it has for me and *should* have for my countrymen." This with a glance at the Mariuses. "You see, I have been abroad for a number of years, largely in Germany as a matter of fact and hurried back to do my humble part."

No one had asked him to sit down, yet he appeared perfectly at ease, standing before them lightly balancing his silver-tipped cane.

"Well I wish you luck," Helena said politely, moving towards the door.

With a graceful bow over her hand and a cheerful *"Au revoir"* to a rigid-faced Monsieur Marius, the Count immediately took his leave.

"What was all that about?" The old man wanted to know.

Helena picked up her dictionary and more or less repeated the conversation. The three of them came to the same conclusions: The man was either genuinely unhinged or, for some reason, deliberately ignorant. Helena was in support of the last view. Those cold green eyes could belong to a ruthless, calculating mind but not to a crazy one. But if all that had been an act, what was the purpose of it? And why come to them with it?

The incident of the plums took her mind off the riddle of the Comte de Baer for a while.

Marian arrived late from school that afternoon, his shirt front stained and bulging with plums.

"Where on earth did you get these?" She demanded.

"I picked them off the trees from the garden up the road."

"You stole them you mean!"

"No I didn't. Madame Marius told me I could go and take as many as I wanted."

Helena turned to the smiling little figure for an explanation and was staggered to learn that she did not consider this to be theft.

"They have plenty, too much. We have none. So, we must share," she reasoned.

"But we cannot share unless your neighbor allows us to," Helena struggled to point out.

Helena felt defeated. She knew she could not convince her but made sure Marian would not repeat the raid. She had already discovered these people's easy-going ways, but had not been aware of their leanings towards a philosophy that bordered on potential Communism.

As soon as the peas were ripe for picking, they all gave a hand in the fields, earning themselves a basketful a day. What they didn't use, Madame Marius spread out to dry in the sun and then stored away.

Stefa's one complaint about the school was the monotony of their midday meal and vowed never to eat another pea once they left France.

To vary their diet, the French children often brought their own *gouter,* a bitter chocolate eaten with a bite of the long loaf. So those items had to be included on her weekly shopping list, and it was while she was buying the chocolate that she had her second encounter with the Count.

He greeted her as if she were an old friend and was embarrassingly insistent that she accept two extra bars of chocolate from him. Her refusal to have lunch with him, on the pretext that she was already late, only resulted in having to accept a lift home in his flashy limousine. There wasn't a person there that did not stare at them as they drove majestically through the narrow streets of Bollene.

During the slow journey home the Count enlarged on his own affairs, telling her that his elder brother, who was in possession of their family seat near Nimes, shared his anxiety over the preservation of the riches of France and was finding it equally hard to pursue this ideology. This nicely explained why their neighbor chose an estate other than his own in which to settle but it still did not make any more sense to Helena and she studied the man with growing suspicion. Misinterpreting her interest, he began to question her about herself. How did she come to be living with the "lower classes"? Where was her husband? How many children did she have, and what were her future plans? And all the time she had the distinct feeling that he already knew all the answers.

When he stopped outside the Mariuses gate, she thanked him and got out before he had walked around to open the door for her. He called out after her that he hoped to be seeing her again soon. Her blond

German admirer in Bielsko had used similar words and in the warmth of the midday sun, she suddenly felt cold.

On a gloriously fine Sunday morning Lieutenant Szumanski drove up to the house with his wife, a plump blonde whom Helena had met only once before. They were followed by another resident Polish family, Mr. and Mrs. Zaleski and their pale-faced daughter-in-law Margareta. They came, they said, to prise the hermit out. They were on their way to Orange from where they intended going some way up the mountain de Lure in the hope of finding signs of pre-historic dwellings. Would Helena and the children like to accompany them? It promised to be an exciting outing and she said they'd love to go.

With the three passengers squeezed into the back of his small sedan, the Lieutenant took the lead.

The road swept past acres of vineyards, with only a handful of women here and there to tend to them.

"What a crime to let all this go to waste," the Lieutenant remarked. "Can you imagine how many bottles of good French wine will be lost through this war?"

"To say nothing of the loss of lives," his wife put in.

"But today, we are not supposed to dwell on tragic subjects, are we, my dear?"

The interplay of covert thrusts in their ultra-polite tones made Helena keep out of the conversation.

A few miles east of Orange, they saw the famous Roman theater and the Triumphal Arch, remarkable for its wealth of decoration. Marian was fascinated by these relics of Roman conquest. He kept adding fragments of pillars and chunks of friezes to his already over-stuffed pockets.

"Just think," Marian's whisper vibrated with awe, "they probably fed the Christians to the lions in this very arena."

The Lieutenant laughed. "More likely they had gladiator contests, plays and dancing troupes here."

"I wish the togas and those heavenly draped robes were still in fashion, don't you Margareta?" Said the blonde.

"What? Oh yes, yes, they must have been comfortable."

Margareta's thoughts had been far away and her detached reply earned her a pitying look. Helena imagined that the pallor and distraction went with worry over her absent husband, fighting beside Adam at the front. How wrong she was proved a short while later when, by chance, she overheard a few potent exchanges between her and the Lieutenant. It was none of her business but she felt put out none the less.

Starting at the foothills, the road up the mountain de Lure was a succession of sharp bends and blind rises. The engine labored, spluttered and eventually refused to go altogether.

"She's over-heated." Their gay Lieutenant sounded cross.

The worn hand-brake was ineffectual against the steep incline, and the car began to roll backwards. Stefa had both hands over her mouth. Mrs. Szumanska screamed. Her husband told her to shut up. He rammed the gears in and the car jerked to a stop.

Mr. Zaleski had also stopped some way behind and was panting up the hill to see what the trouble was. The men placed boulders behind the back wheels of the old car and everyone agreed they might as well do some exploring while the engine cooled down.

It was Marian who spotted the cave on the opposite side of a gorge. At first glance it looked like a small rock shelter but as they climbed closer, they could make out what must have been a table immediately in front of the entrance. It was hewn out of the rock and worn smooth. They all took turns with the Lieutenant's binoculars. An amateur archaeologist, he told them that this was probably a sacrificial altar dating back to the pre-Neolithic phase of early human history.

"How long ago was that?" Marian asked.

"Oh, somewhere between ten and forty thousand years ago, more commonly known as the Old Stone Age."

"Gee."

Preoccupied with their own thoughts, they gazed for a long time at this rare evidence of man's earliest existence.

"Well, time we went back to civilization," Lieutenant Szumanski finally said, "in our so-called reliable modern transportation."

From then on Marian and Stefa were constantly on the lookout for fresh points of interest and often came across a find in the most unexpected places. No more than a mile from the house they unearthed a sacrificial altar surrounded by a strange formation of rock pillars. The Mariuses could not understand their excitement over their discoveries.

Familiarity with their surrounding and their own way of life had made them unaware of any difference between the past and the present.

The peaceful atmosphere, the warm, sunny climate and the beauty of the surrounding countryside all conspired to diminish any real anxiety over the occasional reminder of the war that was being fought out there. Marian was the official radio operator and continually turned the knobs from one wavelength to another, but all they could get were snatches of French, German and English announcements made unintelligible through heavy interference.

It was the Comte de Baer who presented the most pressing problem at that time. Whenever he called, he brought sweets for the children. By now Helena was fully aware of his intentions towards her but she still had no idea why he was so anxious to restore the Chateau to its original splendor. Until his last visit.

Dressed in a light linen suit and paisley cravat, he looked more debonair than ever. He said he had something very special for her and would she please do him the great honor of accepting it over a glass of wine at his Chateau. When she declined the invitation he asked if she would at least come outside with him as he had to speak to her privately on a most important matter. She could see no harm in that. Besides, she was curious not so much about the present, which she had no intentions of accepting, but about the important matter he wanted to discuss. They followed the footpath that led down to a tiny stream bordering on the Marius' property. He gallantly removed his jacket for her to sit on and handed her a velvet box.

"First of all I should like you to accept this, as you are the only woman I know who could possibly do justice to it."

It was a ruby necklace. The exquisitely handcrafted gold lace setting was not of this century and she could only guess that it was a valuable family heirloom. It was beautiful and it matched her bracelet.

"As much as I appreciate the gesture, I couldn't possibly accept such a gift," she said, closing the lid and holding the box out to him.

"Please *liebling*. You will make me the happiest of men."

She shot to her feet, agitated as much by the endearment as by his plunge to his knees and the fervent way in which he took hold of her hand and began to kiss it.

"Ah I see you are cross with me now. Don't you understand how I feel about you?" He stood up, still holding onto her hand. "From the first day I saw you in Bollene and that was long before I had the courage to introduce myself to you, I knew you were the woman for me!"

She backed away from the palely gleaming eyes. He took a step forward and pinned her against a tree. His mouth tasted of liquor and peppermint.

"Please don't look at me like that," he drew back, mortified by her coldness. "I would never harm you. I love you! Now listen to me. There is no future for you here. Your husband won't come back. As soon as the Germans make their base here we can leave. We will go to Italy or Switzerland, anywhere you like." He had taken her hand again and was pressing it to his lips.

So that was it. He was nothing but a pawn, a miserable quisling, busy restoring the "noble" estates of France for German bases. She dared not let him suspect that he had made a blunder in his passionate outburst.

"I, I really don't know what to say and cannot pretend to be insensible to your feelings, but since you speak of love, then you will understand when I tell you that I love my husband and intend to wait for him."

"I see." Dramatically he let go of her hand and picked up his jacket and his present.

"The better man wins."

"There is no question of that in this case," she smiled. "The conquest was made many years ago."

He regarded her for a moment as if to make sure that she wasn't mocking him, then his face softened and once again he extended the velvet box to her.

"I would still like you to have this memento." She shook her head.

"Very well, I shall keep it. The time may yet come when you will change your mind and if you do, I shall be here. No, don't worry, I am not the kind of boor to force unwanted attentions on a lady." With that he raised her hand to his lips with great formality.

After he had gone she stood there for a long time, looking at the clear water, listening to its trickle over the stones and wondering what to do about the whole thing. She could not help wishing that his feelings for her had been less genuine, because she knew she had to report him and the idea was distasteful. She picked up a pebble and threw it into the stream. Why did these men have to complicate her life? She decided to have a talk with Lieutenant Szumanski.

Wheels were swiftly set in motion. Plain-clothed men from Orange arrived at the Chateau. She had no doubt they found more than enough evidence of his activities, for that was the last they saw of le Comte de Baer.

In a way, this seemed to complete her unfinished work in Bielsko. And she knew Adam would be pleased.

*

CHAPTER SEVENTEEN

"The Final Escape"

The shortage of food grew daily more alarming. Passing troops had to be supplied. All the strong able hands had been recruited into the Army and though the women toiled from dawn to after dusk, many fields lay fallow.

The money that Adam had left them was gone, spent on exorbitant prices now charged for everything. Eventually their meals were reduced to Madam Marius' salad and peas, supplemented occasionally with fresh olives picked from the trees grown on the neglected Chateau property.

Helena learned how to make a three-course meal out of the available ingredients, starting with pea soup, followed by either a pea casserole or patties and with local berries for desert. Drawing the meal times out as long as possible gave the impression of eating normally and she suspected it also saved them from a lot of indigestion.

They had finished dawdling over supper and were sitting on the front porch in the quiet of the evening, when Madame Marius turned resolutely to her husband.

"All right. Come out with it man. What's on your mind?"

"Who says there's anything on my mind?"

"I do. You've been brooding about it all day."

He gave a deep sigh. "Oh well, you'll have to know sooner or later, but I wanted to finish the job first." Slowly he filled his pipe. Everyone was looking at him expectantly, waiting for him to go on.

"The dog must go," he said harshly. "We can't afford to feed him anymore."

The old lady caught her breath. Then the full meaning of his words penetrated and both Marian and Stefa rushed towards him with loud cries of protest.

"Stop it you two!" Helena said sharply in Polish. "Don't you think it's hard enough for the old man without you making it worse? It's his dog after all and if he has to put him away then there's nothing we can do. Or would you rather see the animal starve to death?"

Without another word they both ran off, tears glistening in Marian's eyes, Stefa sobbing loudly. Helena tried to apologize for them, explaining that this was their third brutal wrench from a pet in less than a year.

He touched her arm in understanding.

Barely above a whisper his wife asked, "When?"

"First thing tomorrow morning, before the children are up."

Helena knew he did not own a gun and could not see how he was going to perform the hateful task. Yelps of agony the next morning told her soon enough. She looked out of the window and was sickened to see the old man with tears running down his cheeks, stabbing at the animal through the throat with his pitchfork. The second thrust finished him off and the dog was dragged away and buried in a hole already prepared for the body.

No one saw Monsieur Marius for the rest of the day.

That incident seemed to foreshadow the massacre that began to take place up North. Lieutenant Szumanski and the remaining, ill prepared troops had left for the front to once again meet the superbly equipped enemy forces. Marian stayed tuned in to Radio Paris and they all waited for the periodic flashes of clear broadcasting to reach them. Two Polish Divisions won fame on the Maginot Line. Rejecting all summons to capitulate and suffering heavy losses, they covered the retreat of the French troops and the civilian population.

"Sounds like Dad," Marian remarked.

"Yes, doesn't it?" Helena agreed, surprising herself by the chocking pride she felt for the Poles' heroism.

On June 14th, Mr. and Mrs. Zaleski and their daughter-in-law called again, their belongings piled high on top of the car. No sight-seeing expedition this but a timely getaway.

"What about the Lieutenant's wife?" Helena asked.

"She left with some other friends. No point in the rest of us staying on here now. Especially with Petain leading the defeatists," Mr. Zaleski added bitterly.

"Please let's not waste any more time talking," his wife whined. "I hear the air-raids are quite close to us. There's a little space left in the boot Mrs. Polek, but not very much so do take your most essential things only."

"But I am not going with you," Helena said, astonished that they should have taken it for granted.

"Oh but you must!" This from Margareta. "With the fall of Paris there's no hope left."

"Paris? When?" "God, didn't you know? Today! Oh of course, we got the announcement through the Army transmitter. That's why we're leaving. Come on, please hurry."

Helena thanked them but repeated firmly that she was staying on. Shaking his head in bewilderment and urged on by his wife, the man finally drove off.

The idea of an invasion by the Germans did not bother the Mariuses in the least but they were afraid for their friends and would have been happier had they accepted the lift. When Madame Marius' curiosity got the better of her she asked why Helena was so determined to stay on. So Helena told her about leaving Wieliczka, missing Adam and falling into the hands of the Russians. Enough said. Napoleon's *congé* as a result of his fiasco with the Russes made her cluck with sympathetic understanding.

"This time," Helena said, "I'm sticking to our arrangement and I'm not moving until Adam gets here, Germans or no Germans." And wished she felt as strong as she sounded.

The old lady nodded. "Whatever happens," she said, "our home is your home."

Radio Paris became dead for a while and then, as in Krakow, announcements were resumed in German. No need now to be filled in on details not understood. The situation was only too clear and it was Helena's turn to translate the German announcer's depressingly jubilant reports. Nothing could stop the German armies. They were said to be some 60 miles from Orange. Then 40...

The last of the Polish families had left with a final appeal to Helena to go with them. Reason told her that Adam could never reach them in time before the Germans came. Reluctantly she abandoned all hope of freedom and began making plans for their stay in France. Adam was here and he might need her help. She had no doubts that he would make contact, probably in his old man's disguise.

She talked it over with the Mariuses. "If the Town Clerk would help and you are agreeable, I could have my papers changed and become your daughter-in-law. What do you think?"

She was touched beyond words by their immediate enthusiasm.

"We must go straight away before it is too late." As Madam Marius said this, they heard the sound of heavy firing.

"It is too late!" Helena cried, the blood draining from her face.

Then came the roar of engines and she saw a convoy of trucks moving toward the house.

This was it. The first of the occupation troops! Helena felt the familiar twist of the stomach.

"Marian! Stefa! Get inside the house. Quick!"

Stefa started running but Marian called back, "What for? These aren't German trucks, I can tell – look, they're Polish."

With a wild whoop he sprinted towards them. "It's Dad! It's Dad! And he's brought all his men with him."

Adam leapt out of the first, still moving vehicle, while the three that followed ground to a stop in a flurry of dust.

"Thank God you're here." His voice was hoarse with emotion, his face barely recognizable under layers of dust and several days' growth of beard.

"That idiot of a Town Clerk in Bollene said all the Poles had evacuated."

"Just as well you came to check up," she was laughing and crying against him. "I expected you, but not like this!"

Adam turned to a young officer with the wiry physique, beak nose and piercing eyes of a Highlander, introducing him as his right and left hand man. He wrapped an arm around the square shoulders, adding "And don't let his size fool you. This is one tough nut."

Jozef wiped his hand on his jacket. His eyes, level with hers, were smiling as he lifted her hand to his lips. "Your husband is lying to you."

She laughed, liking the man, liking the easy banter between them.

Soldiers were jumping from the trucks two and three at a time, each one as dirty as the other, but all in the highest of spirits.

"Listen you filthy lot!" Georges bellowed at them. "We'll be taking a lady with us from here on, so how about making yourselves more presentable. Last one to the well gets no fag rations for the day." And they were off, shouting and jostling one another like a bunch of schoolboys.

Madame Marius came out to say that she had prepared a basin of hot water in the kitchen for Adam. She gave Helena a triumphant look as if to say, "Didn't I tell you he would come?"

"Adam, do you think we should waste time on washing right now?"

"A few minutes won't matter. The boys need a bit of a break." She followed him into the kitchen.

"But the Germans..."

"They're still quite a way from here. Busy occupying the coast."

"But we heard gun reports just before you came. What's so funny about that?"

Laughing, he explained that the reports had come from his back-firing truck.

"We've had some trouble with it, but the thing still goes like the devil, thanks to Jozef. He's a genius with engines."

She sighed with relief. "So what are your plans now?"

"I've thought of two alternatives," Adam said, drying his face. "We can either make for Marsailles and from there to Africa, or head West, across the Pyrenees and into Spain.

"Can you tune into the BBC on this set? It would help if we knew the Germans' exact position."

Marian fiddled with the knobs and Churchill's voice came over loud and clear. His words, repeated by Poland's own Premier, General Sikorski, provided Adam with his third alternative and final decision. Britain was appealing to the Polish troops to make their way to England via every and any possible route and called upon the Polish Navy to stand by to transport the soldiers. Once again Polish armies were being reorganized. This time to fight side by side with the British. General de Gaulle was also making a valiant effort to save the face of France after Marshal Petain's rapid surrender.

Adam was jubilant. "Good old Churchill. We'll lick the Gerries yet, you watch!"

"So it's England for us?" Helena said, going into the bedroom to pack their things.

"Where else?" He followed her in. "We don't have much space so just take the one case." He began to pace back and forth, beating a fist into the palm of his hand.

"Let's see. Brest is taken, the Germans are moving down towards Bordeaux, that means we'll have to try and reach Biarritz before them. Right! You ready? Grab some food then and let's go!" And he hurried out to pass the good news on to his men, leaving Helena to explain to the Mariuses the reason for all the excitement.

"Then there is still hope for France?" The old man asked, afraid he may not have understood properly.

"It looks like it," Helena said.

"No, no, it not only looks like it, it is so," Georges corrected her, running in and picking up the suitcase.

Helena saw that he had found the only loaf of bread in the house.

"Leave that Georges," she said. "You don't know how little they've got."

"Take it," Madame Marius was every bit as adamant. "Those poor boys must be starving." A twinkle came into her eyes and she added, "We've always got our peas."

"For heavens sake, this is no time to be arguing over a loaf of bread," cut in Adam, hurrying back to embrace the old people and thank them for looking after his family.

Madame Marius kissed the children and held on to Helena. "Wait," she said, fumbling in her apron pocket. "This is for you. It is all I have to give you. No, you must take it," and she pressed the pin brooch into Helena's hand. "God go with you, daughter."

"And you, -mother." She turned to the old man "And father."

Smiling, he said, "I am sorry, but very glad it was not necessary to make it official."

Clutching the precious loaf of bread under one arm, Georges helped Helena up onto the back of the first truck. Other hands reached out to pull the children in and they were on their way. As they turned into the road, Helena caught a last glimpse of the old couple, waving in the doorway and smiling through their tears. She opened her hand and her own tears came anew. The beautifully cut black onyx gleamed as the light caught it. The oval stone was surrounded by chip diamonds. It was now as precious to her as it must have been to the old lady.

With Jozef Zawisza behind the wheel, the truck bumped and shook crazily at breakneck speed, and with each rougher jolt came a groan from a man lying against the cab. Within the darkness of the canvas canopy Helena could just make out the bandaged head.

"Is there nothing we can do for him?" She asked the soldier nearest to her.

"Zygmunt will be all right. With that wound he should have been killed outright. He's got the Polek luck all right."

"Did you say Zygmunt Polek?" "Sure, the Captain's ---"

She did not wait to hear more but pushed past a dozen legs to reach the wounded man. He recognized her and smiled.

"Hi. Good to see you Helena."

"Is it bad?"

"Only when this bloody thing leaves the ground and makes a crash landing. Ouch! See what I mean?"

She felt his forehead. It was sopping wet and she took out her handkerchief to dry it. She adjusted her position and eased his head onto her lap.

"Thanks. That feels better."

"What happened to Jerzy? Is he here as well?"

"No." He looked away from her. After a moment he went on, "He, didn't make it poor kid. A snow storm caught us in the mountains. We got separated and by the time I found him he was finished. Just as well you didn't come with us, eh?"

She could not speak. Wasn't this what she had expected?

They sped on, the truck rattling noisily and back-firing with every change of gear, while the men sang and played harmonicas. This kept everybody cheerful and added to the excitement of the race.

Georges pulled aside the driver's partition and passed along some of the bread. It was only now that Helena saw how hungry they all were. Zygmunt could not be made to eat. She realized his condition was worse than he made out.

They stopped at the French Garrison at Orange, where a heated argument ensued between Adam and the Major in command. Apparently he wanted the soldiers disarmed before supplying them with petrol.

"Tie the fool up before I blast his head off!" Adam shouted, white with rage. "And fill the tanks up. His bloody Germans can release him when they get here."

Covered by the rifles of the grim-faced Poles, the Major's men offered no further protest.

They were now on their way to Montpellier, where they hoped to find something to eat. Helena learned that Adam had been spending what was left of his own money on food, as no one had received any pay in weeks. Rationed out among sixty men, the few loaves of bread that they managed to get hold of in Montpellier did little to assuage their hunger. Over his shoulder Adam looked at Helena cradling Zygmunt.

"We'll find a Hospital in Toulouse. He should make it till then, the bleeding's stopped. Are *you* all right back there?"

"Yes. Not having quite as much fun as Marian is, but I'm fine."

He laughed. "Sure you don't want to swap with Georges? It's more comfortable up front."

"No. Not yet. I want to keep an eye on Zygmunt."

"Good." He smiled at her, liking the calm way she was taking it all. "How's Stefa?"

"A bit dazed, if you ask me. First it was the noise and now it's all the attention she's getting. Not that she's complaining."

Before the harmonicas were out again, Marian started asking questions about the French Campaign. Tears came to Helena's eyes when she heard how one of the men threw himself on top of Adam to take the impact of a collapsing wall. Injured, he now lay in the second truck. *Only a born leader could command such loyalty,* she thought. She wanted to laugh at the expression on Marian's face, knowing that hers must be reflecting the same smug look of pride. She also learned that the reason why Adam had been in a position to have a wall topple on top of him was because he had been the last to leave a bombarded town, having first directed all his men to safety through the traffic congested streets. So the allegiance was mutual.

She also discovered why the truck was in such poor shape. It was a wonder that it went at all, as Adam had rammed it through a brick wall to escape German tanks that were closing in on them.

"All this could have been avoided, of course, had he not been the last to leave the front," Helena put in, interested to hear the reaction to that one.

"It wouldn't have been our Captain if he hadn't been the last to leave," a soldier said defensively.

She looked from one grubby face to the other, thinking they would probably follow Adam to hell itself, and loving them for it.

Unbelievably, Gendarmes halted them at the entrance to the Toulouse bridge across the river Garonne. A machine-gun had been set up to block their way.

Adam called out for an explanation. It appeared that the Major at Orange had telephoned an order through to stop and disarm them. France had capitulated -- the Poles had to follow suit!

"I give you ten seconds to put that toy away!" Adam barked.

He was ignored. Ten seconds passed. A nod from Adam and a soldier pulled back the tarpaulin revealing two machine-guns placed at either side of the second truck. He opened fire, aiming high above the startled Gendarmes' heads. A couple of seconds later the bridge was cleared.

They drove into Toulouse where they were told that the British as well as the Polish Navy was, in fact, evacuating Poles from the ports of France, but no one could tell them which port they should make for. They were however, directed to a Hospital. Zygmunt's wound was attended to in the emergency ward after which the patient was removed against doctor's orders.

To escape the incredible noise and turmoil of the Place du Capitole in Toulouse, they parked under the shade of an avenue of trees on the far side of the city. Jozef spread out the map and he and Adam debated on the next move.

"We've been making good time," Jozef said, "and I think we can beat the Germans to Bordeaux."

"Yes," Adam agreed. "I'll tell the boys we're sticking to our original plan."

Oscar, a cheerful, good looking young Private, who also happened to be a navigator, came up with another alternative that, if the worst came to the worst, they could always take some sort of seafaring vessel by force, an idea that greatly appealed to the rest of the men.

"I don't know about you chaps, but I'm bushed," Adam yawned. "And if we do have to exercise force, as Oscar suggests, then I think we'd better stay here for the night and catch some sleep. Georges, that's your department. See if you can find us some nice beds."

"And innerspring mattresses and feather pillows, I suppose?" He was just in time to duck a cuff on the ear.

There were so many offers of bedrolls for the Captain's family that the matter had to be resolved by a toss of a coin. Georges settled them into a corner partially screened by gymnasium equipment and then got busy on all the cupboard locks. The last closet provided them with soap and dozens of towels.

Helena and Stefa had first use of the bathroom facilities. They scrubbed each other's backs and washed their hair under the shower.

"I won't plait your hair until it's properly dry," Helena said, combing out the tangles.

"Can't we just leave it loose? I'm tired of pigtails, they're so childish," Stefa complained.

"I see, and who are you trying to impress?"

"Well, I thought Oskar might ask me to wait for him," she admitted candidly. "I wouldn't mind marrying him."

"Oh boy! And you think the hair will do the trick?"

They looked at one another and both burst out laughing. Helena hugged her. "Don't rush it my precious. You've got plenty of time."

Later that night she could not resist telling Adam about it. He was silent for a long while. "The crush I can understand," he finally said. "Most kids go through that, but the sense of humor..."

"I know. She's more adult than we give her credit for."

A constant stream of traffic moved past the windows, casting flickers of light over the sleeping forms. Overcome by exhaustion some of the boys were asleep almost before they hit the floor. Others managed to get their boots off. A few showered. The glow of a cigarette revealed those that were too tired to sleep. Helena turned towards Adam, wanting to tell him about the Compte de Baer. His face was in shadow but she could hear his deep breathing and felt the strength that emanated from him even in sleep. She thought of what the men had been telling her about him, of their devotion to him, of that last-minute charge up to the house to pick them up. He was a man in a million and he was hers. She lay back and smiled to herself. She must be crazy to feel such intense happiness with the Germans so close on their tail.

To make up for his lack of success with better sleeping quarters, Georges appeared the next morning with gallons of petrol and a supply of provisions. No one bothered to ask how he had come by this windfall.

By the time they reached Pau, they were penniless. Georges was all for confiscating food and petrol from local dealers. This went very much against Adam's grain but there was no choice and he compromised by signing chits on behalf of the Army. To lend authenticity to the transactions, the men respectfully addressed their Captain as Colonel.

On the last lap to Biarritz the engine began to give trouble again. They stopped next to a river and had a wash while Jozef and Georges worked on the truck. Suddenly, all eyes turned up to the sky. A squadron of German 'planes passed overhead.

Unperturbed, Stefa moved closer to her father. Ever since he had been with them she had shown no signs of fear. As long as she was by his side she felt secure in the knowledge that nothing could harm them. Helena knew that Marian felt the same and to a large degree, Adam had that effect on her as well.

He took Stefa's hand and put his arm around Helena's shoulders. "Won't be long now and we'll be out of this. How's Zygmunt doing?"

"All right I think. He should make it. How did you find him, by the way?"

"He found me. Don't ask me how. Ah, there's Georges doing the war dance. The engine must be fixed. Come on."

At Biarritz they learned that the Germans had already occupied Bordeaux and were some fifty miles from them but that two Polish vessels, the "Batory" and the Sobieski" were anchored outside the port of St. Jean de Luz, close to the Spanish border.

Abandoning his piratical plans, Adam made for St. Jean de Luz.

With the port so close, each man behind his wheel flogged his truck to the utmost. They were bounced about like pebbles in a tide. Georges had swapped places with Helena and she was now sitting between Adam and Jozef. She had not mentioned the ache in her arm but Adam had guessed, and putting his arm around her shoulders, made her lean against him. "All right?" He asked.

"Mm. Better."

"We're nearly there."

At St. Jean de Luz there was only one ship at anchor, while the last batch of Poles and a few French civilians were being hustled into the already overcrowded boats.

Jozef demanded that more boats be made available to take the men across to the ship.

"Sorry Sir," came the nonchalant response from the harbor official.

"There is no one left to take you across and the ship cannot wait until these return to pick you up."

With an oath Jozef pushed the official aside and took some of his men to untie the boats that were bobbing further down the jetty.

"You can't do that!" The man shouted. "Who's going to bring them back?"

"To hell with the boats!" Adam roared at him. "Are they more important than human lives?"

"Can you believe it? What kind of people are we dealing with here!"

The ship's horn gave three impatient blasts. Adam looked at the trucks and gave a final order to have them destroyed. With more than one backward glance of regret at the burning vehicles, the men followed Helena and the children into the boats, armed with the two machine-guns and two cases of hand grenades.

No sooner were they on board the "Sobieski" than her engines began to throb and slowly the shores of France receded from view.

Helena took a last look at the land which she had grown to love. In spite of everything and while it lasted, France and Bollene especially, provided the ideal spot to heal the body and patch up over-wrought nerves. And from what the voice over the loudspeaker was saying, she guessed she would need all her restored reserves to face up to the final lap of the journey.

"Attention!" And again, "Attention! Will all civilian passengers proceed to the main deck without delay, where they will be issued with lifebelts. I repeat: Will all civilian.."

Helena and the children were swept along with the crowd in the direction pointed out to them by members of the crew. As soon as they were all assembled, one of the ship's officers stood up on a platform to address them in a calm, unhurried voice.

"This, as you will have gathered by now, is going to be no luxury cruise. We are overloaded by more than a thousand passengers so that if the service does not come up to standard, I ask you to be a little patient." He waited for the ripple of laughter to subside. "To avoid possible aerial attacks and the submarines, concentrated mainly in the Bay of Biscay, we will be traveling a good distance out to sea. There will, of course, be a few mines about," he added matter-of-factly. "However, the greatest danger lies in panic among passengers. Each one of you will now be provided with a lifebelt which you will please wear throughout the voyage. You are assured that we are well equipped and prepared for any eventuality. So, kindly co-operate with the crew, DO NOT PANIC and you will prevent unnecessary casualties."

Ensconced in yellow lifebelts, the passengers were taken below to their allocated cabins.

Helena told Marian and Stefa to stay in the cabin while she went up to the top deck. She pushed her way through the crowds towards the stern, knowing she would find her husband somewhere in the vicinity of his precious machine-guns, and there he was, talking to a Naval Officer.

"I've just been asking what they've done with our families," Adam said, as she came up to them.

"Demanding, actually," the man laughed, leaving them alone.

"You don't look too comfortable in that outfit," Adam nodded towards the lifebelt. "But it suits you," he grinned.

"I wouldn't mind it so much if I thought it was just an unnecessary precaution."

"Well of course that's all it is. There's nothing to worry about. What with this," his arm swept grandly towards the machine-guns, "and another one at the bow, we'll have ample protection."

"Great! What about the mines?"

Those he dismissed with a wave of the hand. "No problem to a navigator like ours. I hear he's the best our Navy's ever had."

She looked at him and smiled. Adam had not changed much after all. And what was more, she knew that she did not want that side of him ever to change. With that kind of attitude, how could anything stand in their way? He was right – nothing would stop them from reaching England.

He took her hand. "Come on, I'll show you around the Sobieski."

Happily she went with him. They took a few steps and stopped. "Do you feel it too?" He asked. "It's like walking on a stretch of free land."

She nodded. And there, above them, was the white and red flag flying high to remind them that all was not lost.

END

EPILOGUE

Helena and the children survived the London Blitz and three itinerant years in Scotland, following Adam's moves with the Polish Army.

When it became clear that Adam's duties would continue to keep him away from the action, he had himself transferred to the Polish fleet which was then transporting Allied troops from England to France.

Marian finished Nautical College and became one of the youngest Officers in the British Navy. And Liverpool became the family's home base.

Stefa excelled at school and later in her career in journalism.

After the war, the family's fortunes fared better than those of their beleaguered country. The Poleks moved to South Africa, from where they went to seek a more adventurous life in Northern Rhodesia – but that's another story ...

The Poleks – From left to right: Stefa, Helena, Adam and Marian.

The Key Characters

Helena Polek	The main character in the book, and wife of Adam Polek who lived into her 90's, passing away in Durban South Africa, while living with her son Marian.
Adam Polek	Husband of Helena Polek – a true Polish Patriot, who passed away at the age of 86 in Durban, South Africa.
Stefa Polek	The 9 year old daughter of Helena and Adam Polek and author of this book, now living in Hollywood California.
Marian Polek	Son of Helena and Adam Polek retired Naval Officer, and at 84, still living in Durban South Africa with his daughter.
Bronek	Part-time student and the Poleks' chauffeur-cum-gardener.
Lala	The Poleks' Maltese poodle (responsible for saving the lives of Helena and her children)

A ZEST FOR LIFE

SEQUEL TO "A SPECIAL BRAND OF COURAGE"

By

KRYSTYNA LOUW

CHAPTER ONE

LONDON, 1940

Stefa looked bewildered. She was sure that her dancing school was right here, at this bus stop - but there was nothing but rubble. A policeman walked up to her. "You look lost little girl," he smiled. Then noticing the plaque with a foreign name and address hanging by a cord around her neck, he changed to pidgin English. He need not have bothered because she'd been in London for six weeks already and understood him perfectly. She pointed to the ruins and said, "Dance school?"

He shook his head. "Not any more. Bombed." He gently took her arm. "Come, I will see you to the bus. That is your address?"

"Yes," she said, close to tears. She didn't care about the loss of dance lessons she'd been treated to by Mrs. Hart, their landlady. She was thinking of the nice dance teacher, afraid that she had gone with the building.

It wasn't until she got home that she rushed to her mother, sobbing and telling her what had happened.

"I'm sure your teacher wasn't in the school when it happened," Helena said, holding Stefa close.

"Of course not," Marian put in. "The last air raid was late last night, so she wouldn't have been there."

Stefa regarded her 13-year-old brother with some relief. "Sometimes Marian, you make sense."

They had been speaking Polish, forgetting that Mrs. Hart wouldn't know what was going on, so between them and Helena's German they managed to give her the news.

"I also think your teacher is alright," Mrs. Hart said comfortingly, stroking Stefa's cheek with a soft plump hand. Turning to Helena she added, "but it's a shame Stefa won't be getting more lessons. She's so talented."

"When all this is over, she can go on and become a ballerina if she wants to," Helena smiled.

The older woman smiled back. She was glad that she'd taken them in. She had grown very fond of this family, and the extra money that the Polish Government in exile was paying to accommodate them, came in very handy as well. With the coming of the war, her husband's job had become redundant. Who needed a Manager for a non-existent theater? And he was whisked off to serve with the Home Guard. Fortunately her German was passable, acquired during her many years with a German Travel Agency. And so she knew what these people had been through – their horrifying journey dodging the bombs and bullets of the Luftwaffe, only to end up under Russian occupation. Their escape from the dreaded NKVD, the Russian Secret Police; their ordeal in a cemetery shelter; Helena's valiant but futile visit to the Gestapo Headquarters with forged documents to try and get visas for Hungary; her work for the Polish Underground culminating in their unbelievable escape from the Nazis by jumping out of a moving train into Hungary – and jail. Her admiration for this lovely, courageous young woman was immense and the story of the family reunion was enough to bring tears to her eyes.

She had not met Helena's husband, but from the little that she learned of Adam's own escape from a POW Camp and flight into Hungary, she was not surprised that his would have been the last of the fighting forces to leave the French front on the foregone conclusion that no armies at that time were a match for the German might. With his entire Brigade he had swept through the town of Bollene where he had left his family and together, they made a last-minute bid for the port of St. Jean de Luz to board the last Polish vessel to leave the shores of France for England.

As soon as they arrived in London Adam had left for Scotland, to reorganize the Polish forces. Families of Polish Officers were billeted with Londoners eager to help the war effort.

Meanwhile Germany began an all-out air attack on Britain, with London as their chief target.

The London Blitz began in September, a sustained aerial attack with the Germans dropping tons of bombs on the built-up areas of the city. Night after night, 6 p.m. to 6 a.m. people took refuge in air raid shelters and subway stations as fires raged through entire blocks of buildings. Unfortunately for the Germans this psychological strategy did not produce the desired result. Instead of succumbing, the British rallied magnificently under the fiery call-to-arms from their Prime Minister, Winston Churchill. Every able-bodied man was conscripted, young women clambered to be accepted into the Army, Navy or Air Force while the older ones labored in factories, manufacturing aircraft, vehicles and warheads at breakneck speed. Even the ladies of the British aristocracy rolled up their sleeves and pitched in. They could be seen driving Army vehicles or tractors or serving tea to the needy.

Helena learned to knit. Her skill in the use of the crochet hook made it easy for her to adapt quickly to knitting needles of all sizes, and she busied herself making sweaters and socks for the family, the Harts and for the Red Cross, as an exchange for the many articles of clothing that she and the children had received from them, both in Hungary and now in London. The Red Cross had also provided children's grammar books and dictionaries.

"Wish Dad would hurry up and get us out of here," Marian groaned, throwing the English learner down in frustration. What he didn't say was that he felt bad about persuading Stefa to go to an indoor swimming pool that day. He was teaching her to swim when they were caught in an unexpected day time air raid. There was no time to reach the Underground so they huddled together in a changing room. They could feel the ground shake as bombs blasted close by. They were unhurt but he felt responsible for putting Stefa in danger. She hadn't wanted to go but he had insisted. Even if she was only a ten-year-old kid, he should have paid heed to her "sixth sense" which had saved their lives more than once already.

Helena didn't say anything. She too felt irritated by the bureaucracy that was keeping them separated. It had been three months since Adam left them and it felt like three years. Her thoughts were cut off by a loud knock. Mrs. Hart went to open the door.

"Can I help you?" she asked politely, then took a second look at the strong, handsome face and saw the resemblance. "You must be -"

"Adam Polek," he laughed. And that's all he could get out before being smothered by Marian and Stefa. Helena waited her turn, observing the man who meant everything to her, the broad-shouldered powerful frame accentuated by the smart uniform, the square capable hands. She loved the sound of his deep chuckle as he tried to extricate himself from the children, but most of all it was the warmth and vitality in the brown eyes meeting hers, that took her breath away.

His voice was hoarse with emotion when he came to wrap his arms around her. "I've missed you so," he whispered, burying his face in her hair, reveling in its familiar scent. "I've gone to the highest sources to get papers for you to join me in Scotland. It won't be long now."

Mrs. Hart decided this was an occasion to take out the precious leg of lamb from the freezer. Helena helped with the meal while Stefa laid the table and Marian went to draw the black curtains over all the windows, to conform with the Blackout regulations so that German bombers would find no speck of light for their target. They ate early, before the expected sirens began to whine and they'd have to run to their allocated shelter.

No sooner was the table cleared than there was the usual sound of sirens, dead on time. 6 o'clock, and with that came a loud banging on the door. Adam opened it this time and after a few sharp words slammed it shut.

"The fool!" he exploded. "Expecting us to go into that ready-made grave down the road he called a shelter."

"But that's where we've been going every night," Helena explained, clutching pillows and blankets.

"Well no-one's going there tonight. Can't you see, it's nothing but a hole dug under a bus shelter. We're a hundred times safer staying in the house."

Mrs. Hart agreed to stay only if Stefa slept with her. Not a Catholic herself, she nevertheless found the child's pious telling of the rosary reassuring and had more than once referred to her as their guardian Angel. Touched by the woman's faith in her child's protective aura, Helena gave her a spontaneous hug.

Always ensconced in the impregnable darkness of a shelter, they had not been subjected to the full spectrum of a mind blowing blitz by night, until now. The frantic groping search lights and anti aircraft gunfire, the sound of the enemy planes swooping down, the accelerating whistle of bomb after bomb before exploding, followed by bursts of fire that lit up London like a gigantic fireworks display, all that, coupled with the tremors that shook the earth, took on a scene from Dante's Inferno.

Helena stood at the window. There was no point in drawing curtains. They were useless against the constant burst of light. *How could this be happening to a city like London?* She felt her stomach knot every time she heard a bomb close by and marveled at Adam who could sleep through it all.

She went to see how Marian was taking it and found him also standing at the window. Before she could speak he said, "Don't worry Mom, they won't get us."

Stefa too was wide awake, clutching her rosary but strangely calm. From their flight in France, Helena knew that as long as her father was with her, Stefa felt completely safe, but then his own men had referred to their Captain as "indestructible". Now, Stefa's composure had the right effect on Mrs. Hart who didn't seem as agitated as she was at the beginning of the raid.

Helena went back to her room and slipped into bed next to Adam. Somehow she too, felt that they would be spared that night.

It was only the next morning, when they went out to look at the devastation all around them, that the full meaning of the word spared, hit her. For the shelter where they would have gone to, was no more. It had sustained a direct hit. There were no survivors!

Adam had to leave early that morning but urged Helena to go and see his friend at the Polish Embassy. "I think they open at 9 so be there early, and wait for your papers if you have to. I can't have you stay here any longer!"

"Nor do I want to!" she retorted with feeling.

The day turned out exceptionally warm and sunny, so with just the handbag that she always carried since it held all her jewelry, and light jackets for all three, Helena and the children set out for the Embassy. When told that their papers would be ready that afternoon, she decided to spend the time waiting in a nearby park. Finding the little kiosk open and serving tea and snacks – rationed to one per person- was an unexpected pleasure, a pleasure that was cut short by the unexpected wail of sirens.

Instinctively all three rushed to hide under the nearest tree, as they had done in the attack by the Luftwaffe in Poland. But these planes didn't have the same kind of freedom to swoop low to mow down pedestrians, for squadrons of British and Polish fighters flew out with lightening speed to engage the enemy.

The sound of the All Clear sirens had more than the usual effect of relief on Helena. Her voice shook as she murmured, "Let's get out of here."

They went straight to the Embassy, picked up their papers and headed for home, to pack.

When they got there, they stood looking in stunned silence at what had been the Hart's house and the one next to it. Both were razed almost to the ground. Stefa's sobs stirred Helena to action. "Stay here," she commanded, already running.

"Stay here!" Marian echoed, following his mother to the ruins. They scrambled through the debris, calling and calling but there was no sign of life, and the dead would have been buried under mounds of mortar, twisted steel pylons and cables. "It's no use," Helena said finally, realizing that the firemen had already been there, judging by the charred wooden beams that still felt hot to the touch.

Bereft of all their belongings once again, except for Helena's precious jewelry, and with nowhere else to go, they made their way back to the Polish Embassy. The bus was practically empty. After a while Marian broke the silence. "Do you think Mrs. Hart was in when it happened?" he asked, his eyes glistening with tears. "We'll never know," she murmured.

The friendly Embassy clerk who had taken care of them three months earlier on their arrival in London, escorted them to the newly formed Polish Citizens' Committee for Refugees and introduced them to an elderly official who took them to the Red Cross warehouse. He waited while they were fitted out with some warm clothes and helped them board their train for Scotland.

*